The Edge of Silence

by

Mark Sikorski

ISBN: 979-8-35667702-1 (Paperback)

First printing edition 2022.

Front cover image and Book design Erin Sikorski.

Editor services by Stephenie Magister.

Printed by Amazon Publishing, Inc., in the United States of America.

Any references to historical events, real people, or real places are used fictitiously or to the best of my recollection. Names, characters, and places are products of my fading memory.

Note: Parts of this work are pure fiction as I have no idea what the greater minds of this particular decade were thinking about. Since I had to guess, I used my better judgment which I have been told is sometimes not good at all, so buyer beware. As well, I need to point out that because of a fading memory, I probably put myself in the best light possible, so, its up to you to figure out what really happened all those years ago. I also put into character's verbiage (mouths?) words that they may or may not have been said (see above regarding memory). Any resemblance of persons living, or dead should be apparent to themselves (unless they are dead) even though I changed most of the last names to not embarrass them or myself.

For David Sikorski
My brother.
My hero.

Foreword

When I asked my father Joe Sikorski to tell me some of the things he did growing up and about his time in the military—specifically Vietnam, given it would be my turn to join the front lines soon enough—he refused me any details.

The reason he gave didn't just feel wrong, it didn't make any sense. At least not back then.

He said, "Not interesting, Marco." (Marco is my family's nickname for me.)

I couldn't believe him. *How on earth could it not be interesting to hear about your hero?*

He became a star athlete, joined the Air Force, went to interesting places, had a tour of duty in Vietnam, and he didn't think this was interesting? *Give me a break.*

I didn't know until I was older that he had told me as much as he could. War does that to people. Some of us, it shuts us up. Others, we're a dam waiting to burst. Wait until you see which one I am.

Me trying to talk about my dad's life by word of mouth doesn't have the same impact as if it were in his own words. Not only that, but I also have a hard-enough time remembering my own life. I see now what it would have meant to me if my dad had been able to give me more of his own story. Son of a gun cracked the door open a little every once in a while, but otherwise kept it closed and no amount of oil would break it open. I guess one side of me was hoping he was this huge hero and in his mind he probably felt he did nothing at all. Most of the really good men kept quiet and truly felt they just did what any honorable person would have done. That's the kind of man my Dad was. So, what should I do?

I want my kids to understand what things were happening during the time I needed to make critical decisions and the impact those decisions had on me; and, on them. If I pass this on verbally, my kids will forget or just make up stuff and my grandkids would be deprived of knowing that their grandfather lived an amazing life, went to interesting places, met interesting people, and, well, had to kill some of them. I not only did all of the above, but I also happen to be the cranky old guy that loves my kids and grandkids unconditionally.

Like me when I asked my own dad for what he could share, I began this journey of writing about this sliver of time on earth at the request of my children. They wanted me to tell them stories about my life growing up as a child, what happened in high school, places I've been, and the things I did in both the Marines and the Army. I did share with them some of the fun stories and hid others from them because I felt they were too young to understand. Some of the stories are just so intense, they became too much for me to relive, as you will soon see. I started to see what a challenge it might have been for my dad to open up. I have no idea if he went through some of the things I did.

I just couldn't tell those stories regardless of

my kids age because it would mean opening up areas of my life that were best left hidden to the outside world. This is one of the reasons I have the title "The Edge of Silence." I did not want to tell this story and so remained silent, but now, as I tell my story, as my personal dam breaks, we are all at the *Edge of Silence*.

My father died on 24 December 2009, without passing on his stories, only small bits and pieces. With several cancer scares under my belt, and knowing I won't live forever, my kids began showing that same desperate need to know me better before the chance left us forever. I had better start writing.

Looking back on my life, I saw a lot of my father in myself. He was an uncomplicated man; most everything was black and white and very little grey. I inherited those traits and world view as well. I kept putting off telling my stories to the kids much like he put off telling me his stories. Our reasons may be different, but the outcome was going to be the same.

It would have been helpful had my father at least told me some of the things to expect in the military. The experience he had in a combat zone and the things he dealt with ethically might have helped me frame a better understanding of what I might face. Even though none of my children decided to enter the military, my feeling is that maybe by letting them see what I went through and the feelings that coursed through my body and soul will help them navigate the tough environment of being parents and hopefully have a place for those that sacrificed much more than I did to make the United States great.

This period between 1974-1979 has a lot of history. Vietnam ended, Nixon got impeached, Arabs attacked Israel, again... and were defeated... again, and Carter became the President of the United States. Iranian revolutionaries took over the U.S. Embassy in Iran and the President of Egypt, Anwar Sadat, made peace overtures to Israel, and then, something happened that was never expected to happen: a peace treaty with Israel. Israel invaded Lebanon because of terrorist attacks and the Middle East became a powder keg once more.

Central America became ruled by dictatorships that were U.S. sponsored and the Red menace led by the Soviet Union expanded its tentacles throughout South America and slowly trickled upward to engulf Central America. The Iran-Contra Affair happened shortly afterward as did the Marine barracks bombing in Beirut, Lebanon. Not only did I live through all of this, but I was also an active participant. Can you imagine, I was eighteen years old and signing paperwork that requires, under penalty of perjury and worse, that I not talk about the missions for thirty years? I had to sign what the government called "Non-disclosure Forms." How cool is that? Cool enough that I get to tell you now because I am way past getting in trouble for telling. We're well past the Edge of Silence.

Please do not take this as a factual account of

anyone's history but my own. This is my attempt at making a memoir that is an enjoyable read as well as keeping a factual account of my life during this time. After over 40 years, unfortunately, I don't remember all the names of everyone, so I took the liberty of making up some of them. I also had to guess at the big picture because none of the higher powers sought out my expertise or advice regarding how to prosecute world domination issues. I don't doubt that I made the correct assumptions, but still, I needed to guess. Therefore, this might make for a fictional account in some areas.

To get a real feel for the Marine Corps Boot camp, you should watch parts of two movies–*The Boys in Company C* and *Full Metal Jacket*, both of which were produced after I attended boot. When I watched these movies, I about shit my pants, I became so scared the D.I.'s (Drill Instructors) were going to come through the screen and clasp me by the short hairs! I made sure that I added my bent to what the movies showed or failed to show regarding the enjoyment the D.I.'s derived by the issuance of the pain and suffering that became part of our everyday experience.

I also should mention that this memoir happened to be easy to write in some areas, might bore you in some others, and caused me to have some sleepless nights, because I brought up old memories that are heart-pounding and mind-blowing. I had to walk away from writing at one point because of the sheer intensity of what I happened to be writing. Those memories are all here as best as I can remember, and I hope to put you in the dirt right next to me.

The things that I write about do not rule my life; they are just part of my being. I've accepted them and hide them in a special box, in my brain. I would like to think of them as learning experiences to help me grow into a better person.

As I love to tell my kids:

"What we have here is an opportunity to excel."

I'm still waiting for them to correct my *Cool Hand Luke* quote, but it's part of my joy as a father and a former sniper to keep giving them easy shots at me.

Here is what I want for my grandkids to take from this—when you read my story, remember, it doesn't matter where you came from, how bad things look, how difficult the journey might be. You can rise above it, make mistakes, and keep getting better. Hold and judge yourself against yourself, don't compare yourself to others, don't worry about what's fair and what others get that you don't, be the person you want to be, and work like hell to accomplish your view of yourself.

"Tell me I'm a good man."

From *Saving Private Ryan*, the ending at the cemetery.

Mark Sikorski, 2022
The Few, the Proud, the Marines
Semper Fidelis

Prologue

"Those who cannot remember the past are condemned to repeat it." –Santayana

The past. It sits on your shoulder like a hawk patiently waiting for its prey. You can learn from it or die of it. I chose to learn one excruciating lesson at a time.

Could my father have passed on his experiences to help me learn? No, I guess not. For whatever reasons he chose, he would not or could not disclose much at all. Getting tidbits from him was like pulling the teeth of a bull. I know I would have heard him - problem is I probably wouldn't have listened.

All the same, I wish he would have given me the opportunity to hear his stories and maybe some of my future life decisions would have been better. I hope I will learn by watching others. The truth is, up until now, I went out and made mistakes on my own. I was one of those young men who didn't believe what others said and would do stupid things to prove I could and suffer the consequences.

Much as I want my kids to avoid the same path, I guess there's a generational cycle to most of this. We face the same struggles until each of us breaks free. As they say, "The apple doesn't fall far from the tree."

My learning about real ethics in our world begins with my Bar-Mitzvah. What I learned in studying for my Bar-Mitzvah speech is that humanity sucks. We kill, maim, and hurt to get what we want. We need defenders of the innocent and a process to shape and form them to be the barrier against evil in society. The problem is: who makes sure the defenders don't become the problem?

Being Jewish, with a synagogue full of survivors of the Holocaust, I need to be mindful of my facts. My research takes me down a dark tunnel to view horrors that a thirteen-year-old should not see but needs to. The final solution of killing all the Jews the Nazis could get their hands on. I can't stress enough the pictures that will stay as nightmares in my mind. Neighbors pointing out neighbors and marking them as different. Abusing and hunting Jews down and transporting them to death camps. Confiscation of all they owned and the dehumanization of the victims. And then: death. A horrible, torturous murdering of people just because a madman and former Army corporal had convinced an entire country to deem them subhuman and to extirpate them.

As I look over the one hundred or so people sitting in the synagogue, I'm thinking two things, *who the hell are these people, and this had better work Dad!* My heart is in my throat and it's choking me to death. I've listened to all the prayers, traditional talks, and the Rabbi's commentaries. Everyone is staring at me, some faces with smiles, others with some intensity and others, waiting for me to screw-up. Now, it's my turn and it is scary.

Why do they put thirteen-year-olds through this? It's crazy, don't they know we don't know shit! As I get up and trudge to the pulpit, all I can think of is, *"Don't trip, eyes up, smile, don't trip!"*

Now my hands seize onto the bema and hold on for dear life and I begin to utter my speech. My Torah portion is about the Sin of Commission and the Sin of Omission. My father and I went through some of the things he faced in Vietnam[1] in the hopes of explaining how the two sins are different. Learning what my father had to do and the risk he took in saving lives made the point more personal. I can understand better what others should have done as a group to help our people in Europe during World War II. My father put his life on the line by making sure he avoided the Sin of Omission when several soldiers tried to execute two Vietnamese men for no other reason than "they looked wrong."

He came across the situation while walking to work at the Air Base. On the street, three U.S. soldiers were pushing and making two Vietnamese men kneel. He asked what they were doing and was told to mind his own business. When one soldier raised his weapon to possibly fire, he stepped in. My father

---

1   (P. 415) Staff Sgt. Joe Sikorski at Tan Son Nhut Air Base, 1969

pushed one soldier down and grabbed the other two and threatened to kill them if they tried to shoot the two men. As luck would have it, the Vietnamese Military Police came by and assisted my father. After some translation, the two men were only trying to find food for their families. By my father's actions, he ended the Sin of Commission by these three soldiers and also avoided the Sin of Omission by stepping in and taking responsibility for someone else's life, a stranger in a strange country who he didn't know.

Imagine if the world in 1939, or sooner didn't turn their collective backs on the Jewish people. What if a defender halted the Sin of Commission of murder? This is what Israel is. This is why I will accept "Never Again." This is why accepting the requirement of Bar-Mitzvah is so important. I want to be like my hero, my father, in helping others by stopping or avoiding those two sins.

At the time, I had no idea just how close to war this lesson would bring me. Other people, other places, other conflicts would damn sure wrap me up in that black hole of death and destruction where I would have to make life and death decisions for others.

I go on to talk about the examples in the Torah and how we need to open our eyes to the discrimination that goes on in the world, not to accept it or condone it, but change it no matter at what level. I want the survivors of the Holocaust that are present to understand that a new generation is growing up and will continue to defend not only Jews but all people who need assistance from the two Sins. My watchword, I promise, will be "Never Again."

As I end my speech I look out and smile.

Didn't screw up. Yes!

I look down at my hands, white, guess I gripped pretty hard. It takes a supreme effort to let go of the bema. I had successfully navigated my Bar Mitzvah! I wish I had thought of the future children I might have, it would have brought an evil smile to my face knowing that their future would bring joy to me watching them go through this trial and suffer just as much as I did.

Time rapidly advanced and just two years later, the Arabs attacked Israel for the sixth time, and this time, the United States almost blinked. The greatest country on earth actually thought about turning their back on Israel. The United States came close to committing the Sin of Omission.

Never again.

On 9 October 1974, I went to religious school, and we were told the school was canceled. Half of my teachers had disappeared, and I asked, "Where are they?" The principal told us that the teachers bought their plane tickets and left to fight for Israel. The Arabs had attacked during the holiest day of the year for Jews, Yom Kippur. That was on Saturday, 6 October. The Israelis backs were against the wall and needed fighters desperately. What went through my head is, *"I can't wait to make that kind of commitment."*

This drove me. It made me want to hold up the watchword "Never Again" to the world.

When my teachers came back and school resumed, I listened to stories of bravery and sadness and the determination of the fighters. I secretly wanted to be one of those fighters, a Maccabee. My Jewish name is Mordechai. It means warrior.

Never again.

That had been my watchword. My promise. I owed it to my family and my people and myself to do something.

Chapter 1

8 May 1978

Six years after my Bar-Mitzvah, I am nineteen years old and have arrived at a point in my life I never imagined. Without understanding how fate may have played a role, the warrior imagined in my thoughts is now embodied in my life. I have the training and the experience needed to be a soldier should Israel ever call upon me to fight. A hop, skip, and a jump by aircraft, but a million miles away from reality, Beirut, Lebanon is where my boots land. A Jew armed with a weapon of destruction, dropped in the middle of over one million people hell bent on killing me, my people, and my religion. I think the Marines knew exactly what they were doing with me.

What kind of sins will I have to atone for?

It's about a three-hundred-yard shot, maybe a little closer. The world was supposed to be done with this kind of horror, to learn from the past and live up to our promise to never let this happen again. And yet here we are: where all of our targets threaten my watchword.

Why are these men doing this now? Fuck them.

As I focus on the first man, Danny pats my shoulder, "Ski looks like the last guy has a long gun. Not sure, so take a look."

"Roger that."

Slowly moving the rifle and attached scope to the left to try to track the last man we see, I have to move slowly otherwise my sight picture will be lost.., the point where the bullet locked and loaded in my rifle will enter his body and terminate his life. He is in my sights. The heat from the cement blocks sends a mirage of shimmer in front of my position. My whole environment is calling to me and letting me make the calculations needed to deliver death. I see something is sliding over the rocks next to the men, like a small snake, it might be a scope. Another oversight, no intel on whether the Arabs have scopes to make the long shots effectively. Now we know they might.

"Danny, I don't see a long gun, but it looks like a scope. Too dark to see in the shadow of the rocks. Lock-on that for me and watch, okay?"

Danny looks through his spotters' scope and says, "Shit Ski, can't see it either, what about you, Sarge?"

Gunny Ornelas is the third team member keeping us out of trouble. He isn't a sniper and mutters, "You shitbirds are the experts, move Danny, let me look."

Danny responds, "Never mind old man, your eyes suck anyway."

No rifle yet. The temperature feels like it's 100 degrees even though I know it's not. Sweat drips off of my nose and onto the stock of my rifle. *Close your eyes, breathe, relax; open your eyes...wait for*

Danny. The Deadly Sin of Omission, the Arabs could be pointing the long rifle at me and I wouldn't know that they could hit me, Danny or Gunny. We don't know what weapon they are shooting with, if they have scopes, what their egress area is. The list goes on.

Danny is so close to me our bodies are practically touching. I can feel him tense, he sees something. He whispers, "Hey Ski, the Ahab in the front has a rifle. It looks like he is putting a scope on. They must have passed it up to him."

Damn, I'm tracking the wrong guy and need to shift to the first target. I move the barrel slowly. Got him.

"We've taken incoming from that area a few days ago, I say light them up Ski." That's all the permission needed from the Gunny.

Target acquired, I pinpoint the rifle, and it looks like he's getting ready to line up a shot toward the embassy—

My focus is on the target, and forgetting everything around me, and yet I can't help but lose it for a second—

My mind runs back in time to my high school rifle team. It's a Springfield 1903 .30-6 from WW1. It has a clip with 5 rounds and is a bolt action. This weapon, when I was fourteen years old, is the exact rifle I learned to shoot with. The one that had been almost as tall as me. Fantastic rifle, also good in the right hands out to one thousand yards.

I snap back into the present and understand

my first lesson. The past informs the present. The present shapes the future.

Just as I did at fourteen, I will myself to breathe deeply, but my throat is already closing, and a film of sweat coats my skin.

Stick with what you know, practiced this a thousand times. Train the way you will fight; you will fight the way you train.

The crosshairs are on the side of his head. Air is now filling my lungs. Breathe in, let it out, relax, squeeze slowly. Let it be a surprise. Pull, slowly pull the trigger. The crack of a weapon firing echoes off the buildings and shatters the edge of silence.

Chapter 2

June 1976

There was a lot of time to think about the last few years and the promise I made during my Bar-Mitzvah. I can't answer that I held up my end completely. The enjoyment of high school took over my brain, and hormones being what they are, I forgot enough promises to count.

I made my first promise in 1961, a decision that opened the world to me.

My father, Joe Sikorski met my mother, Rachel (Kiki) Pimenta[2], in Casablanca, Morocco in 1959, courtesy of the U.S. Air Force. The marriage resulted in the production of a wonderful, at least in my eyes, little boy.[3] I was born in Casablanca and we stayed in Morocco till 1961[4]. My first move was to Spokane Washington (Larson AFB) with the USAF, where my brother, David, was born. I knew from the moment I saw him that my heart and my soul had already made a promise to him. I would take care of him in every way a human as precious as him deserved.

Unfortunately, he was born with severe

---

2   (P. 415) Joseph Sikorski and Rachel (Kiki) Pimenta
      wedding in Casa Blanca, Morocco 1958
3   (P. 416) Kingdom of Morocco Cert of Citizenship/Birth
4   (P. 417) Joe and Mark Sikorski, Casa Blanca, Morocco,
      May 1959

Cerebral Palsy. What this meant was that he could not walk, talk, or control his body. He needed twenty-four-hour care. Rather than put him into an institution that the doctors recommended, my parents elected to keep him at home and work with him to give him the best life possible.

Our first test of that commitment came when my father received orders in 1963 and we made our next move to France. We spent several years in France and I remember touring several countries. I learned my first language, French, and worked on English. After four years in France, the Air Force reassigned my Dad back to the United States and the location was Tucson, Arizona (Davis Monthan AFB) in 1967.

My first real memories of the United States were around 8 years old. The new school in Tucson made me understand that I was different. I quickly learned to fight because I couldn't speak English very well and kids in school were not nice to anyone they viewed as different. I qualified as very different. I didn't speak English; I had a disabled brother that I took everywhere with me, I am Jewish which no one understood, and had a mom that looked different than all the other moms (Middle Eastern.)

Most every neighborhood we lived in on a military base had the same type of kids, just different names. Our last move, in 1970, brought me to Riverside, California. (March Air Force Base.) My best friends here were mainly black and Hispanic because the military neighborhood we lived in was all enlisted, which made it more diversified than the population of our city as a whole.

I think because of this diverse group of kids, my brother being disabled and my father's guidance, I became blind to the differences in people. Didn't matter where you came from, what you spoke, your religion, or the color of your skin. If you did right by me and were honest, then I gave back equally.

So when I tell you my dad's refusal to talk about the war would years later strike me like a slap in the face, you'll understand what came next.

I'm at home waiting for my father to show up from work and had made up my mind to have the "talk." How long is he going to let me live at home after graduation? There was an inkling of an idea of what I wanted to do but decided it would be smart to get his opinion. He grew up in a tough neighborhood in Pittsburgh and made some hard decisions of what he wanted his life to look like so maybe he could guide me. My Dad retired from the Air Force as a Senior Master Sergeant. He traveled the world and served one combat tour in Vietnam. He raised two sons, one who needed constant care and then my brother.

No, I think I have that reversed. David needed the constant care, but he will tell you different! How strange here to see that it is in the telling that I've rediscovered a memory I thought I knew so well.

At this time, dad was now working at the

Accounting and Finance office at March Air Force Base, California. I know that his career choice in the Air Force helped him get a great career outside the Air Force. When he left the military, the base commander offered him a job to be the head of the accounting department for the base under one condition. He had to get a bachelor's degree in two years while working in the job. He accepted the position, started school while in the military, finished year one and then used his veterans benefits to finish the second year while working at his new civilian job. Four years of college in a little over two years. He knew something about sacrifice from this as well, his deployment to Vietnam, his 21 years in the military, and devoting his life to my brother. The military had been a great choice for him as well as being good to him.

I spread out my homework on the dining room table, for the first time in a long time, so that when he gets home it looks like I had been studying. (I am in summer school.)

If I had been studying this whole time, I might be going to college instead of being a deadbeat, too late now.

In comes my father, all tired from the drive home and expecting his usual. Read the paper, eat dinner, use the bathroom, and watch the news. Surprise, your son wants to talk to you about real adult shit. Ready?

"Leave me alone," he says.

"It's important, Dad."

"Someone die?"

"No, Dad. I want to talk to you about my future."

"Why? You leaving soon?"

"Uh, no, I don't think so, why?" Now I think, *Maybe this might not be a good idea, is he going to kick me out?*

"Then leave me alone. We can talk after dinner."

"Okay, Dad."

It wasn't supposed to be this hard. Maybe he had a rough day. Well, he did promise to talk after dinner. Dinner goes fine and he pulls his chair away from the table and relaxes. I'm guessing he is ready to talk so now I have to figure out a way to convince him to let me stay here after graduation. He sounded like he might be looking forward to me leaving.

How could that be? I am his favorite son, right?

It isn't like I didn't think about what to say, but I butchered it anyway.

"Dad, I'm not sure what I want to do going forward. What I'm good at or how I can fit in the real world. My options are limited, and I guess I could have done better in school. I'm not that big of a dumbshit, I swear."

"You are a dumbshit, but that's okay. I guess I was too. If you're asking, I think you should join the Air Force. You know I left Pittsburgh to see the world, and I did[5]. I've gone places and seen things none of my friends ever have or will. I learned a lot and now I have a great job, and on top of that I get a check every month from the Air Force because I retired at thirty-nine years old."

"I understand, Dad, but what do you think I'm good at?"

"Well, ROTC, you love it and enjoy being in charge. The military will be good for you. The other thing you're good at is working on cars. You have a mechanical ability because of rebuilding engines, transmissions, and carburetors. You're a natural grease monkey. You could do that in the military and get certifications and that would guarantee you a great job after the military. You also make friends easily and love to talk, so maybe being a politician?" He pauses long enough for me to think he might be paying me a real compliment. "Just joking Marco, no one would listen to you."

"Thanks, Dad." I want to call him an ass, but that would be stupider than talking to him about this in the first place.

At that point, dad gets up and smiles, and as he wanders away, he mutters, "Let me know when you figure it out, dumbshit."

----

5   (P. 417) Leaving Pittsburgh

Chapter 3

July 1976

I joined the Army JR. ROTC program in high school to get some training for two purposes. One was in case the military drafted me for Vietnam, I would be ahead of the curve, but since the war was at that point over for the United States, that would not be a consideration. The second was that having some military experience would be handy if I had to follow in the footsteps of my religious schoolteachers and go to Israel to fight.

I decide to talk to my high school friends over the next couple of weeks to see what their plans might be. Secretly, I'm hoping one or two of them want to join up with me in the school's Buddy program. It would be the first step to entering the military.

In high school, most of my friends are in the ROTC program. My closest are Bob Kingman, Tim Saccucci, Pat Gonzalez, and Gary Liswood. I've known Bob and Tim for four years. The four musketeers, plus Gary the resident computer nerd.

Bob is a handsome guy, good shape, and could get the girls with just a look and a smile. Great for him, bad for us if we wanted one of the girls for ourselves. Well, until I learned to give him a little competition. He had a nonchalant manner that made it seem he didn't care about things, but I knew him well enough to know that wasn't the case.

Case in point, once I turned on the charm, Bob had to play catch up! The two of us always competed to see who could date more girls. Mad as he was to lose, we evened out in the end.

Tim is the big guy of the group. To state Tim was intimidating is an understatement. He has the size but never tried to see if he had the talent for football. I bet he would have been great. It was good to have Tim lurking in the back of our group in case my mouth opened up to the wrong people—and I hate to spoil things, but my mouth will soon get me into trouble like I'd never seen.

Pat is the small guy and, for some reason, just fit in. He stayed excited and tended to be high strung, but had a kind word and smile to reveal his true self lurking underneath all of that anxiety. He thinks things through and tries to keep us out of trouble, which is surprising because he moves at the speed of light.

Gary is always lost in his little world of electronics. His mom would give me money to get him out of the house so he could hopefully meet girls. It was a losing battle with him. He loved his new computer toys more than anything else. He had these floppy drives, kilobytes, green screens, and games.

Have I conveyed just how much I loved these guys? How much I *still* love them? It was a great group of friends and we all got along pretty well. I felt sad thinking it might come to an end, but maybe I could convince them to join up with me. I usually led the group due to my "controlling nature," so maybe

I could control this. That went about as well as it usually does, but that's the heart of a Marine. Never take defeat for an answer.

Since Tim and I work together, I will ask him first about his plans. We are working at the Texaco gas station on Arlington Avenue in Riverside, California. The station is owned by his stepdad so getting a job there with Tim was easy.

"What are your plans after graduation, Tim?"

"Its all worked out. I get to go to whatever college I want because of the gas station. They have a scholarship program for kids of owners so that's what I'm going to do."

This didn't help me. I figured since he is a slug, we would be in the same boat. Maybe we could do something together. Nope, he had a plan because of his stepdad.

A few days later I met up with Bob and we had a long conversation.

"Bob, what are you going to do after graduation?"

"You know my brother is at the Air Force Academy and my dad knows some people. I'm starting to write to the representatives to see if I can get a nomination. If I can't, I'll just go to Cal Poly for engineering."

WTF? Bob, engineering? Who is he kidding, he isn't that smart. Great. And I thought Bob was stupid. Two down and I still end up last.

I am afraid to meet with Gary because he is

the smart one. No telling what he is going to do. Later in the week I met up with him and asked him the same questions.

"I'm in the CAP, Civil Air Patrol and I can get an ROTC scholarship with the Air Force and go to school in San Diego. Plus, I think these computers will be big in the future so I'm going to keep working with this stuff."

Computers, right. All you do is play stupid text-based games. How are those plastic boxes going to do anything? Loser. All those electronics and floppy discs, just like him!

Damn it, three down and they are all going to college.

Looks like my last bet is on Pat. I met with Pat the very next day and low and behold, he isn't going to college. I figured he and Gary would be the ones going to college.

"Why not?" I ask.

"Don't have to. Dad's getting me a job at the Stater Brothers grocery where he manages. I can work there, then start school later and have the company pay for it. I probably will just stay there and work, and one day maybe manage it."

Maybe he can get me a job there? No, it's on the Mexican side of town and they only hire Spanish speakers.

This is no help either.

It looks like I am on my own to decide what to do going forward. Not a hard decision. I had nothing, no money, and didn't want to borrow money for school. This meant the military, but which service? At this point, the Air Force won out.

As the summer wore on and my senior year came closer to an end, there had to be a decision made. I tried to talk to my Dad as much as I could, but he seemed somewhat distant. I know he wanted the best for me but only two words would ever come out of his mouth. Air Force. Back to the black and white. No gray area. No matter what I asked, how I tried to point out the pros of the other services, it was a moot point. I know that I was a disappointment because I wasn't this star athlete, and I didn't have any kind of brains or a personality that drew people in other than girls. Not exactly star material for my dad.

I felt like making this decision, one he could be proud of, one I could point at and say I finally made the "right choice", would be his reward for being my Dad, my hero and mentor. Figuring this out, I felt confident I could finally say, "I made my decision, Dad, and I am going to go Air Force blue." Most important was that I had decided that learning something useful would be smart and after my commitment was up, I could take that training to the real world and use it.

I am pretty excited to sit down with my dad and tell him the news. I look into my mind and imagine his chest puffing out, a big smile on his face, his hand reaching around to pat my back as he says,

"I'm proud of you, son."

I'm not a big dreamer, but this one felt so real that I convinced myself it would happen.

As five o'clock nears, I once again put out the homework charade and wait for the door to open. In he comes, perpetually discontent about *something*, but the normal look on his face will turn into a bright glowing smile once I tell him the news. I'll no longer be the loser son!

"Hi Dad," I practically shout. "Can we talk a few minutes?"

"Why?"

"Umm, made my decision and wanted to go over it with you."

"What decision?

You got to be kidding me, right? Here I am, agonizing over this and he doesn't know what decision?

"What service I want to join up with, Dad."
"Talk to me when I get out of the bathroom." Off he goes with his newspaper. Crap, (pun intended), now I have to wait another half hour or more!

I'm never going to do that to my kids, if I ever have any.

Even worse, homework is out, and I bet I'm now expected to actually do some. Oh well, such is life.

Around a half hour later, Dad shows up and sits down across from me. No happy face. He knows something is up, and he isn't looking forward to it.

He sits there, his cold steely blue eyes looking right through me. It's as if two lasers are pushing their way to the back of my brain to see if I'm lying and I haven't said anything yet.

This is child abuse!

Here goes.

"Dad."

"What?"

So, all the speech thing I had thought about, the words and smooth talk all disappear. His eyes are boring like drills into my skull. I think my mouth is moving but it isn't. Shit.

"I'm going to join the Air Force!" I blurt out.

His mouth moves like he wants to say something, but nothing comes out. Not yet. He's staring straight at me, and he leaves me in silence long enough for me to think I've gotten him wrong. He's not in a bad mood. He's just thinking of what to say. The words of pride and acknowledgment are coming!

"Good. You're not as dumb as you look," he says. And he gets up, goes to the TV, turns it on, and sits down on the couch.

Hmmm.... That went well. What did I expect? A trophy or something?

I don't blame him for not being proud of me yet. All I've done is announce what I'll do. I haven't actually *done* anything yet.

Things will be different once I'm in uniform. He'll see.

###

It is now time to get off my ass and get this ball rolling. The first step is to get to the recruitment office for the military. But before that happens, Tim sends me bad news that opens a new opportunity. That new opportunity would be meeting Mr. Williams.

It's 22 July, and as I drive into work the radio is playing "California Girls" from the Beach Boys." I noticed that all the pumps were locked up at the station. That didn't make any sense. I went into the office and Tim is there along with his mom and brother. Things didn't look good because it appeared Tim had been crying and everyone looked like a fire had swept through the station.

"Tim, what's going on, what's wrong?" I ask.

"Shit hit the fan, Marco. My dad died of a heart attack and we found out some stuff. He had a lot of debt and we can't pay any of the bills."

"Fuuccck... Tim. I'm so sorry. That's messed up. Do you want to get out of here?"

Tim broke down again and cried he has nothing left. No scholarship, no job, and no future. I felt so bad for him and told him,

"We'll get through this; we'll find new jobs."

Before the courts locked up all the financials, Tim's mom handed me my last paycheck and hugged me and asked that I help Tim as best I could. I told her I would.

I quickly gave Gary a call because I knew

his dad worked at the Van Buren Drive-In Theater. I am hoping both Tim and I could get an interview and get back to making some money to pay for our date nights—with girls, not each other! Things will change once I'm in the service, but until I step into that recruitment office, the most important thing in my life is girls.

Fortunately for us, Gary's dad got us the interview with this really big man named Mr. Williams. I had no clue this man ran the theater. At first blush, he looked like those Italian guys who killed people, like a hitman. He reminded me of one of those movie gangsters with the slicked-back hair that smiled and asked you which knee you wanted to be broken first. This is a man you didn't screw around with. Mr. Williams decided to hire us. I guess we were just a couple of new warm bodies so no risk on his part.

Chapter 4

August 1976

I am now on the back edge of seventeen when I strut into the recruiter's office on Brockton Street in sunny Riverside California. It is a nice day and I had driven my Fiat 850 sport spider[6]. A yellow/tan two-seat convertible that had an engine you could wrap your arms around and pick up. It is a really small car but at the time, cool for a kid and better than the Pontiac station wagon with the fake wood sides (my first car). Believe me, the Fiat helped with the chicks - even though my good looks and charm usually did the trick, it is nice to have that ace in the hole! Into the gates of heaven or hell, I crossed that threshold of the recruiter's office and just stared into my destiny.

The services are all lined up along a shiny hallway in a lit-up row. Army, Air Force, Navy, and Marines.

Who will get the chance to claim my loyalty?

Well, I go up to the Air Force counter and take a seat. There are probably 15-18 men ahead of me.

WTF? How long am I going to be here? I am hoping to go out on a date later and this is going to cut into things.

It isn't every Saturday night I had off from work! Who am I kidding? I probably will stay home for pizza night. As I looked down the line, the Army

---

6   (P. 418) Me and my 1970 Fiat 850 Sport Spyder

guys were doing good business; they had their dress green uniforms on. They looked okay, for Army guys. The Air Force guys were in dark blue pants and light blue shirts, kind of casual, but what would you expect from the Air Force? The Navy guys didn't have too many people around them and they had white uniforms and one guy in a black and gold dress uniform. Imagine trying to keep the white uniform clean—no way.

And at the very end are the Marines.

Well, two of them.

Hmmm...

I take a little stroll down to the end.

Couldn't hurt, right?

These guys look sharp. Dark blue pants, red strip down the side, and tan shirts that were so crisp, a razor might not have been sharper. One Marine, guessing it had to be the officer, is wearing his dress uniform. I figured with Bob gone that I'd be the sharpest looking guy in the room, but it looked like it would be me who had some competition against other Marines. I'll have to learn fast how to make my own uniform look just as good, or better. Anyways, sauntering on over and acting cool, shuffling around, picking up literature, and trying to act as if I know what I'm doing, I take it all in. I probably looked like an idiot, so I probably am just what they are looking for.

As I glanced at the floor, and it gleamed, some big Marine came over and put his hand on my back. I thought his hand covered my whole back, that's scary. I had been in lots of fights, but this guy looked like he could snap my neck by just looking at me. Then he smiled...that didn't look good, it appeared the smile is hurting him and that he might just rip my head off with his teeth to feel better. I couldn't move, wanted to, bad, really bad but happened to be afraid that he might hit me, so I just smiled back. His voice is what you would imagine a grizzly sounding like if it could talk.

"How can I help you?" he pronounced.

I looked at his name tag and it revealed his name: Smith. Perfect, the most common name you can think of. How can I remark, "Smith" convinced me to join? Why couldn't it have been "Thor" or "Undertaker" or better yet, "I kill you now'?" Nope, had to be Gunnery Sergeant Smith.[7]

As I stood close to him, not because of wanting to, but he just got close, I could smell stale cigarettes and aftershave. Not a winning combination. I think smiling back at him made him mad. Most everything seemed to make him mad, but he had to play nice, which made him madder. He removed his meat hook of a hand and again asked how he could help me.

Shit, how do I know? What am I supposed to stammer, "I am here to join the Air Force and made the mistake of walking over here?"

Believing he might have killed me, I decided to answer in my cool voice (probably sounded like a

7   (P. 418) Marine Corps saying

10-year-old girl,) "I want to fly Airplanes."

Oh God, that smile again. He knows he's got me hooked. Gunny Smith commented, "Oh, you want to be a Zoomie? Let's get you in front of the Colonel. Sit here, now."

He can get me a flying spot. Really (really Marines have planes that they let 17-year old fly? As I stated, stupid, right?) Okay, I am ready to bite.

I feel the sudden urge to run. My feet dance in place, but I don't dare let Smith see, so my feet dance in my shoes. He puts his 150-pound hand on my back to help me sit. I thought, *"He could probably chase me down if I ran."* So, I sat.

Next up, I meet another Marine with the curious name Colonel Smith... Naw, just joking, I have no idea what his name is, just Colonel. He is so nice, he had me escorted to another desk by my new buddy, the Gunny, and again, the 150lb hand assisted me in sitting. The Colonel made some small chitchat about the Marines and what my plans were after high school. I didn't impress him too much by working at the Drive-In. If he only knew about all the girls I met there, and all the extracurricular activities that were enjoyed, maybe he would be a little more impressed, but it wasn't the right time to bring it up. He probably had a daughter my age and, well, let us announce my life might have been forfeited at this point.

My heart is beating a thousand beats per minute, one of those "be careful what you wish for, you might get it moments." Did I want this? Maybe if I leave myself an "out" in case things are not really what I want would be smart, even if I have no clue what I want. It's one thing to say you want something, another when it's offered and you get buyers' remorse. It's almost like someone is cheating you and you think they are, but then aren't really sure.

"Sir, this is what it boils down to, flying airplanes is the most important thing I want and if you can make that happen, I will join." There. I am thinking, *No way he can answer yes, and my freedom would be guaranteed.*

The Colonel gave me this nice smile, not like Gunny's, and added, "I believe that is something we can work on for you."

My thoughts were, *"What a salesman! He must be a millionaire by now. Oh, crap. Now what?"* He just ripped the arms off of that "out."

"Okay," I finally said, embarrassed that this was all I could think to say. Then I mumbled, "Tell me more."

My dad told me to mention "tell me more" to the Air Force people when they described some jobs I might qualify for. That would make me sound smart. Hopefully, it would work with the Marines. The Colonel mentioned that if my performance in the Marines was superior, the possibility of getting a scholarship to go to college and then become a pilot would be a probability. Signing up for three years, he could guarantee me that I would be looked at very hard for a college scholarship. (Little did I know that everyone had that opportunity.)

What is going on in my head? All I heard is that the nice man said I could fly, didn't he? Look at those uniforms, that is sure to get the girls even faster. Look at how many muscles these guys have, betting I will look like them too. What a deal.

Next thing you know, I'm signing this piece of paper.

What am I signing?

He added, not to worry, it's just an indication of interest and there are two options. One, my parents can sign the paperwork to let me in early. Or two, waiting till my eighteenth birthday in April. All I need to do is choose which option and sign.

Then he asked something strange.

"Are you in trouble with the law, did you happen to get a girl pregnant, or do your parents want you out? If so, the Marines can arrange for you to join earlier and get you to boot camp faster if needed."

"No," I declared, though it may have felt like that last one sometimes. "None of those things, and I think my parents love me, maybe, hopefully?"

I quickly gathered up my copy of the paperwork and explained I would probably come back after my birthday. Thinking, *that worked well, right? I get to fly, wear cool uniforms and be with lots of girls!* I could not wait to tell my Dad. I am such a stud!

Chapter 5

It was a nice day, warm weather for August, and cruising with the top down. Since it was a Saturday, I decided to go over to the Tyler Mall and check out the girls. They were always enough 16- to 17-year-old girls running around in shorts and tank tops, and sometimes the gold standard, 18- to 19-year olds!

Bob and Tim would be there waiting for me, and after we roamed around, we were going over to Castle Park. That is where the real action was. Castle Park had some games you could play on a screen, about the size of a small TV. Gary was always getting these games for his Franklin Computer but mostly they were text-based, these were entirely different. These things moved on the screen and we could control them to shoot and move. That was way cool. We had Asteroids, Lunar Lander, Tempest, Depth Charge, and of course, Pong! I don't know why, but the girls always liked watching us play games. At 10 cents to a quarter for the bigger games, it was worth it.

I met up with Bob and Tim at the food area, got some ice cream from Zipps and I told them what I was planning.

"Well guys, I decided to join up with the Marines. What do you think about that?"

Bob starts laughing and answers, "Your dad is going to have a shit fit!"

Tim looked at me and shook his head. "Your dad is going to kill you, but have fun!"

I asked them how their plans were working out so far or are they going to join me in the "brotherhood?"

Bob comments, "My plans haven't changed yet, either the Academy or Cal Poly. Whatever I can get."

Tim states, "I don't have a fucking clue. My world is still upside down and it sucks. Maybe I'll look at the military."

That was a change, maybe I can con Tim into joining with me. After all, we do make a pretty good team at the Drive-In. Now I had to talk Bob into maybe enlisting. Then I told Bob, "Who wants to spend four years going to a military school, and then have to be in the military for four or five more years? Why not just join up?"

Tim thought that was a good point, but Bob, probably smarter than both of us, observes, "It's better to let the military pay for school, moron, then when you graduate, you can be an officer and make more money rather than go enlist, get paid nothing and then still have no college when your time is up."

"Bob you're a dumb shit, how about getting out of Riverside and starting your life rather than just sitting on your ass?" He didn't have a good answer to that, and at least at the time—funny how fast that changed—it looked like I won the argument.

We finished off our Ice Cream at Zipps and took off to Castle Park, home of more girls than the mall! I met up with my girlfriend at the time, Janet and some of her friends. Janet Reddington was a four-foot 11-inch powerhouse of a girl. All of sixteen years old and on fire every time we were together. Long silky straight brown hair and a tight little body that was made for holding. I met her through some friends and although I was attracted to her, I knew we wouldn't be together. She is a head-spinning, foul talking, cigarette smoking (and weed), tattooed girl in great shape. Not the all-American blond hair, blue-eyed girl like my last four girlfriends. Janet proved me wrong, we did end up together. After we were together a couple of times, she came up to me and announced, "I choose you."

I asked her, "Choose me for what, exactly?"

Janet was not shy and announced, "Why, to be my new boyfriend."

That shocked me, but everything she does is shocking, I have never been with someone as active and constantly moving everywhere all at once as her. Most of the guys wanted to be with her, she just had that attraction. I probably showed little interest, so I became a conquest of sorts. Fine by me, I was conquered.

We talked a little bit about me joining the Marines and I must have hit a hot button. She was all for it and asked when we could be alone to talk about it. I replied, "As soon as possible!" Unfortunately, we had to stick around for a while. We all played a few games and the conversation turned to going to the beach as a group soon. Loved going to the beach and finding more girls wearing bikinis. I probably will be hit a few times by Janet, but she looks really good in her suit and also had a good sense of humor, so no problem.

There's more to life than this, more to me, but I'm young, and the part of me that knows better understands that however likely I think it is, this could be the last chance I have to see these girls. To talk to them. To remind myself I am alive before I so gleefully offer to sacrifice myself if it will keep people safe and free.

Now just imagine how well that kind of proud talk went with the girls. Joining the Marines quickly seemed like the best decision I'd ever made.

I knew I had to eventually face my dad and let him know that the man he raised is joining the Marines, not the pussy Air Force! Telling my friend's good-bye, I spring into my Fiat like a stud and yell, "Expect a call from me later tonight and if you don't hear from me, I'm dead."

Fortunately for me, I had to take Janet home, so she flies into the seat next to me and gives me that look. We definitely are not going home. I drive Janet over to the One Tree. This is an overlook high up on a small hilltop that overlooks the city. That little bundle of energy was happy to show me her thoughts on me joining the Marines.

Chapter 6

I get home and start thinking about how my dad is going to take all of this. We had a few conversations and he pretty much hated most politicians. His view of the world was changed after coming home from Vietnam. It was a tough time for him watching all the news and the animosity the general population had towards the military. Especially the poor guys that were in the field and could not order a change of anything. He felt that the politicians let the military down by running the war rather than letting the soldiers fight it the way it should be. Lucky for me, we were not discriminated against too much because our school had a lot of military kids going to it and we stuck together pretty well.

Guys coming back from Vietnam were called baby killers, murderers, and much worse. Jimmy Carter is the Democrat nominee and the current President, Ford, the Republican nominee for President. Ford took over for Richard Nixon, who resigned because of Watergate which was some sort of spy scandal the Republican Party put together to get Nixon reelected. Such was the depth of my understanding at the time.

In listening to the debates, Carter is more into Pacification and healing the nation. All this Kumbaya stuff and can we all hold hands and pray type of guy. Somewhat surprising since he is a graduate of the U.S. Naval Academy and was part of the design team for atomic power submarines. He left the military when his father passed away and went back to Georgia to run the family business—a Peanut farm. Somehow, along the way he became president. It's rumored that when he told his mom he was running for president, she said, "President of what?"

I know my father is going to vote for him because he doesn't trust the Republicans. The only part my father has a problem with is Carter wants to pardon all the draft dodgers from Vietnam. Dad feels betrayed because he did his tour of duty and was on the front lines. My Dad's feelings were that those who left for Canada or other places didn't deserve to get the freedoms of Americans. Ford, on the other hand, declares he is healing the nation and will be a strong hand militarily because the Soviet Union is still a threat. My dad is worried we will get into another war we can't win because of the politicians.

That is the reason my dad is not going to be happy with my decision, because I am going to join the Marines or Army. Anything that has to do with direct combat. He does not trust politicians and feels after what he saw in Vietnam, they don't care about the troops, only votes. Well, it was good to understand a bit of that, but it wasn't going to sway me one way or another at this point. All I cared about were girls, cars, and food, in that order!

Off to see the old man.

"Home, the place where, when you have to go there, they have to let you in."

46

I remember that from one of my English classes, and the author is Robert Frost. One thing for sure, I was happy that was true. As I came in the door, the aroma of freshly baked bread and tomato sauce overwhelmed my senses. Pizza from scratch was cooking. Saturday is pizza night and tonight was a night off. Usually, I work Friday, and Saturday nights and Sunday swap meets.

Here we go again, as soon as I came in the door, Dad stands up and comes over to me. He asked, "Did you sign up?"

"Sure did, Dad!"

"Let's see the paperwork and information they gave you. Any idea what you want to do?"

Well, we both knew I couldn't sign up because I was too young, but he is ready to help me research.

"Let's go over this tonight and get some direction. I'll help you understand all the different opportunities"

"Not a problem, Dad, but I asked to fly airplanes and they said that wouldn't be a problem."

Silence. Pause. Then he exploded. "Who is the lying son of a bitch that said that? Because I am going to go down on Monday and talk to them."

Uh oh, now what?

I figured that telling him I would be flying would placate things. Nope. So...

"Dad... Don't get mad—," stupid me, whenever you stammer that to any Dad, you know he's going to get mad "—but... I want to join the Marines." I hate how weak my voice sounds. I say it again before he can notice. "I mean, the MARINES!"

He looked at me and smiled. He rather looked like Gunnery Sgt Smith with that smile. Again, the smile got bigger. Those two cold steel blue eyes once again are drilling into my skull and he does not look happy even though there is a smile on his face.

"Marco, Marco, Marco, thank God I didn't raise two idiots." *Well, that was a surprise because we knew my brother was the dumb one.* "Yep, David got the brains. Only one idiot in this family, you!"

Wait, Dad just called me what? "Come on Dad! What's wrong with the Marines?"

"Cannon fodder."

"What the hell is cannon fodder?"

"In a nutshell, First to Die. You know how many Marines were wounded or died in 'Nam? One in four! That's 13,067 Marines killed, 88,633 wounded. Almost all my friends from high school that went into the Marines are either dead or wounded. You think that's what I want for you?"

"Dad, you don't have to worry about me being shot, I know how to duck!"

Well, he is pissed. I mean really pissed. How did I know? When Dad was upset, he yelled. When Dad was pissed, he wouldn't talk; his jaw would just start moving. He looked at me and growled, "You give me tight jaws."

Once upon a time, I asked him when he was in a good mood, what were tight jaws? He explained it was when someone got him so mad his jaws hurt because he kept them closed so tight, they hurt. Here I thought maybe he would be a little proud of me, but nope, I thought he was going to kill me.

He never let himself get too out of line when Mom was around, so I was glad to see her join the conversation, even if she was upset along with Dad.

"Why are you doing this to me, Marco? What's going on?"

This was one of the few times I ever heard Dad raise his voice to her. He just hissed, "Shut up Kiki and leave us."

Wow, am I going to get an ass-kicking from my father?

I was ready to run. I had no idea where, but I thought I might be able to get to the door before he got to me.

Maybe I can snatch something and hit him... No, bad idea, he would probably rip my arm off and hit me with the bloody end...

Okay, run it is. I got up to get the head start I needed and then he got up. Oh oh, shit.

Wasn't going to make it to the front door, now what?

In the drill sergeant tone, he yelled, "Sit down, now!"

I remember hearing that voice once before the Datsun dealership. The sales manager of a car dealership asked him to sit down. This was *after* he told them he didn't want to buy the car they showed

49

him. If there was one thing you had to know about dad, it was that when he said something, he meant it. You didn't question him like he hadn't already told you no.

Dad stood up, clutches one guy by the shirt, picked him up out of his chair, dragged him across the desk, smiled and roared, "Tell that asshole to get my keys!" (They took his car to check out what they would give him for it). The other guy ran off and I think the sales manager shit his pants.

When I told Dad I was joining the Marines and he told me to "sit," I wanted to react like those car dealership guys—shit my pants and run—but once again, I saw my life flash before my eyes, so I decided to sit. May as well be comfortable when he kills me.

About a minute went by and he sat down. He seemed a little deflated and sad.

I sure as shit am not going to whisper anything.

Maybe he forgot already. He was old, close forty-one-years old. Ancient to a teenage punk like me.

Now, he looked at me and speaks, "I'm sorry Marco, I just want you to really take some time and think about what you're planning on doing. It's great you have the time to think this over so don't rush to get in. I spent my time in Vietnam getting shot at, mortared and scared to death more times than I can count. I did my part so that you don't have too."

Even though he was Air Force, he told me stories of when he went out to several Special Forces base camps and FAC (forward air controller) areas as part of his job. He told me years ago about some firebases he had to go to and how he was sure his death was imminent because of the attacks he was defending against.

"Marco, I chose the Air Force because I needed to leave home. My dad was abusive to my mom and me and Norbert. I couldn't fight my dad back then, so I had to get out. Also, the town was a steel mill and coal mining town. You died young and I wanted to live. I told you my friends went into the Marines and Army, but I didn't want to get shot at. I needed a career and something that would make me money even if I left the service. You are a lot smarter than I was and you don't have to go into a combat branch. Your problem is that you just don't apply yourself."

What was I to say to that? I told him, "Don't worry Dad—," another stupid thing to babble to a dad "—I will give this a lot of thought."

That's about it. (Many many years later I asked my dad why he was so pissed. He was embarrassed and comments it was because he thought how selfish I was, what if I did die, or became injured, who would take care of David. Then he thought better of it and decided he was the selfish one. I needed to live my life and it wasn't fair to make his burden, my burden. My Dad was and is my Hero. He was never in his life selfish.)

I was supposed to call Tim and Bob up and tell them that I was still alive, but after all that, I just couldn't do it. Guess they could just figure my dad killed me. It was a quiet night, watched something on TV, kicked my little brother a few times, ate my pizza, and went to bed. After all, I did have to get up early for the swap meet, and my dreams of Janet were still waiting. The day wasn't a total loss!

Up until now, my Dad is always around to help pick up the stupid pieces of my life, but if I made the wrong decision, it was mine alone to face. Can't fix stupid!

This means that my biggest worry was that as much as I wanted to prove my dad wrong, there were no take backs if it turned out he was right.

Chapter 7

September 1976

"You cannot exaggerate about the Marines. They are convinced to the point of arrogance that they are the most ferocious fighters on earth–and the amusing thing about it is that they are." –Father Kevin Keaney, 1st MarDiv Chaplain, Korean War

The days wore on, getting cooler. Work, friends, girls, food, fixing up my car to go faster. I rebuilt the transmission and carburetor. I did think a lot about what my dad said. Made sense. Janet and I had talked a few times and she liked the idea of me going into the Marines more than any other service. I let her think that I would because the rewards were great. I talked to a lot of other people and most all observe the Marines were not the way to go, but they were some of the best fighters, pound for pound, anywhere in the world. I asked if they had to choose one military person to be next to them that they could count on, to a person, all declare, the U.S. Marine.

So, it's stupid for me to join an organization that almost everyone tells me not to join but if they ever needed what they considered the best, they would pick someone from that organization. Makes sense, right? Conflicted.

It should come as no surprise that the man I

admired more than any person on this earth is my father. So many of my friends didn't like their father or didn't want to be around their father. I wish I could be around my father more than I am, but he would not let me. Dad felt I needed to get out from under his shadow and make my separate way.

Hmmm...was he being nice but really kicking me out? Never thought of that till now! No, he didn't.

He is everything I wish to be. The things he gave up to take care of us and especially his devotion to my brother makes him a saint. I just can't say enough good things about the man.

There was another man at the time that was cut from the same cloth as my dad. After my father, he is the second most influential man in my life. I look up to him almost as much as I do my father. Both are about 6'1" or 2, and I am 5'9", joke!

His name is Fred Williams. He is the manager of the Van Buren Drive-In Theater in Riverside. Mr. Williams is the guy who interviewed me and Tim for the job. Although he is older than me, he is younger than my dad, so, he is like an older brother even though he is my boss. Talk about a mean, big, gruff bear of a man with a look that could make your crap your pants—and the biggest teddy bear and softy you ever met. Little girls would wrap him around their little fingers in a New York minute. When he really wanted to know something, he would stare at you with these penetrating eyes that looked right through to your brain. You did not lie to this man; he did not suffer fools well.

My first day on the job was a Friday night—both Tim and I worked our first week together there—and we asked what we were supposed to wear.

Mr. Williams comments, "What do you think? Black pants, white shirts, and bow ties."

Hmmm...never saw anyone wear that but okay. We stuck out like the proverbial sore thumb, but we didn't notice. Then I asked what we should wear to the swap meet the next morning.

He adds, "Why, the same thing."

Okay. Like I thought, I will make the perfect Marine, and I believed everything he said. We wore our black pants, white shirt, and bowtie to the swap meet. I finally caught on... Twiddle Dee and Twiddle Dumb! We looked stupid! He had a good laugh, as did everyone else.

I stuck it out and enjoyed working there. And Tim? He hated it. One night, Tim and I were working and had to go under the screen to get some cups for soda and tubs for popcorn. The maintenance people must have left the top off a large tub of paint. It was dark and before I could get the light on, I heard, "Shit! WTF did I just step in?"

Tim stepped into the yellow paint barrel that was used to paint the lines for cars. He walked around and left yellow footprints where he stepped. It was funny as shit! This wouldn't be the last time I saw yellow footprints, but that would be much later and not as funny. This is how he got the nickname "Yellow

Foot." Tim's attitude left something to be desired after that, and Mr. Williams decided Tim would be better at some other place of employment, but I survived!

(I was later fired three different times but told to make sure I came back each time for the next workday, a story for another time.)

I valued Mr. William's opinion, and as time went on, he put things into perspective quick. My dad pointed me in the right direction, gave me the tools to be a good and honest boy to man. Mr. Williams gave me a good mental shove whenever I slowed down more than I deserved. He taught me that persistence matters as much as focus, like holding a shot until the perfect moment.

It was one day in mid-September when the keys to the box office were locked in the trunk of my car and we couldn't open the theater. Mr. Williams just stared at me and then comments, "Scruntski, you better figure this out otherwise we will have to rip open the trunk"

"No, Mr. Williams, I'll give my Dad a call, he has a spare set."

"He better get here quick then!"

I called my dad and after calling me a few nice names, made his way to the theater. I think my dad liked Mr. Williams from the start because of all the stories I told about Mr. Williams, and believe me, there were a lot!

"Now, Mr. Williams, understand my Dad may talk to you about calling me Scruntski. I don't think he likes it. You know my name is Sikorski, so just warning you."

Mr. Williams just shrugged his shoulders. When my Dad showed up, they shook hands and then started having a conversation and I think with all the smiling between the two of them that my ass was grass. I realized that the conversation probably was not going my way, so I stomped up to them both.

Mr. Williams: "Pleased to meet you, Mr. Sikorski"

Dad: "Call me Joe, and good to meet you too, I'm here to see Scruntski."

Damn. My own Dad.

Mr. Williams, with a smile: "Call me Fred."

Dad continued, "I understand the dipshit locked the keys in his trunk and the cash registers?"

Mr. Williams replied, "Yep, too bad you got here in time, was looking forward to watching his face when we broke into the car."

Dad: "He wouldn't have learned, not the brightest bulb in the box. Did you hear he wants to join the Marines?

Mr. Williams: "Yea, maybe he will have a clue and pop his head out his ass about it."

These two, talking as if I'm not here. It reminded me of when I was in the principal's office in elementary and junior high after getting into fights. He told the principal he had permission to beat me if that's what it took to put some sense into my head. Guess what? I took a few beatings… and no surprise to any of us, it didn't work.

It still wasn't working.

Anyways, Mr. Williams sat down with me several times and told me a bit about himself and how he got to where he was. He believed that the service was fine and had a lot of respect for the men who went in. He also remarks to listen to my father, but in the end, I need to make my own choice and that if I ever need a job after, he would make sure I had a place with him and he would help me be a manager.

His original feelings were that I join the Air Force like my father said. We spent a lot of nights at the box office talking when it got slow, and I explained the reasons why I thought the Marines would be a good idea. It mainly played out that I thought being a tough guy and in the presence of real men might make me like them. I wasn't ready yet to discover who I was separate from the men my father and Mr. Williams told me I needed to model myself after.

I guess I still felt like my father was disappointed in me. I hoped there would be no way he could feel that way if I was a Marine. The few. The proud. Me.

Mr. Williams explained a little more of his background and why he didn't go into the military. It wasn't that he regretted not being able to join up but more so that something passed him by that may have made him "more" than what he was. In the end, he didn't agree with my decision but felt that if it meant that much to me, I would probably regret doing anything else. He finally told me to join—The

Few, The Proud, The Marines.

After that, he decided to help me become prepared for the Marines–that's what he claimed he was doing when I complained. To make sure I would get used to all the things the Marines would have me do, he promised to give me "shit jobs." I had no idea how literal those two words would be.

Let's see, I had to run whenever I put the poles that blocked the entrance up. I had to clean out the women's restrooms—you don't want to know, but here is a little taste. Women can be filthier than men. Not that men aren't filthy and often filthier than women— but I got abused of the notion quick that women are dainty and magically clean at all times.

Imagine having to walk into a place that you're afraid of going into because it's the den of what you desire most. As you enter, the competing smells overwhelm you and the sticky sweet smell of Pine Sol emerges as the winner.

Pine Sol? Why?

Because you're spraying the fuck out of the place. The things you find on the floor are appalling and you become very careful of where you put your shoes. No telling what you might step in. This is no longer the place the girls go to and put make up on and giggle and talk about their dates, it's the dungeon of hell that no man should ever have to enter.

There is also plenty of stocking up on stuff like candy and cups, tubs, moving food everywhere and carrying things to work out your gluts and biceps. When a customer was going to get upset and complain, he made sure I was the guy they yelled at so I would get used to someone constantly yelling at me. He made me work the back gate so when people tried to sneak in, I would get to confront them.

"Mr. Williams, are all of our customers this mad?"

I wasn't being entirely insincere. I was a little confused how he stayed in business if everyone felt like the people who threatened to tear my head off.

He laughed. "Mark, 99% of my customers are too happy or don't care enough to say something. Don't think that just because you get the 1% mad enough to say something that the rest of the people aren't happy."

Almost as though to prove how mad those few enraged customers were, one time a guy came in the exit driving a white van. The guy's arm was dragging along the ground, that's how long it was. His head was bigger than the door window.

I stopped him at the exit and roared, "Hey, Melon Head, (no, I just politely said, excuse me sir, but melon head sounds better), you need to turn around and head back out the way you came. This is an exit."

His girlfriend pipes up, "Melon Head, why don't you just get out and beat the shit out of this little boy, and then we can go watch the movie?"

Melon Head spits, "Little boy, want me to get out and beat the shit out of you?"

Little boy, I mean, I stutter, "Umm... have a

good night sir."

Usually, I don't shy away from a fight, but this guy looked pretty big and when sparks came from his knuckles as they dragged along the ground, I figured my life was more important than a few dollars.

They went and parked. I decided to let Mr. Williams know what happened in case he wanted to do something about it.

"Mr. William's, this orangutan came in the back gate and parked his van. He was a little too big for me to handle so just want to let you know."

He snatches his flashlight, smiled, and goes, "OK Marco, show me where they're at."

I pointed out the van as we got close and he gets excited and says, "Come on", nope, I was happy standing right here. That's when Mr. Williams put his 150 lb hand on my back and laughed-

"It'll be okay, just watch." Oh, man.

Mr. Williams tells this guy, "Excuse me, do you have your tickets? If not, you need to leave, NOW!"

The melon head responds, "How about I get out and kick your ass and the little boy's?"

I've had just about enough of this! Go ahead, Mr. Williams, kick his ass!

Now Mr. Williams snarls, "You're welcome to get out of your van and we can see what happens next, otherwise, you need to leave."

Little did Mr. Williams know I had on my best running shoes. Thank goodness I wasn't put to the test. The guy rolls up his window and drives towards the exit. Then brakes. Then he turns the van around and drives fast at us. Mr. Williams just stands there, unscrews the flashlight, takes out the four batteries, and starts throwing them at this guy's windshield! Crack! Crack! Busts the windshield. The van halts, Mr. Williams reaches behind his back and pulls out a gun! Melon Head spins the wheel and hits the gas and rushes away in a cloud of dust.

Mr. Williams turns to me and states, "See, I told you everything would work out just fine, just part of the plan." Just so much fun.

Working for Mr. Williams made me understand that you never ask the people working for you to do something you would not do or have never done. He understood to be a good leader, you needed to discover what others went through and be willing to go through it with them. Much like I wanted when I asked my father to share his past. Much like I'm asking you to do now with me.

I was to learn a few years later, a leader doesn't jeopardize his men just because he has personal feelings that something is not right. He cannot put others at risk without them knowing the risk. Mr. Williams would take the risk himself versus making others take the risk. He is the type of person who would give you the shirt off his back if he thought you deserved it, no questions asked. He had helped a lot of people.

I kept waiting for my father to tell me he was proud of me, but up to this point, it never happened (it did eventually). Mr. Williams was the first man who verbalized it. He is the generation between my dad and myself. I don't really know how he talked to his kids, Dawn and Shawn, but he gave me some of the "Attaboy" that I needed.

Dad just knew you had to not worry about what others thought and praise was something for heroes. Mr. Williams had to work around a lot of teenagers and probably developed a manager's mindset that you had to reward good results, even if they were expected.

I think it was something in my dad's generation of men and how they were raised to not really show emotion and to just assume you knew what they felt. It was hard to hear my dad telling me he was proud of me if he refused to say the actual words. I had to remind myself how he felt. I had to tell myself he meant it, even if he wouldn't say it.

It might be that Mr. Williams's generation embodied the transition of wanting that feedback and never getting it, so they started giving it. We hopefully work on being better to the next generation. (He was lucky that he also had a great wife, Rhonda, who kept him in his place and made sure he didn't do too many dumb things either. I was too young to want one for myself, but if not for Mr. Williams's example, I might never have found the great wife that keeps me in line, too.)

Chapter 8

October 1976

One of the things I enjoyed the most in the Army JR ROTC program was the Rifle Team. Command Sergeant Major Klinger is our instructor. CSM Klinger had been in the shit and he liked to tell stories. He wasn't a tall or large man and had become a little rounded at the edges if you know what I mean. There was no intimidating look or killer attitude that he exuded. He was just a nice, easy-going, smiling man until you did something wrong. Then an undercurrent of rage would slowly seep out until you corrected your mistake, or he reigned in his intent on killing you. Other than that, he was at peace with himself and the world.

At 14 years old, during my freshman year, I signed up for the rifle team. When I showed up, I was laughed at. I was about 4' 11". Small for my age, I guess. Just a little taller than my mother. Let's put this into perspective, 59 inches is my height. CSM Klinger handed me the rifle I would shoot to qualify on. The Springfield 1903 A3. It is 44 inches long. I was about a foot taller than the rifle. Yep. Sarge decided the team needed a mascot and I would be it. That sucked but whatever I had to do to make the team was fine by me.

As all military does, you needed a nickname. There wasn't a huge thought process that went into it so naturally, I got the nickname Ski. Real genius. I guess better than what could have happened like squeaky or something.

I learned how to shoot well over the 4 years and became the Team Captain and lettered all four years. I qualified as a top shooter at quite a few events and was an 'Expert' marksman on a 1903A1, the M-1, and the M-14. I also qualified expert with the M1911 Colt .45cal pistol. The M-16 rifle was not available to us, but it didn't matter, it wasn't a match qualified rifle. It is more of a rapid-fire infantry weapon than a real quality rifle. What would you expect from a toymaker—Mattel?

Oh, you didn't know that the same company making toys for tots for a brief time made the handgrips for those plastic pieces of junk they called an M-16? The government grunts figured that since soldiers in Vietnam were fighting in close quarters, they didn't need the sturdy guns that had secured victory for America in other wars. No, now it was time to make the guns out of plastics and alloys.

The government must have saved a dollar or two, but so many guns jammed in the field—one record showed as much as 80% of surveyed troops experienced at least one terrifying malfunction while engaged in combat—that the panicked soldiers saw the logo on the handgrips and blamed Mattel. To this day, people still believe Mattel made the guns, even though they only briefly supplied the logo-embossed handgrip.

I learned close to most everything about rifles from CSM Klinger. We did a lot of out of town trips and many competitions. He was always helping me and keeping my spirits up when I was teased by other shooters. I found out about his calling me dynamite at one of the shoots in my sophomore year. As I walked up to the line carrying my Springfield, I noticed some other competitors elbowing each other and pointing at me. I was clueless as to why and when "Sarge" came up to me, he whispered, "Beat the shit out of these assholes, okay?"I intended to but didn't know why he called them assholes.

It must have been quite a sight, this kid with a rifle as long as he was. I settled in and did all three positions. Standing, kneeling and prone, ten shots into each target. Thirty points and this would be one of my better days, fired a twenty-six. Most everything went into the center. I took second in the competition and actually beat all my team members for the first time. When we went up to get our medals, he went up and said the line, "my smallest shooter who packs the most dynamite." From that point forward, he would introduce me as the smallest shooter but the one who packed the most dynamite. In my senior year, I grew about a foot and stood 5'9" which that meant Sarge didn't have to talk about his smallest shooter - only his best.[8]

_____

8   (P. 419) Varsity Rifle Letter Team (1 yr JV, 3 years Varsity)

After growing in height and winning tournaments at 250 yards with the M-14, he sat me down and mentions, "Ski, if you're interested in joining the Army, after basic I can talk to some people about getting you into the LRRP's (Long Range Recon Patrols)."

Sarge told us a lot of stories about Laos and Cambodia- places we were supposedly never at. From cutting off ears to torching places down. His biggest complaint was that the media and the REMF's (Rear Echelon Mother Fuckers) chickenshits that ran the war from afar and didn't know their ass from a hole in the ground. He did not like President Johnson or Nixon and wished the military could just fight the war and be done. He ran a lot of LRRPs in Laos and Cambodia and knew most of the NCOs (Non-Commissioned Officers) in charge of the programs stateside. He had the pull I am sure at MILPERSEN, the Army Personnel Center to get me whatever assignments I wanted after basic. Sarge retired as a CSM for a Division Command–that's like a two- or three-star General for the enlisted ranks.

I don't know why, but I asked, "Sarge, tell me about snipers. And do you like them? It seems everything we do is to put one round at a time into a target versus using fully automatic to just hit everyone. That's what a sniper does, right?"

Sarge sat back and put his hands on his stomach. He waited for a beat or two and then comments, "I think most of them are cowards and what they want to be are glorified infantrymen. The best thing the Army can do is not waste money on some sniper but spend it on maximum firepower to kill as many enemies as possible and as fast as possible. That's not what a sniper does."

Hmmm...didn't expect that answer, especially since he is teaching us how to kill through a scope.

I asked Sarge what he meant by that. "Sarge, didn't you tell us about some guys in the Army and Marines that were sent out to kill North Vietnamese generals and politicians? I heard you observe they were some hellacious killers."

"Okay Ski, it's like this, we can send out these snipers to kill one or two people, but it's not going to end war or change anything except for the short term. The best bet is to kill them all with whatever weapons we can bear on the target. I'm not saying there weren't some badass MF's, there were, but they didn't change shit."

"How can you call these snipers cowards when they go out by themselves, past enemy lines and kill someone. After that, they have to come back through the jungle while being pursued. Seems to me they are the best of the best."

"Your right Ski, but these guys were far and few. I remember this Marine, his name is Carlos Hathcock, and his nickname is the 'White Feather'. He's still active duty and teaches snipers for the Marines. The thing is the enemy died if Hathcock was around. The rumor is that Hathcock killed another sniper in Vietnam from one thousand yards out."

I rolled my tongue under the inside of my mouth. That seemed...less than possible. And impressive if it was true. "A thousand yards?"

"Yup. He put the bullet through the other sniper's scope and into her eye and killed her. Yes, you heard me right. Her. This sniper was one of Vietnam's best and was tasked with killing Hathcock."

I found out later that this story is true, but it has two halves. He did put a bullet through a scope of a sniper at one thousand yards that was hunting him, the Cobra. This Vietnamese sniper lured Hathcock to his killing field, but the hunter became the hunted and was shot first, through his own scope. Hathcock stated that he believes that the other sniper was just moments away from pulling the trigger on him.

The other half was the woman called the "Apache" who derived pleasure from skinning captured Americans alive. She would hang them up on a post and then shoot at Americans that heard their screams and tried to bring them down. After Hathcock witnessed her work firsthand he went and hunted her and killed her. She was taking a dump in the weeds when he spotted her, one shot to the throat and two to her body. He stated that it was the finest shot he ever made.

I then asked, "Sarge, did you use any snipers?"

"Nope, the Army didn't have designated snipers as the Marines did, but I did have some good shooters I used as snipers when needed. Matter of fact, I would go out sometimes and hunt ahead with my little team."

Then, of course, I add something stupid. "Sarge, were you and your shooter's cowards then?"

"Shut the fuck up Ski and get the fuck out!"

Oops. I guess if it isn't Army Green, it isn't right. I never turned him down about helping me get a job with the LRRP's, but again, I wasn't sure the Army was the right fit.

A few days later when he had calmed down, I figured I would tell him my thought about joining the Marines and what was his opinion. Secretly I enjoyed watching his eyes go wild as his face turned red. I could work him up and then leave, and then the next person would have to deal with him. Kind of like little kids, feed them sugar and give them back to the parents!

"Sarge, can I ask you a quick question?"

"Sure Ski, shoot."

"I think I'm going to join the Marines, think it's a good idea?"

"You little asshole, get back here so I can beat you!"

I ran like hell.

That answered that question. I am going to stay away from him for a few days!

The other half of the dynamic duo is Major Bob Sagona. He is the Senior Military Advisor to the High School ROTC program. He mainly is an administrator, even though he retired with the Armor (tanks) MOS (military occupational specialty). He served during Korea and Vietnam but was lucky enough to never have deployed to any combat areas. He never had the draw that CSM did because of missing combat time. Not that he isn't cared about by the kids he teaches, he is, but seeing firsthand and participating in warfare as an example to future warriors became more important than theory or guessing.

Major Sagona was willing to write letters for me to get me into college. That is what he expected me to do. No amount of explaining that money wasn't available would change his mind. Major Sagona was more into teaching the Officer and Gentleman parts of the Service than war. I would have loved to hear his thoughts on me joining the Marines, but when I approached the subject, he smiled and just said, "Why would you ever do that?" and "They are a good outfit."[9]

---

9   (P. 419) Graduation from Jr. ROTC

Chapter 9

November 1976–March 1977

The next few months were a whirlwind of activity to soak as much fun out of civilian life as I could. Dances, shooting championships, wrestling, dating, and living the dream of high school. I steered clear of Sarge until he calmed down, worked a lot at the theater, and met quite a few young ladies, and enjoyed myself immensely.

It wasn't just that I sensed my life was about to permanently change. I'd like to tell you it was fear of death and all of that, but the real reason I went wild over those months is that somewhere along the way, I lost Janet.

She had gone off to visit her father in St. Louis and told me over the phone that she was breaking up with me. Unbelievable! This girl tore me up. I had finally settled on this compact box of TNT believing my future was set. What she mutters next made me decide that I had dodged a bullet. She was driving back to Riverside with three guys she had met, and she decided to make some changes. No more foul-mouthed, tattooed, cigarette/weed smoking girls for me, no matter how hot.

The decision going forward was to absolutely not give my heart to another girl and to just enjoy as many young ladies as possible. My buddy, Tim, was there for me. He talked me through this difficult time and helped put things in perspective. For such a stoic guy, he has a lot of heart. From that time forward, I would make sure anyone I dated knew beyond any doubt that I was going out with them with one thing in mind. Stay clear otherwise. Funny thing, it wasn't a problem, I became a little bit of that bad boy your mothers warned you about.

The election occurred and Jimmy Carter is elected as the Thirty-Ninth President of the United States. His politics were somewhat anti-military which made me wonder about my choice of joining the military. He had talked about downsizing the number of soldiers, even though we downsized a lot after Vietnam, cutting the military budget and closing bases. I heard the Major and Sarge became upset, but my father thought differently, he believed it was a good idea because we didn't need to be in any more wars.

Tim went to work at several places and ended up working at a supermarket in groceries as some sort of stock person. Pat went to work in the same industry as well and went on to be a manager. Bob had it made, his parents took care of him until he moved out and decided not to go to the Air Force and wanted to study engineering at Cal Poly. Gary was still in the clouds with the CAP program and his computers. No telling what he would do.

For quite a few months I dated every girl who came my way. Love them and leave them or pass them on was the new model. Janet broke that trust and like

I said, I would be damned if another was going to even get close enough to break it. My reputation wasn't the greatest, I have no idea why these girls were willing to go out with me but like a moth to flame, I was on fire! A little bit dangerous. The closest any young lady got to my heart was Olivia Lopez. Her Dad and brother put an end to that relationship when they promised to do bodily harm to one young man one evening. I promise, my car did break down and to this day, I have no idea how my father found me on the side of the road with a busted radiator hose. Stay clear was the message and heard loud and clear! Time went on and as usual, what happens next is always the bat that came flying out of left field and hits you right in the head, bam! Next thing I knew was that I met another young lady that captured my heart. I was determined in no way was I going to actively commit to anyone, but this gorgeous girl just wrapped me up.

Tamese Neal is as beautiful as they come. She is fifteen years old, dark brown skin, big brown eyes, and a smile a mile long. I had met her through a mutual friend, Tammie, who had a crush on me, but I fell for Tamese hard. She is stunning and my mind turned to mush the first few times I was around her. There's something irresistible about girls who speak their minds. I don't think at that time Tamese realized what a strong and independent woman she was or better, would turn out to be. And when so many men are intimidated by strong women— particularly if a woman is stronger than that man—

without understanding, Tamese was delighted to find a guy who appreciated her power.

Tamese has no problems explaining how or what she thought of things, but she always smiled when she tore people apart, so you were never sure of what just happened. Her parents are divorced, and her father is a large, strong, well-built man of color who is also a Sergeant in the Army. Scared the hell out of me as I guess he should have. Her mother is a pretty lady from England that her father married and brought to the U.S.

Me and Tamese went to some dances, movies, lunches, and dinners. She is most everything I wanted in a girl. She supports my decisions, gives me great feedback, smart as a whip, and helps me be a better person. As time went on, I believed this was a girl I might marry, and my mother was becoming a bit difficult as time went on with the relationship. My father liked her a lot, but my mother wasn't as keen. I think a little bit of racism showed through and that surprised me. Tamese would be the second girl I fell in love with, and after voicing that love, it would never happen again.

I was also introduced to a game my father played, Racquetball. I liked it because it relied on my skills and no one else. There was no one to blame for a loss other than myself. I am starting to find out that even though I enjoyed large groups, the small, tight-knit team or individual competition was more enjoyable.

I may have left out that I also wrestled but did not make varsity. My one claim to fame was that I did take down last year's state wrestling champion in a scrimmage and pinned him. Just because I used an unsanctioned move and surprised him with fat boy speed doesn't take away what I did. He was after all, a state champ, right? He wanted a rematch, but I told him I had nothing left to prove. I was better and to leave it at that. Pissed him off but good. I did stay away from him the rest of the season because there was no reason to tempt fate.

As winter moved into spring, I became more in tune with what was going on in my thought process. I enjoyed being part of a team, but not to the extent I had to rely on the team to make me win as an individual. The shooting competition was an individual sport, but the numbers added to the team total. Wrestling was one on one, but the win counted to the team. Racquetball was all as an individual unless you played where a club score was needed to help the club. Many examples defined me in this capacity, and I needed to figure out how I could best achieve this type of individual/team merger.

The Army, you were part of a large organization, but the Army defined the soldiers. The Air Force was a loose-knit group of individuals all working in the same direction but no real esprit unless you were the warrior- the fighter pilot. Don't get me started on the Navy.

The Marines though? Ah, the Marines.

Each Marine was part of a small team that had each other's back. Those small teams made the larger organization stronger. You were part of a larger organization, but each member was a team unto himself. They were told to go do something, not how. I needed to talk to my dad some more, because try as I might to find a better target, my mind kept returning to the same bull's eye: the Marines.

Chapter 10

7 April 1977

If my Gunny ever saw me fail to fire on this easy of a shot, he'd make me his next target. You can't rely on a sniper who hesitates. It may be the only chance he gets.

Yet here I am stuck deciding between the Air Force and the Marines.

Where am I going to go? I still had my doubts about it and told others I would join the Marines, but that wasn't true. I hadn't decided on the Marines. I hadn't decided anything.

What the hell anyway. It was time. Time to let the Marines know they were number two in my selection. Jeans, nice shirt, clean underwear, check. Clean underwear was because my mother always said- "what if you die, don't you want to make sure your underwear is clean?" Where did that come from? Sure, figured if I was going to die it would be from something scary and big and I would probably shit my pants! Gunny Smith fits that bill just right and would now kill me, so clean underwear it is.

If I didn't do this now, I would keep on vacillating until my father beat the shit out of me for joining or my friends would because they were tired of hearing about it. I did realize that joining the Air Force meant that my real desires of combat and learning to fight would be out the window. My promise to learn what I needed to help Israel would probably be gone as well. It was like I decided on avoiding risk and becoming what I hated, someone who talks big but goes small. I had no choice; it was time to get it over with.

I drove on down to the recruiting office and entered. Nothing had changed. A line for the Air Force and zero for the Marines.

If I were going to a restaurant and this is the line I saw, I would probably not go near the Marines and wait for the table at the Air Force.

This looked bad for the Marines. Too late now, I trekked down the shiny floor towards purgatory once again.

Smith wasn't there, and some other large Marine was, and he didn't look as mean but still had that voice that made me croak.

"SIT," he quietly bellowed.

Down I went, just like an obedient dog. The Colonel shows up and here is that big smile.

Gonna disappoint you, buddy. You don't have Smith here and I think I can outrun you!

Yea!

I allow myself to be led back to his office like were, old friends. He had me take a seat and showed me some pictures of an airplane. Okay... Then he asks, "Ready to go out to the airport and fly today?"

"Umm, yeah, I mean, sure!"

"Let's go!" He snags his cover (called a hat in the civilian world)—he is wearing Utilities (the Marine olive drab uniform) and we go out to his car. I don't remember what kind of car it was, but it must have been nice because that's the only thing I remember, the overwhelming impression that it was a *nice* car.

Off we drive to Riverside Airport. We drove through the gate and onto the flight area. I looked around and didn't see any military aircraft, so I wasn't sure what we were doing. We pulled up and parked near this gleaming white airplane with the overhead wing and front propeller. It had two doors and what looked like a hatch in the back. The Colonel explained that this is a Cessna.

On the ride over, he was telling me all sorts of stuff about airplanes. He is the real deal. The Colonel is an Aviator as he called it, and he flew the A-4 Skyhawk and the F-4 Phantom for the Marines in Vietnam. He flew a lot of mud work missions as he calls it. Close in Air Support for Marines.

He explained, "You see, the Marines don't rely on anyone but other Marines; we know that we will never let each other down. That's why we have our own planes, tanks, infantry, artillery, and borrow the Navy to get us where we need to go. We also borrow Navy Corpsman because they are almost Marines. (They are our 'doctors')."

Wow. This was fantastic. He talked about blowing the shit out of everything and saving the ground pounders who got in over their heads. I started to worry because there wasn't anything to kill here in Riverside, and I could see the veins on his forehead and neck starting to pop out. Now he looked exactly like Gunny Smith.

What is this crazy man about to do?

Doesn't matter, I'm all in!

The Colonel gave me a paper coated in plastic and we glided around the plane.

He told me, "Read each item off and when I note check, go on to the next item."

Check!

After the walk around, we hopped inside. Buttons everywhere and a steering wheel kind of thing. I thought planes had "sticks," not a wheel, so I asked. These guys must go to the same school to learn this "I kill you" smile. He gave me a "you are a dumbshit" smile worthy of the last guy. Great, they must all go to the same school. He let me know.

"This is a civilian aircraft and a trainer," he says. "But yes, military fighters had a 'stick'."

Okay. He gave me another paper coated in plastic and said to read them off the same as before. Seemed like a waste of time, just start the damn thing and let's take off! I knew better than to vocalize that, so I just read off the entire checklist.

Surprise, everything works. What did he expect?

Now he got this puppy started and did all these other things with his hands. He was explaining it all as if I was going to understand. Right. He passes me the headset, plugs it in, and says, "This is so we can talk to each other."

Sounds good to me.

Not that I give him a response, not even a thumbs up. He isn't asking for one.

Then we taxi out to the runway. He's talking to what was called ground control. These individuals would guide us to the correct runway and make sure everything is cleared before we take off. So far, so good, except for all the things he was doing with his hands, I didn't see a problem. He pushed the engine faster and let off the breaks and off we went. Into the wild blue yonder! That's Air Force, but who cares!

This is awesome.

Unbelievable. The plane did all sorts of things-- twists, turns, drops, straight up, and stalls. I am having a blast! Then he lets go of the wheel and tells me to fly! I clutch the wheel and stare hard in front of me. I can't believe this guy is ready to die!

He speaks into the mic and states very clearly, "Don't touch the fucking pedals or I will kill you before we crash."

I have no clue what they were for, so, no problem. I go up, then down, I do a hard-left turn and then a right. I complete a figure eight and then a stall. What a rush!

The Colonel says, "You are going to make a great fighter pilot."

No shit! I was born for this!

He explains, "Some kids I take up, start to cry or croak that they are going to puke, you just laugh and want to do more. I weed most out quickly this way and you passed."

Well, I just want more. Unfortunately, time was up, and we had to go back to reality. Flying out over Riverside I could see forever, even with the brown cloud of pollution. The vista and views are wonderful.

This is some bodacious shit!

I want to fly more than anything else at this point. Once we land, the Colonel gives me another paper encased in plastic and has me go over it as well.

Fine. If it made him happy, it made me happy.

Checklists, always making sure that you check on each thing that can mess up a good day.

I probably should remember this.

After we get through all the checklist, we tie down the airplane and zip back to his car for the ride to the office.

It is unbelievable, we spent almost the entire afternoon flying and it seemed like 5 minutes. By the time we get back to his office, he was relaxed. The veins weren't bulging out and the regular salesman smile is back. The Colonel asked, "Are you ready for the CORPS?" "Hell Yes!" He had the paperwork ready and mostly filled out. After another hour of sitting in his office, and a "checklist" of things I needed to bring back to him, I was ready. I hoped my parents had this stuff, I was born in Casablanca Morocco and I don't have a birth certificate. I had all the other stuff though.

Hmmm...didn't I just go there to tell them I was going Air Force? What just happened?

As I think back, I never did see the Air Force recruiter. Never stepped into their offices. I can only imagine the conversation.

"Hi, I'd like to fly airplanes."

"Sit down son, how about we pay you good money, let you drive fast cars, never have to go into the field, you can live in clean quarters, we take care of your food and healthcare, and to top it off, you have most weekends free for dating all the girls you want, after all, what girl doesn't want to fly?"

"Where do I sign?"

Now I wouldn't even get to see the piece of paper.

Yea, Dad was right, fucking moron!

Chapter 11

Oh God. I have to face my father again.

What did I do??? I was tricked!

Well, I wanted to fly, and the Marines will let me fly, so I have made up my mind, this is what I am going to do. No two ways about it.

Dad is going to kill me.

I thought of all the things I was going to mention to my dad and how I thought he was going to react.

Maybe I can convince my mom to tell him? No, she will be upset with me once my Dad tells her what I did and what it means.

Glad he is at work! Maybe I just won't go home. This waiting is going to kill me. I think there must be a dad school that teaches them how to make sure their kids know the world is about to end without them even being around to torture you. You do something stupid; dad knows somehow. You demolish something, he knows. You tell a little untruth—not a lie, just one little detail tweaked, and he knows. You scratch the car, he knows. You lost something of his, he knows. The list goes on and on. He probably knows I joined the Marines and is just waiting at home right now to kick my ass.

Enough! Home I go. I get home early enough to get my brother from the Handivan when he gets home from school. I wheel him into the back yard and tell him I am joining the Marines! Since he is unable to talk, he starts to yell at me, all upset until I shout, "David, you get a room all to yourself when I leave. Your own TV and don't have to share with anyone."

He shuts up. A little smile creeps onto his face. So much for brotherly love, right? I guess that went well.

His room is a shared room where we had the TV and ate our pizza night meals. It is the family room, even if it is his bedroom. I just realized my brother had a TV in his room all those years and I didn't. I know he warmed up to the idea now of having his own room that no one else could come into. Add to that he probably would get a new TV, probably a color one! So unfair.

And for a moment, I got him to see that. We were in a race, and he was going to come out the winner with all sorts of new stuff.

But after thinking a little longer, he became upset again. Then he started to cry. Not hard yelling crying, but sad emotional crying. Of course, my mom comes outside and hears him. That always happens when you make your little brother cry, even if you were not the reason, your parents always are ready to beat you because it must be your fault! I explain to her that David was just sad, and he would get over it.

"Why is he sad?" she asked.

"Because he's stupid! That's why!"

Well, that got a reaction; he ceased crying and started kicking at me. Ha! Back to yelling. Much better! I was lucky at this point that he couldn't walk or talk otherwise it might have been fist time! Wait, I mean he was lucky because I would have beat him down!

I mentioned earlier that my brother David has Cerebral Palsy and is unable to use his voice to talk or control his limbs for movement. This happened at birth and his life revolved around everyone having to do things for him and take care of him. Still, no matter how bad things were for him, he pressed on.

Although David is not on that list of mentors that helped me along, he is my best friend that showed me that the absolute worst day of my life was better than his best day. He would trade that best day for my worst in a heartbeat, so I had best make the life I have worth something and not bitch about what I don't have. Even though I joked about him being a pain in the ass, don't get me wrong, he is, he still is the best friend I could ever have. I will always be with him and no matter what happens in the military, I will be back for him.

Maybe the fear that this time I won't come back is why my dad can sense something is wrong as soon as he comes home.

So, the old man shows up at home. It's my birthday so maybe a happy birthday? Nope. That's okay. Maybe he will just be happy and eat dinner, go to the bathroom, read the paper, watch his news, and off to sleep. Then his voice echoes toward me.

"Marco, come in here!"

No hiding out in David's room now. I made sure to give David a quick kick before I left to make sure he was awake. "Yes Dad, I'm on my way."

David's screaming again, don't know why. Maybe he senses what's coming. What I won't admit.

"What did you do to your brother?" Dad says.

"Nothing!"

"You did something."

"Why do you think I did something?"

"David is screaming."

"He always screams."

"Why don't I go ask him?"

"Go ahead."

Well, this is going well, wonder how else I can mess things up.

Let me stare at the ceiling and pretend I'm on drugs, no, fall on the ground and have a seizure.

At least then he might see me as something other than the brother who failed to take care of David. Another day, he might have a point, but today, that is most definitely not the point.

Let's just preempt this. "Dad!"

'What?"

"I joined the Marines today."

Silence. Total silence. You've heard the song by Simon and Garfunkel, "The Sound of Silence"? That is what is going on in my head. Now he's laughing.

"Marco, you are one stupid son of a bitch."

Now, my smart mouth wants to ask him, *what*

did you call my Mom? Instead, my brain freezes up and I say nothing. Dad goes on to explain how I should be careful about what I wish for but since I made my decision, he is fine with it. He wants to know when I am leaving and where I would be stationed.

"San Diego or Parris Island?"

"MCRD San Diego," I said. (Marine Corps Recruiting Depot.)

"When?"

"I don't know."

Those steel blue eyes burrowed into me once again, then, more relaxed as if a decision had been made, stated Let me know when."

I let out a slow breath. Was this really happening? "Okay," I said in quiet disbelief.

Guess what? Dad forgot all about David! I win! I went and put David into his wheelchair, called him a name or two, and brought him out to the dinner table. I had a date with Tamese, so I told everyone goodnight and to not wait up! Dad did remember to mumble happy birthday before I left and also to be careful.

He remembered after all. That was nice, right?

I went out and picked up Tamese for my birthday dinner and dessert. We had a nice time and a great dessert. The past few weeks with her were amazing and the weeks leading up to graduation were equally wonderful. We went on lots of dates, movies, dinner, lunches, and just hung out.

One of my favorite memories was that we went out to the Military Ball, but first to dinner. I was driving my dad's Ford Mustang, an underpowered POS, 1976 with no horsepower, not the 'stangs of old. Bob and Tracy were dating and going with us. I was driving and my attention should have been on the road, but my wonderful date kept moving her hand around places I am embarrassed to mention. Not paying attention to my driving, I made a lane change and bumped another car. The lady driving that car pulled over as did I. The accident was reported in by a neighbor on the street and a police officer shows up.

The officer providing the ticket said, "Young man, why didn't you signal your intentions?"

"I have no idea."

"Did you look to the side and behind you?"

"I don't even remember driving."

"WHAT?"

The Lie of Omission may be a sin, but so is coming home with a ticket on top of a banged-up car, so I scrambled for a worthy way to get out of this. "I did look, I didn't see anyone..."

That probably wasn't the first lie he'd heard that night. "Here is your ticket."

Well, it was a small price to pay, and with a big night still ahead of us, at least I wouldn't have to pay up until long after the fun was over.

With the cop gone, we were off to the Ball, pun intended. "Tamese, keep your hands to yourself till we get there!" That smile...

After a great night, and forgetting about the accident, dropping everyone off and going home, I decide to let my dad know later. The next morning there is this hysterical madman at my bed.

I wake up to my Dad shouting in my ear, "What the hell did you do to my car?"

"Umm, nothing?" Wrong answer. He hauls me up in my whitey tighties and marches me outside to look at his prized possession. "Oh, that..."

"Yea, Oh, that."

"I bumped another car by accident, but all is good, the insurance will take care of it."

"The insurance you pay for?"

"I guess?" He had me there.

His jaw tightens and the veins in his forehead prepare to explode. As his hands bunch up, I decide to just run, in my underwear, grab my clothes, climb through the window, run around to the back of the house, jump the fence, and leave for just a little bit until he dies of a heart attack or he goes somewhere to tell his friends what a dumbass he has for a son.

I did end up paying for the repairs myself, so no insurance had to be involved. See, took responsibility for my actions, or rather Tamese's!

I'm not sure what was going on in my mind, but I started becoming a jerk to Tamese. The girl I fell in love with, and who treated me very well was now getting treated poorly. On one hand, I felt I needed to

93

be free from her as I started my next journey and the other hand was how I could ever leave her. She was sixteen now and still in high school so maybe I knew subconsciously that being away from her wasn't fair to her. Great way to justify what a dick I am.

When she hugged me, I didn't hug back, when she called and wanted to see me, I said she was too clingy. I didn't make jokes with her and when she wanted to cuddle, I made excuses. We broke up a little later, or I should cry, she decided to, and I couldn't blame her. My friends couldn't believe what a dickhead I became as well. I was an asshole and just lost one of the best friends I probably would ever have.

A week before I graduated, I went out to the garage and did my weekly routine of putting the trash out. I lifted one of the lids to toss the house trash in and had to back up in shock. You will never believe what I found. Not in a million years. There, lying in a tangle of trash were my father's ribbons, medals, awards, and certificates from his military career.

I panicked and started picking the stuff up and putting it aside like they were pages of the bible. This had to be some mistake my mother did and didn't understand what these things meant. I piled them up in a corner of the garage and that evening, when my father got home, I pulled him aside. I asked that he not get mad—I know! Should not have said that!—but Mom threw away his stuff. He wanted to know what stuff, so I showed him.

He just stared at all the stuff. "I meant to throw that shit away, toss it back into the trash."

I asked him, "Why? Isn't it important?"

He answered, "To who? That box and a quarter will get you a cup of coffee.[10]"

I could not understand why he said that. I told him that I was going to take them, put them in my room and they had better stay there till I got back from boot.

I understand his ambivalence now. My medals and such mean nothing to anyone but me either, but I try to keep them, and I still have all my fathers. His medals, certificates, and awards mean something to me. I was proud of my father. Of the ambition and sacrifice that drove him to make a difference.

Years later, he confided that he was glad I kept them. He wanted to get rid of them because the world had changed and being in the service was no longer viewed as a noble calling. He was not embarrassed by anything he did but felt let down by the people he was protecting in some way, which meant the awards to him, were meaningless. A lot of veterans of Vietnam felt that way, but now, they stand proud to say they served. My father was one of them.

To unfortunately add to what a real asshole I am, I dated one of Tamese's best friends, Theresa, for a couple of weeks before I left for the Corps. Then, of course, I dumped her. Tamese did get back at me by dating Pat Negrete for a time as well. I confronted Pat

---

10   (P. 420) Joe Sikorski's Medals

and at first, he denied it. I told him I wouldn't beat him up, so he confides, "Yes, I'm dating her." What could I add? My loss. Talk about feeling depressed, one of my friends stabbed me in the back. Wait, I guess Theresa did the same to Tamese, but again, I was the idiot.

Time passed quickly and before you know it, I graduated in May and was on my way. Fat, dumb, and happy and ready to make my way into the world and join the greatest fighting team on planet earth, the United States Marine Corps.

Chapter 12

June 1977

My parents, along with my brother, drove me down to the MCRD in San Diego. The drive was about three hours long because of heavy beach traffic. Rather than take the bus that was offered, my dad insisted on driving me down so he could watch me walk the walk of shame and be able to wish me luck in enjoying my next eleven weeks in the warm sunshine of San Diego.

His parting words were, "Have fun, Marco. Hope you feel good about your decision."

Shit hot is how I felt, of course I would enjoy this, what was he thinking? This was going to give me wonderful memories that were just mine. Eleven weeks of sunshine near the beach, bars, clubs and most of all, girls. Fantastic.

The training used to be nine weeks during Vietnam and now it is moved to eleven weeks. The reason for this is during Vietnam, they found that they needed more warm bodies quicker so dropped time off some of the training and figured the troops would get it in the field. My dad was quick to point out once again, "Cannon Fodder." After completion of basic, we would be sent somewhere else for our additional training for our MOS (Military Occupational Specialty). This would be for the job we would have in the Marine Corps.

The truth is that every Marine is a Combat Infantryman first and then whatever the Corps decides. The good thing is you could be a cook, a mechanic, Pilot, anything, but when the shit hit the fan, you were an Infantry Marine and every Marine could count on you. This is completely different than all the other military services.

How did I know this? It became apparent over time. My future military experience in dealing with the Army, Air Force and Navy proved that no one had your back like a fellow Marine. When there is one Marine in the room, you have everyone where you want them, two Marines? You have everyone surrounded!

In all the other services, once you were out of basic, all you qualified for was in whatever job you were doing at the time. You never had to go pick up a weapon or worry about Infantry tactics. That was someone else's job. Not in the Marines.

In the Marines, each person qualified every year with their weapon, and Physical Training standards. Each person went through Infantry skills training each year no matter what your job, it simply didn't matter what you did.

I knew my future MOS would be flying as a pilot just like the Colonel promised, so all this Gung Ho Infantry stuff didn't matter to me. *Sure, I would learn it but who wants to lug around a rifle all day and get shot at? Not me!* I knew at the end of all this training, I would get Aviation as my MOS, and on to pilot school. Sure, I would do all this other stuff because completing it would get me to the end game. All the recruits were set to arrive by air, car or train to the depot and report in. What happened from that point forward is it was all a blur. As soon as the D.I.'s saw you, he owned you, your life was done.

I am seized and tossed in with 50-60 other guys. Lined up and standing on yellow footprints. Don't move, don't breathe, the Corps will tell you when. We are told where to go, what to do, how to do it. I don't have to think of anything, except I was in the wrong place. I looked around but didn't see any airplanes.

The D.I.'s yelled. And yelled. And for good measure, yelled some more. The Corps found the most maniacal, sadistic, extremist psychopaths they could find and blessed them with the name D.I. Some of them are Hispanic and yell in Spanish, but if you get yelled at long enough, every bark starts to sound the same.

The more excited the D.I.'s were, the less I understood them. Imagine someone spitting in your face, talking as loud as they could (not shouting, I was told), and spitting on you the whole time. It started with one saying, "I am going to take a shit in a box and send it to your parents for sending me theirs!"

This is the most scared I have been in my life.

"I swear I will punch your mother and rape

your father if I ever meet them."

"You want to make me wash my mouth out with a revolver?"

"You look like you got smacked in the face with a hot shovel."

On and on. Guys to the left and right are crying. Others are just storming away, then nabbed and thrown back into line. Some are puking in the bushes.

As God is my witness, the main job of the D.I. is to destroy your life and everything you ever believed in. Even harder to believe is that judging by their looks, they all have the same birth mother. All of them have muscles on top of more muscle. None of them have necks and all have flat faces that look like bulldogs. Different heights, but that didn't matter, all that mattered is they could kill you however they wanted to, and no one would ever find the body.

We are told that we are all morons because 50% didn't finish High School which I took to mean I was smarter than at least 50% of these guys!

This is starting to look promising.

The D.I.'s start fast by smashing us down and making us look as much the same as possible. Haircut time. I am in a long line, and then the barber plops me into a seat, shavers in hand. The smart-ass asked each of us—especially the long-haired hippies—how we would like it styled. He took the request with the gravest seriousness.

Then, of course, all the barbers laughed. Faster

than a speeding bullet, flying hands like a magician, all my hair is gone in under a minute. When I get up out of the chair and see myself in the mirror I stopped, paused, and ran my hand over my shaved head. Now I look like a moron or an escaped convict. Don't tell that to Dad or he'll say, "Your obviously both?"

The next thing that I feel is a D.I. running up, grabbing me, and propelling me outside while asking obscenely, "What the fuck are you looking at?"

Next, I find myself in another line for shots. Not the alcohol type, no sir. The ones that are painful right away, not the next day! The D.I.'s gently explains to all of us that the Corps has no clue what type of diseases we might have, and since the Corps didn't give us the disease, the Corps would make sure it is killed. I have no idea how many shots I received that afternoon.

At the same time, the vampires came by and drew blood. I heard some Corpsman betting on something. They were asking each other about the distance each of us could drift after we had our last shots and blood pulled. Then it was my turn, and I hear "How far do you think this guy will make it?"

I look down a long hallway that had a lot of bodies lying down in their underwear on the floor. These guys weren't dead, I think, because most were moving, and some were getting up after falling. Other Corpsmen were helping them up and out.

Me? I am a wimp when it comes to shots. I hate shots. I will do anything to not get a shot. Shots scare the hell out of me. My body is one big bag of pain and the relief I feel about being done with the shots is almost as good as a sweet kiss from a beautiful girl.

As I got my last shot and last vial of blood drawn, I made sure my eyes were on the door.

There is no way I won't make it into the hallway.

I hear the response from the second Corpsman. "Down before the door."

Fuck you, I thought. Dizzy as shit I start on the long journey into the hallway. I start bumping into the walls on each side and then.... No more walls! The next few feet are critical!

I made it past the door and a couple of feet further, thank you very much! Then my world went white, not black, and I fell on my ass. I hope the first Corpsman made some money off me!

This also brings new meaning to the phrase "bend over." No one gives a damn about my delicate sensibilities. I was in an assembly line, like robots just moving forward. I could hear a glove being snapped on, told to bend over, spread your cheeks, owwweey, NEXT. Then came a long row of urinals and we are all told to piss in the bottle at the same time, turn it in, and line up outside. Not a problem for me, I don't have a shy bladder, especially since someone just pushed on it hard. The poor guys who have shy bladders never stood a chance.

We all had to wait for the last guys, and Drills decided to help things along. They are yelling, "What?

Can't find you goddamn dick? Grasping the wrong hair? You don't need two hands; it's not like your writing your name! Look at the size of that, you're never going to have kids."

It never ends.

More lines, the Marines live for lines. Next up, uniforms. I am looked at, not measured, told Medium, and they throw the uniforms at you. I asked what happens if it doesn't fit and the guy behind the counter lets me know this isn't Sears, if it doesn't fit, trade it.

As I walk through this it becomes obvious that the first steps of taking away our civilian persona and replacing it with a number. After the haircut starts the indoctrination of non-discrimination. It doesn't matter what color, height, weight, background or language, we all start looking like each other and become part of the machine. We have a number and a name tag that means nothing. As I continue, I notice that all the stuff we get are interchangeable and exactly the same for each. Only small things prove it belongs to a certain individual but can be taken and used at any time by the team.

Boots, I get mine, stencil my name on the inside of both, and am then commanded to put them into a big boiling fifty-gallon drum of water. Let them boil for an hour and fish them out. Why boil them? I had no clue, but it is explained to me that it would break them in, and I would not get blisters on my five-mile run every morning.

I'm ten steps away before I realize what I just heard.

Wait, five-mile run? Every morning? Shit.

Next line, TA-50 gear. What is this? This is a belt system to hold the entire universe on your hips and then add your Ruck Pack on your back. Toothbrush, paste, floss. Better have those or you will regret it if your breath is not squeaky clean when the D.I. is half an inch from you. You will also need those as cleaning instruments for the head. What the hell is a "head?" Bathroom!

I didn't know I could have asked for a second toothbrush. Making us clean the toilets and floors with our toothbrush is awful and I wish someone would have told me to get a second one. It was horrible having 'shitty' breath after cleaning the toilet, or maybe that why my mouth always tasted like shit. Hahaha, sometimes I crack myself up. Aft, Starboard, Keel, give me a break!

A helmet that weighs 50lbs after an hour of wearing it. Helmet liner, stenciled. Flak jacket that you will never use in training except to have extra weight to run around in. Flashlight for when you have fire watch duty. What's fire watch? You watch for fires from 2200 hours (10 pm) till 0430 hours (4:30 am). You better have that red lens on. Shoeshine kit. Need to have a spit shine otherwise you will be in the shit line. Put your name on every piece of equipment they give you. You do not want to lose it, or you are so fucked.

Next, the D.I.'s got us into a constant stream

of consistency. In the mornings we usually woke up at about 0400 or 04:0 hours. This happens typically with a D.I. throwing a trashcan down the bay (the center of where we slept).

We lived in something called a Quonset hut. It was a half a metal barrel cut lengthwise and stuck into the ground. When that trashcan banged its way down the center aisle, we jumped up and lined up as fast as we could. Next was more yelling and throwing things. After that, we got dressed as fast as we could and started our day with running, calling out cadence and Jodie's (songs we had to sing as we ran).

A Jody is the worthless shit of a guy that all of us hate because he is the one guy that our wife/girlfriend is cheating with while we are away. Most of the Jodie's were about how our girlfriends were now free to screw all our friends back home and not worry about us. Luckily, I had no girlfriends. I had broken up with the last one, Theresa, about a week before I arrived here! As I said, I was a shit of a person and it was Tamese's best friend. I just didn't want to leave any attachments that might cause me problems while I was at boot. As awful as it was being alone, I saw how much worse it might be the other way.

The D.I.'s are about the most proficient users of the English language. Never have I heard curse words used in the manner they used them in. It is unbelievable. I never wanted to be the center of attention, but bad luck sometimes happens. I became the center of attention when this short D.I., wish I could remember his name, was yelling at me for some reason. I struggled to keep my eyes just over the top of his head like I am required to do. This time, he takes issue with this and wants to know "why the fuck aren't you looking at me maggot?"

Okay, so I look down and he asks, "Don't you like me?"

Uh, no, not really, but I had no clue what to say. I decided that the best response was "Yes Gunnery Sergeant!"

He questioned, "Really?"

I could tell by his tone I'd fucked up, so I didn't utter shit.

Then of course he said, "If you like me so much, do you want to fuck me?"

What? "NO, Gunnery Sergeant!"

Then he spits, "Then you don't fucking like me, DO YOU?"

Easy answer now. "NO Gunnery Sergeant!" I swear, I couldn't plagiarize this, yes, it was in one of the movies, but the movies were made after I attended boot and it was bellowed very distinctly to my face. After this encounter, my future was set, I knew what I had to do and made the resolution to do it right then and there!

After that exchange, I was done with the Marines. I knew exactly what to do. Whatever these people called themselves didn't matter, they should all be labeled crazy as fuck. I was mentally exhausted, physically abused and had my head so far up my ass I could see out of my mouth. There was no doubt in my mind that I was going to die in this place. Corrections needed to be made. On my first Sunday, I call my parent's house and get my mom on the phone. As logically as I can, I tell my mom, "These monsters here are trying to kill me. You need to call our Congressman and get him involved as well as the Rabbi in getting me out of here!"

I need to enlist as many people as I can to support me getting out! I must have lost control because my mom became calmer than me, which never happens. Next thing I know she is yelling for my Dad and telling him to get on the phone and help me.

No mom, don't tell dad!

"Hello? Marco?"

"Yes..."

"What's wrong?"

"Nothing, except... they're going to fucking kill me." (My Dad hated it when I cursed.)

"Really? Tough huh?"

His matter-of-fact tone made me lose it again. "Dad, you have to help me, these people are crazy! Crazy, Dad!"

"Yep, Cannon Fodder." Then I hear laughter and he hangs up. HE HANGS UP! The man I looked up to, the man I wanted to be like, he just lost that privilege. Not my hero anymore! I had no other plans. I knew it was a last-ditch effort and my plea for help came out of nowhere. I could just hear his laughing at me the rest of my time at boot. I guess in that way, he kept me company the whole time. Thanks, dad. You're a real giver.

After our morning run, we would usually go and get breakfast at the Mess. The Marines never skimped on breakfast. There are always good, hot meals, cereal, bread and lots of fruit. Lunches and dinners were no different. Eating is the best part of each day. We were naturally starving for some reason, and the amount of food we put away was amazing. We had everything we wanted, and as much as we wanted. The Marines made sure we worked for our breakfast and dinner because we have to do exercises while we wait for our turn to go inside.

Usually, for lunch, we receive a break from working out because we had a full schedule to keep. At each breakfast and dinner, we visit the monkey bars which seemed to be a mile long. Start there, climb across hand over hand, then drop, then run in place until the D.I. said drop, then pushups and all this while waiting for the last guy to get done. One thing unexpected is that the monkey bars were like rollers, when you jumped up, grabbed, they rolled. Quite a few guys landed on their asses when they first went up. No one told us they would spin, and we were up eight to nine feet.

No talking, looking around or anything otherwise the D.I. was 1/8 of an inch away from your face and spitting on it as he spoke. I can tell you that one morning as we were going through the line, I saw what looked like steak in the warming tin. That was odd for breakfast.

I approach the server and whisper as best I can, "Is that steak?"

He whispers back, "No, it's liver."

About three or four people ahead of me froze up. You could see them start to quiver and shake. You see, whatever we took, we had to eat. A nice little sly smile crept up slowly on my face. Too bad for the guys ahead of me, I am happy I was able to ask the question without any Drills around. A few people behind me started whispering the dreaded name for the meat.

Liver.

I froze the liver delivery for a short while! I noticed that some of the guys in front of me threw the meat away before they left, and others tried to hide the meat if the D.I.'s were watching. Better to throw it away and get caught than to hide it and get caught. The guys that were caught throwing it away were lucky because the D.I.'s would not make you eat it. They would give you an ass-chewing and push-ups, but that was normal.

The guys who were caught outside with extra meat in their uniform (extra if you get the hint!)? They were lined up and waited until everyone was back outside. Then the ass-chewing about how the Corps has decided what they will eat and not eat. It is not up to the individual to decide. After the ass chewing, they would have to eat it whatever it was. I remember watching one guy throw up and then three others gagging and the fifth one tossing his cookies. Damn if that was gross as shit.

You can get used to anything if it goes on long enough. This is why it became much worse for us all when the drills changed things up.

One change up was the first time they had us eat before the run. We all thought that we would have the morning off from running and go straight to some classes after chow. We all thought wrong and that was the last time we made that mistake. After we left the chow hall, we started marching away, and then, off onto the dirt road, then at a double pace.

Crap. How long were we going to run?

We all drank a lot of milk or water and even coffee. Plus, we had some pretty good food that morning. As we went along, we were singing away our usual Jodie's, and one of the guys in the middle started getting pale. His buddies next to him yelled for the D.I. and we all had to stop. Next thing anyone knew, this guy is puking his guts out all over the place, and then another guy starts to puke. Were all backing up and thankful for the halt so we could keep our meal down. Oh man, the smell! This will make it hard to keep breakfast down.

And then the Drill has this great idea. He gets us all around and starts shouting, "Who wants to be a Marine?"

We all yelled "Me, Gunnery Sergeant" again, and again. We meant it, and even if one of us didn't, we knew better than to say so out loud.

Then he smiles the Sgt Smith smile. "Then get over here and pick this shit UP!"

We all complied. What the hell, just pick up a little and toss it when we can? Nope. Again, he gave us the "who wants to be a Marine" shit.

Okay.

"Me."

That smile again...

"EAT IT!"

Nope! Not going to happen. I saw some of the smarter maggots just drop the puke and start doing pushups. That was a great idea, so I tossed what little I had and wiped my hand clean and started doing pushups. I never looked up, but I think that some guys put it in their mouths. That is unbelievable.

Then I hear the Drill yell at all us who didn't eat. "Get on your face. Begin! FOREVER!"

Not a problem here. C-Rations became much more eatable after that. I always get pork, but someone was always ready to trade. It's not that I ate Kosher, that would be impossible, but I tried my best to follow tradition. If I was hungry, and I suspected something had pork, I would just ignore it and not ask the cooks. I assumed it was beef unless it was obviously pork. The Marines didn't give a rat's ass. If I was hungry, I would eat. I figured that between the two, letting myself starve to death would be the greater sin.

Other memorable things that happened were climbing ropes, poles, logs, and obstacles over and over. One day it got to the point I couldn't make it up a rope. I thought I was the only one. You didn't look around, so you didn't always see the bodies lying down exhausted and not caring about who was yelling.

And there I was about 15 feet off the ground. I couldn't go up anymore and refused to come down. Shithead.

D.I. started swinging the rope back and forth and calling me names. I am telling you, it was like I was in a tornado and he was whipping the rope up and down as well. I fell. On my ass. He ignored me and the next guy started up. That's when I was able to see lots of guys just laying there.

Going through obstacle courses with live fire going on over your head was another interesting drill. Talk about your "pucker factor" going to zero. What is a pucker factor? It's when your asshole closes up so tight a fart can't even make it out. And let me tell you, the only assholes that wouldn't pucker up faster than a hedgehog in a thunderstorm must be drinking milk of magnesia by the bottle.

The D.I.'s of course had targets up about four feet high and a gunner would shoot at that level. There were explosive pits that had things blowing up in them. All this to add realism to keeping our heads down and moving through as fast as we could. A few guys balked at getting started, but when you had a drill right on your ass, well, getting shot was the last thing you worried about.

I remember another time when they had a

seamstress come out and put name tags on our Utility uniform. We all lined up and waited our turn. I forgot what side the name tag went on and which side the Marines went on, so I quietly asked the guy ahead of me where it went. Just as he turned to tell me one of the Drills started yelling, "Who the fuck is talking in my line?"

No one said a word. He then explained all the wonderful things that would happen to the entire platoon if the person who spoke didn't pull themselves out of line and get their punishment. Crap again. I knew that the Drill would be good to his word. We had seen other platoons out late at night doing extra duties because someone wouldn't take the blame. Usually the culprit became a victim buy having a blanket party, so it was best to throw yourself on the blade and accept the punishment. The old "take responsibility for your actions" thing.

I stepped out of line and waited. He escorted me to the front of the line, which was nice hoping I would get to have my stuff sewn on first but instead he placed me directly in front of a large fan that was blowing at full speed. He then explained that I needed to convince the fan that I truly deserved the opportunity to be a Marine and I had better be convincing.

I don't know what the hell I rambled, but I was yelling at the top of my lungs and getting windblown in my face, so my voice sounded weird. Someone laughed, thank God! Next thing I look down and see two recruits doing pushups for every word I spoke. I tried to talk slow, so I didn't kill them or myself.

This lasted for about five minutes and then he stops us, puts his finger in his mouth, and pulls it out making a loud popping noise. He then yells and asks, "Do you know what that sound is, maggots? It's your heads finally popping out of your ass! Now, get the fuck back in line."

I need to remember that one. The job continues to break us, but maybe it's worth it for what we'll turn into when the Marines put us back together.

Their goal was to tear us down until we either quit or allowed them to shape us like a soft piece of clay. Sometimes, we didn't know which we were until it was too late.

The major exercise we constantly do is pushups. You did them every time you looked around. The Drill's favorite quote is, "Go do push-ups till I'm tired." Your brain at some point turns off. As an example, we were doing pushups and here I am, up, down, up, down, next thing you know, a D.I. is standing on my back. Instead of just lying there, not trying to kill myself, and faking it, I am trying to do pushups with this guy on my back!

The whole time this D.I. is yelling at everyone, "Pain is weakness leaving the body." What a moron. Marine material right here.

I remember one guy well. James Ditmore, he

was one of the smartest in the platoon, but he decided he didn't want to be in the Marines. He did what he was supposed to but would always give the D.I.'s shit. I asked him what he was doing, didn't he know that these D.I.'s would get together and beat the hell out of him?

That's when he asked me if I had ever seen a Drill hit anyone.

Hmmm...no, I hadn't.

He told me that last year a Drill had hit a recruit a few times and then when they were in a building, he went to hit him again and the recruit leaped out a three-story window and died.

Not everyone was as soft as clay.

Also, out on the field during Pugil stick training, a D.I. forced recruits to beat on this one kid who was having problems learning. The recruit died of head injuries and both the D.I.'s were convicted of manslaughter.

James told me to look around sometime and we would see an officer or two out on the field. That never happened before. That is a new regulation the Corps put into place to stem the tide of recruits getting beat to hell by the Drills. We were now a kinder and gentler Corps.

Okay, he could test them. No way in hell was I going to. I'd smelled bullshit enough times on my own toothbrush to know better.

The next day we were on a five-mile run and he decided he didn't want to run anymore. Then he quit running and started dawdling. Holy shit! The Drills made us keep running but we all looked back from time to time.

James yelled, "The more you yell, the slower I will be!" He had some balls!

They finally kicked him out because they declared he was gay. He wasn't. The story circulating was that he was cornered and told several D.I.'s to leave him alone. They started pushing him, not hitting, and then called him derogatory names. He finally told them that "yes, he was gay." Then they wanted proof and made him drop his pants and told him what they were going to do. No one knows what happened, but he was in the hospital, and then he was discharged for diminished mental capacity and deviant behavior. You don't mess with the D.I.'s.

I'd call them bigots if they weren't cruel to everyone regardless of race, religion, or sexual orientation. They had the art of discrimination down to an art form. It was just discrimination against anything human. Just like Vietnam soldiers were handed faulty M-16s, drill sergeants were handed old style tools to shape modern Marines and then told abuse was the only way forward, because abuse would prepare Marines for war.

There was another guy, Chuck, who constantly fucked up, not in the same way James did. This man, Chuck Billings, just didn't get it. The Drills told the platoon it was up to us to either fix it or see to it he left. I heard one Drill yell at Chuck, "You are so fucking dumb, if you fell into a barrel of tits, you'd come out sucking your thumb!"

If we didn't fix things regarding Billings, then we would all share in recruit Billings punishment, whatever that ended up being. After seeing what they'd done to James, none of us were eager to find out what they'd do to us. We were ready to obey.

I had no idea how to fix it or how to make him leave. I found out one night what the drills meant when I heard him yelling and crying. It's true, they do give blanket parties. Some of the recruits put soap in their socks, tied a knot, and at about one in the morning went and pulled his sheet over his head, held him down, and beat him.

It's hard to keep to yourself in a group like that. I am outgoing and well liked. But that put things in a different perspective. Here I am, trying to think of ways to help him and never noticed that the D.I.'s not only wanted him out but would endorse all manner of cruelty to make sure it happened.

I had a few friendships that I developed, but these guys were not people I wanted to know well. Most of these guys were truly crazy. James had left already, and I couldn't admit that he was my friend. I'm secure in who I am and wasn't so much worried about them labeling me as gay as whether they'd once again weaponize the accusation.

As much discrimination as gay people continue to face today, those days left even straight people afraid to be mistaken for it.

Back then, it was a very real fear that regardless of your branch of military service, you couldn't afford to be seen as gay. You ran the risk of being beat, shamed, and discriminated against.

Chuck decided to leave rather than get beat again. I know a scene was in Full Metal Jacket like this, but it happened in real life. Instead of killing the D.I. and himself, Chuck did the smart thing and left.

I know these things may make it look like the Marines are an awful place to be, and there were a few more things that we just took in stride or discovered was enough to break us, but the whole idea was to make you into a soldier that would blindly follow orders and do what was best for the team. You were no longer an individual; you were part of a well-oiled machine. A lot of the Drill Instructors came out of Vietnam and had lost a lot of friends. They weren't there to torture us but make sure that if we went to war again, they could count on us, and we could also count on us.

We were told time and time again, you may think you fight for God, Country, and the Girl Next Door—I mean, the American way—but that's not true. You fight for the guy to your left, right, in front and behind you because that's all you got when you're in the shit. You fought for your shipmates and they fought for you. A Marine never leaves anyone behind. Ever.

There was still a lot of anti-military sentiment from the late '60s and early 70's that made things difficult for everyone. We were given classes on ethics and unlawful orders and case studies of things that happened in Vietnam to help us understand right from wrong. Most of us understood the lesson but still had a hard time believing that the United States committed some of the massacres like My Lai in 1968. It was eye-opening, that's for sure.

###

The positive areas outweighed the negatives. We were given instruction and class time to understand our roles as American Fighting men. These were new concepts that were taught to Marines that were excluded from training before. When I heard the NCO's talk about this, it seemed to me that the politics were more of covering your ass rather than doing what's right. It seemed the blame would be shifted from leadership to the last guy on the totem pole. This is just a hard subject to wrap our heads around.

We are trained to kill with overwhelming firepower and now told that we have to be certain about where we shoot and who we're killing. It's great in theory, but not in practice. I can understand disobeying unlawful orders, not allowing indiscriminate shooting and trying to not harm innocent civilians but to prosecute us if we're under fire and returning that fire to save our lives and our team's lives is just stupid. What next? Tell Police Officers that if someone is pointing a gun at them or you or a knife and threatening to kill. You must not use lethal force to protect? Crazy.

Our abilities increased exponentially day by day in hand to hand fighting (Judo, primarily), marksmanship, and marching orders on the field. We had beach assaults, ambushes, reaction training. We all remember the CS Gas training and taking off our masks and then reciting our names and spelling them backward to make sure we got a good lungful of gas, then running outside flapping our arms with drool, snot, and burning eyes. I learned real fast to spell my name backwards—Iksrokis—and how to pronounce my name backwards quickly. Nothing beats watching someone puke up inside their mask because they didn't have a good seal. We ran obstacle courses every day and did night training exercises. We had our Drill Instructors around us all the time, Sergeant Instructors were people that were not our Drills giving us classes.

I remember throwing my first hand grenade. Scared the shit out of me. I remember the training as if it was yesterday- hands at chest, pull the pin, cock back arm, do not drop the pin, release spoon at the same time you throw overhand, drop!

"Why not drop the pin?"

"That's because, Maggot, if you fuck up and don't throw the grenade, you can put the pin back into it so it's safe, moron!"

That was my Sergeant Instructors' mild way of explaining things. The process sounds easy but they always tell you of the recruit who kept the grenade in their hand or dropped it in front of themselves or the one who forgot to let go soon enough and it hit the wall in front and bounced right back at him. You know we were each terrified and thought that we were going to be the one that the D.I.'s would talk about in the future because we killed ourselves. A damn Hand grenade was nothing to fuck around with! Never happened to anyone I saw but it was a rush all the same.

When we were not throwing, the larger group sat in a dugout like you use for baseball but it had a Plexiglas front so we could see what was going on. One weird thing was that there were lots of little pieces of metal shrapnel embedding in the plastic. How did shrapnel hit back here when the grenades were thrown the opposite direction? *One of those things that makes you go hmmm...*I bet some poor trainee (more than one) threw the grenade in the wrong direction!

When we weren't avoiding our own grenades, we ran around the desert areas in Armored Personnel Carriers and Amphibious assault vehicles. The military knew that trouble was brewing in the Middle East. We knew that our biggest threat was still the Soviet Union but after the oil shock in 1973, all eyes were turning to the desert areas.

I could tell we were now training for desert combat. We still trained for jungles but the desert seemed to be taking priority. There was a fun time when they closed off part of the Camp Pendleton beaches, and the civilians were able to watch us assault the beaches. We had our lanes set up and would have to stay within the lines. It was tough training because the areas that were not closed had women in bikini's watching us. Had to focus, focus, focus!

This was harder than you'd think. And speaking as someone who'd already seen firsthand how hard it could be, even I was still shocked.

There was one training exercise when we had the beach assault, and a storm had hit the area prior. The beach was littered with seaweed all over the place. As I jumped out of the landing craft and slogged through the surf, I was paying more attention to the young ladies than I should have. I dropped on the beachhead, pointed my rifle at the imagined enemy, and landed on some squishy seaweed. Not knowing what it was because I didn't look, and my imagination quickly kicked into gear, I believed it was a large jellyfish and it was wrapping itself around me.

As I screamed and rolled away, I noticed laughter, by girls. Damn, and as I rose to attack the beach once again, I finally noticed it was seaweed and I was dragging it along. So here I am, screaming first because I thought it was a giant killer jellyfish, now I'm running with this shit wrapped around me and look stupid hopping along trying to get rid of it. It must have been funny if it wasn't happening to you. Glad no one could see my face. Later, as we went through the after-action report a couple of guys were laughing about some jarhead that panicked and screamed when we hit the beach, I smiled and laughed with them. Thank goodness we all look the same and no one ever knew it was me!

Of course we weren't always running from grenades and wrestling seaweed. Digging foxholes is also fun.

One of many times (the old hurry up and wait trick) we arrived at our objective early and had to dig out our foxholes. Five feet down so if they had to bury us, it would be easy. (Do foxes dig that far down? Don't know) So, I dig this beautiful foxhole and set it up. The Sergeant Instructor comes up and chews me a new ass. "Why in the fuck did you put that hole in the wrong spot, shithead?"

I put it exactly where you pointed.

But I decided that it was better to not say anything.

"Move the fucking hole where it's supposed to go, shit for brains!"

How in the hell am I supposed to move a hole?

I just didn't get it, so I asked him (mistake), "How am I supposed to do that, Sergeant Instructor?"

He picks up the shovel and started throwing dirt all over me and snarls, "You will move the hole by digging the new one where it should be, you will put the dirt from the new hole into the old hole thus correcting your mistake. If you fuck up again, I will personally dig a new hole to bury your sorry ass."

Oh. I understand we need busy work because

we got here too soon. Yep, that was obviously the case as he went up and down the line yelling at us morons and telling everyone to move their goddamn holes.

I think the part that caught my attention the most was the Air Assault. They are called the Air Cav in the Army and the Marines just call everyone Infantry. Every Marine is qualified to do Airmobile operations. This is what I thought I might be able to do if I couldn't fly fighters, maybe helicopters. When fulfilling an Airmobile objective, we load up and head over the ocean, land, mountains, cities. The views are awesome and if you enjoy roller coasters, you'll love this.

I mean, you're skidding through the air and moving up and down. The nose goes down and you're on a never-ending zip line. The back end drops down and you stop on a dime and drop into a landing zone. You name it, we do it and down we come and spring out like rabbits and go onto the attack.

I remember the first time in a chopper. The smell of the canvas, the oil and JP-4 fuel. The rotors turning like crazy until they became a blur. Up and then nose over and accelerate. The feel of the wind in your face going 150 miles an hour, the noise and the vibrations shaking apart the aircraft. And just as suddenly, quiet because you no longer hear the noise, your mind takes you away and you dream the dream of what it's like to truly fly on wings. I like it.

The other area I enjoy is the rifle and pistol

range training[11]. Understand, we never call our rifle a gun, and you will never lose your weapon. We had to tie parachute cord to our rifle and then attach it to our body. This way there happens to be no excuse for losing your weapon. It still happens and the poor soul who leaves his rifle alone pays a heavy price for the next week. The rifle range training ends up being pretty easy for me since I have qualified expert in High School and know just about every weapon.

Gunny Garza is the range master and seems to have a soft spot for me. Besides yelling at me all the time, he somehow makes time to get me out of additional duties to help him at the range. His Hispanic heritage comes out sometimes. It is so funny when he gets pissed, he starts yelling in Spanish and only about a quarter of the jarheads can understand him. The jarheads that understand him just start running around doing what he wants and the rest of us just stand there with our thumbs up our ass. We eventually learned to just follow what the other guys are doing and then ask them questions.

It's nice that Gunny Garza takes an interest in me. He'll just tell my Gunny that he has additional duties that suck and wants me to be assigned to do them. No problem there, my Gunny was happy to give me up thinking I was being miserable somewhere else. I did a lot of shooting with the Gunny Garza and we have some good conversations. He wanted to make sure I applied to OCS (Officer Candidate School)

11   (P. 420) Rifleman's Creed

when I got out to the fleet.

I found out that OCS is officer training and I knew I wasn't smart enough, but Gunny Garza observed I was smarter than 50% of the people out here, maybe more! Not hard when the bar is so low. I told him I would think about it but couldn't pay for school. He explains there are ways. After that, there is just one day after another of training with no end. We are like one of those hamsters in a wheel going around over and over and going nowhere.

I know I brushed over it but another area we had a lot of concentration in was hand to hand fighting. The D.I.'s were very patient with us during this training. Didn't yell at us, helped us with positions, and worked hard to make sure we understood what and why we did the drills. We were told that a lot of guys lost their lives when the units were overrun by the dinks in 'Nam. The Gunny's wanted us to know how to fight when our rifles were not going to be enough. We had a lot of Judo training because some of the cadres had come in from Japan. Another large block of training was from guys that came in from Okinawa. They were not D.I.'s, just Jarheads (nice Sergeant Instructors) that had a lot of training in what they called martial arts, they called this Karate. The two other interesting things I learned were knife (bayonet) fighting skills and, surprise, the e-tool.

The e-(Entrenching) tool is better known to civilians as a shovel. This is no ordinary shovel; it is a little more than two feet long unfolded and about two pounds. It has a serrated edge and a knife-edge if you kept it that way. You can defend yourself very well with it if you learn the techniques. Most of these guys were damn good and told us that no matter what, the best thing we could do is continue the training no matter where we were stationed. Self-defense was needed for all Marines because even civilians were not always predisposed to being nice.

Overall, we just learned that yesterday was the easy day and tomorrow will be a harder day. I think the Marines took that from some football saying at training camps. It isn't always that way but if you had that mindset, you can't be disappointed. Graduation neared and we did a lot of practice of Drill and Ceremony to get ready for marching around and impressing everyone. Every D.I. has their language that we have to learn and understand. On the drill field, they have so many people marching and so many commands being given, if the voices weren't different, then how would you know whose voice and commands to follow? We learned quickly the voice of our God.

My parents came out with David to see me for graduation. Instead of being excited, I soon became embarrassed because my mother started crying when she saw me. In front of everyone. I thought she missed me, but it was more of that she could not understand how I could be so thin; she was sure I was starving to death! I was about 160lbs and 5'6" when I went in and about 5'8" and 138lbs when she next saw me. I grew taller and thinner. I was in the best shape of my life! We did our marching and parade, we were looking good and you knew all the women wanted us! After that, we received our orders for the next training assignment, and I was very lucky. My Drills did like me and recommended that I get my first choice after all. I was assigned Aviation and I was sure I was now going to fly! What I was hoping for in the very beginning was a victory at the end. I was a certified crayon eater. (It's a joke the other services refer to new Marines as.) Nothing in the way now—at least nothing I could see.

Chapter 13

August 1977

After graduation and a week off, it was time to go to my first assignment at Camp Pendleton.[12] I wasn't accepted to Aviation per se, and though the particulars are lost to time, I think it's because someone fooled me. I'm still just a Jarhead. If I want anything better, I have to go after it. What I needed was a job I could dominate like no one else.

I could apply for a job where the competition was fierce and only the best rose to the top.

Or I could apply for a job you'd have to be dumber than hell to want to do, but at least I'd be the best.

So I applied for a position in Machine Guns. Not too many people wanted to hump a .50, .30, or 7.62, so it was easy to get in. Gunny Garza had told me to get MOS 0331 and ask to be a door gunner on a Huey (UH-1, Iroquois helicopter). He explained to me that they were begging for people. Sounded great! Like everything else, I should have asked why they were begging when we had so many recruits. Another lesson learned. I later found out that the life expectancy of a door gunner was 5 minutes in combat. He is the one person, hanging out of a helicopter, shooting at people on the ground that has usually up

---

12   (P. 421) 1st Battalion, 5th Marines, 1st Marine Div

to 100 people on the ground shooting back at him. Not the best of odds.

I didn't want to be carrying around one of the big guns, or ammo for that big gun. So, I hoped I was able to stay on helicopters. You had to look like a gorilla and be built like a monster to handle the .50 and .30, but not so much the 60.

During training, we were able to shoot all these weapons so I was very familiar with what they could do and what they weighed. Also, flying around in a helicopter sure beat being a ground pounder so the two went together perfect. Ground gunners operated in a 3-man team because of the equipment. On a chopper, not a problem, you were a one-man team unless there was another gunner on the other side of the chopper. All we had to do was load it on the chopper, strap the gun in, and link the ammo belts but after that, rock and roll. We started with ground training, so we were familiar with the .50 cal and .30. Those two could eat up most anything that it came up against except a tank. Shooting these were a kid's dream. The feeling of power behind those machineguns is something else.

The M-60, 7.62mm, the light machine gun is what I familiarized myself with.[13] I know that is what is on most choppers so I learned everything I could about it. It is a very simple weapon and easy to fire. As long as you had your "headspace and timing" all was good! Headspace and timing only apply to the

_____

13   (P. 421) M60 info

M2, .50cal but is used to mean if you set things up correctly, you won't have a problem. Qualification was not hard on any of these machineguns. The rounds went a long way and the tracers helped you track and hit anything you pointed at, and whatever you hit was usually destroyed. Next up, getting helicopter rides. Everyone in the Marines rides helicopters. Vietnam proved that it was the fastest way to get you into hell. Since Marines always were welcome in hell, we had the fastest machines to get there! I will admit, as much as I enjoyed flying, helicopters took some getting used to. I am told that the machine was built of 3000 parts all going in different and opposite directions and aerodynamically was proven to be unable to fly. It is built by the cheapest builder that won the contract and to top it all off, these all were the hand-me-downs from the Army that stated their useful life has expired. Welcome to the Corps once again.

I enjoy the flying and we had several options on our 'birds' to use when we were setting up. The first is a fixed option. A mount is on the floor and set with interrupts so we could only safely fire up so high, down so low and so much to each side. I know the pilots liked that one best. It was sure to stop some private from shooting down their own helicopter or killing the pilot.

Next, the bungee system or strap system.[14] A top mount had several straps or bungee cords set

14   (P. 422) M60 Bungee system

up and it took the weight of the M-60 so the gunner had a lot of flexibility to where he could shoot. A good system, but the pilot had to deal with someone who may not be the sharpest tack in the box and lose situational awareness. If this happened, the gunner can shoot up his aircraft. The last was the most stupid but still used from time to time. Big guys like to do what was called "free 60." Yep, just shoot from the hip. Do you know how hard that is? I don't because I never did it. It's scary enough being on a roller coaster that can throw your sorry ass out at every turn. Now imagine holding a machine gun while twisting and turning. And then trying to shoot during all this without losing control of the gun. No thank you.

That was the next thing, staying in the damn bird when the pilot and co-pilot were jazzed up and trying to twist your guts up because they were getting shot at. You could use the lap belt and be very secure, but it didn't give you the ability to see where you needed to shoot. The seat was adjustable, so you could be looking out the side of the bird, not out the front, but it still wasn't as flexible as the second method known as a monkey harness.

Ah, the monkey harness. It's like you were tied to the aircraft but could bounce pretty much anywhere you needed to. You could still fall out, but not very far. Your ability to lean out of the aircraft and shoot was a lot easier. Most everyone used this along with the bungees. I was told that this method was preferred in Vietnam because when you needed to take on bodies, you could hop out and help if needed but be dragged back in if you were hurt somehow.

We went up every two to three days practicing missions and getting target practice in from the sky. Other days from the ground. It was fun, exciting, and being in the "real" Corps or Fleet was much better than being a recruit. You still were yelled at, and officers didn't notice you- or you tried to not get noticed which was smarter. It is an art form to not be noticed and I tried to be a master of the ghost persuasion. We had barracks which were apartments. Two people to a room, desk, shared bathroom with the other two guys on the other side. Not bad at all. We still went through inspections which were usually the OD (officer of the day) having to look for drugs.

Each time the OD inspected my barrack for drugs, my heart raced. It didn't make sense to me. My drugs were booze and girls, but when it came to the illegal stuff, I was a straight edge. They'd never catch me with any of it.

But my heart raced. I couldn't think straight. I couldn't remember. But once it finally slowed down, I remembered why. For you to understand what happened, first I need to tell you about the man who almost destroyed my brother's life.

Chapter 14

Drugs were there alright, usually marijuana. I never used it or tasted it because of what happened to my little brother David.

The story from my father is that my brother, David, was born on a U.S. Air Force Base and the Doctor that delivered him was a user. The Doc was "high" on Marijuana and used the forceps too hard during delivery on my brother causing a brain injury. His motor skills were destroyed and his ability to communicate verbally was hurt as well. Yes and No is all he can vocalize, and it was hard for him just to say those two words. He is as smart as any of us but in a broken body. I helped take care of my brother since we were young kids. I never let his broken body get in the way of our relationship, nor let him get away with not doing stupid things I thought up.

I probably caused more injuries to him than he would have on his own by all the stupid stuff I cooked up. He didn't have a choice because what was he going to do? Run away? Nope.

The stuff I did to him would make any brother hate me. I never really thought of him as disabled, so when my friends went skateboarding, well, his wheelchair was just a big skateboard. I would jump on the back and we would start at the top of a very long road and all of us went rushing down, laughing all the way. As we neared the end, I could see a large curb and as my friends hit the curb, they leaped up and ran on the grass, saving themselves. Oh oh. I could leap but David was tied in with a seat belt. He was so fucked. So was I.

If I came home with less cuts or bruises than my brother, my Dad would beat me. Only choice, hit the curb with him, fly through the air and get crushed by the wheelchair. It was monumental, bent the wheels and broke the Plexiglas tray he had in front of him. We learned how to do it better in the future.

Next up, racing my Fiat. I used to do something called ridge racing. We would race along dirt ridges with steep drop-offs on both sides. Anywhere between fifty to two-hundred feet. The one time we really almost died was when David, who I strapped in the seat next to me, decided to reach out and grab my damn steering wheel. He has a spasticity that can't be controlled, and I guess the excitement produced the perfect timing so that it made him reach out and grab the wheel. Here we are, going about forty miles an hour into a turn and David decides we don't need to make the turn but fly off the hillside in a blaze of glory. This gave the term 'drifting' a whole new meaning.

I'm screaming at the top of my lungs for him to let go, but unfortunately that only tightens his grip on the wheel as he pulls it toward himself. As my life flashed before my eyes, he suddenly let's go. That created a new problem; I was pulling with all my strength the other direction. Lucky I was braking all that time and we did a three sixty on a narrow ridge and ended up in the right direction. A big smile from both of us and off we went. From then on, I strapped his arms together as well!

One last story about my poor brother. I must have been about eleven years old and David nine. I had the brilliant idea of climbing up about twenty-five feet up a ladder and on to a diving board. Yes, I put him over my shoulders, told him not to move too much otherwise I might drop him. He might have been a little scared.

As I walked out to the edge of the board, I scanned the numerous amounts of people below us. In my loudest voice, I yelled, "Mom, Dad, watch this!"

The crowd was hushed to silence and all eyes locked on to us. Can you imagine the looks I got from everyone? David is screaming at the top of his lungs and I have this big smile on my face as I leaped off with my brother. I hit the water so hard that I lost him somewhere in the bubbles. All I could do was think about how pissed my Dad would be if I didn't find my little brother. There he is, at the bottom of the nine-foot pool! Got him, grab him and up we went, ready to do it again. Guess what, I didn't get to do it again. That day. Lucky, he lived, but he has a life![15]

---

15   (P. 423) My brother David

Chapter 15

This Doctor ruined David's life to be normal for no other reason than to make his own shitty life go away for a little bit. That's the excuse I hear from all the young guys here: MJ makes their stress go away.

Fine, but go into another line of work. You can't hold someone's life in one hand while you've got a joint in the other.

This is why I have utter contempt for users of this drug and most any other drug including alcohol. Drug users observe it gives them clarity and calms them down. It helps them see more clearly or take away the stress. They have so many excuses as to why it should be legal. Sure, a bunch of BS and I will never forgive anyone who hurts someone else because they used drugs or alcohol.

I won't trample on a person's right to drink or smoke, but when it comes to endangering another person's life? I will not be guilty of the Sin of Omission.

I have seen it go wrong firsthand on the firing ranges where guys were "high" and thought they were the "shit." They couldn't hit the broad side of a barn but thought they were freaking John Wayne. It was fun watching the safety officer pull them off the line and having the NCOIC beat the fuck out of them. Remember when I said recruits could not be touched because officers were usually around watching? Not so in the Fleet.

The danger didn't stay with them on the

ground. Can you imagine going off to fight and having someone you needed to rely on being fucked up? How about a helicopter pilot flying around or a tank commander turning up high?

Needless to say, I made sure my roommates understood I didn't care what they did, but that was one thing that if they used in the field, I would personally kill them. Fortunately, we all got along. I would note that more than half in the unit were probably users, but as far as I could tell, that didn't include anyone on my team. It would have been very hard for them to hide any usage because the smell would have given them away. I was very paranoid to any new deodorant or aftershave. I didn't want my career or life ruined by some drug user.

Some of the fun we had was in dropping off infantry in the field. We would light up an area after artillery had pounded it, drop the poor suckers off, and then fly off to pick up others. We got to hear stories about choppers that went into "hot" LZ's and picked up wounded during firefights, which is some brave shit. I did not want to be one of those guys but would do whatever I was told. The position for door gunner was a volunteer position so we usually got pretty good people. Sometimes a little mental, but I think we all might have been slightly bent.

We all were able to visit San Diego and the surrounding areas now and had our weekends to ourselves, mostly. The Gaslamp Quarter of San Diego had most of the bars and women around so that was the usual destination. We had to be careful because the Navy liked to go there also and sometimes, we would find ourselves at odds with them. Rambling down the street proved to be difficult because the squids thought they should occupy the same spot we were occupying, so, we usually made them move.

Most times I was the smallest guy at 5'8" and my buddies would usually push me out front to start a fight. I never remember not starting one. Well, I didn't start it, I just helped move it along, but it usually broke up pretty quick when we heard police were on the way. We even helped each other because no one wants to go to jail and then explain to the Chief or Gunny what we were doing. Chiefs existed in the Navy which was like our Gunny's.

I do remember a time where I hit someone, and they just stood there. That was not a good sign of what would happen next. I got my share of beatings, but I am sure I gave more than I received.

The worst beating I never got was when we all went in to get our Marine Corps tattoos. I decided to put "Chesty" the Devil Dog on my arm. Different guys with different tattoos. There were four of us at the time and I watched the first guy get started. There was blood. And a needle. He was getting the Marine Corps flag. I don't know if it was blood or ink, but it was a lot of red. This is not what I expected. I didn't think about how the damn thing is put on your body.

It's not a peel and stick, is it?

He had tears running out of his eyes and

his face looked like someone was torturing him. Sometimes the biggest guys are the pussies, so I discounted him. My next buddy sits and it's the globe and anchor. I remember that vividly. A big ass needle and more blood. I don't think this is going to happen at this point for me. He looks as if someone took a hammer to his head. The third guy seals it for me. He just starts to curse and looks like he is going to either puke or shit. Don't know which but I head out the door and waited for them to come out. They prattled a few words to me but I told them to shut up or I'd hit them in their tattoo and end the discussion. I never did get the tattoo and have no desire to ever have one. I hate needles.

The other part of Gaslamp besides beating squids was the girls. Southern California in San Diego. We just hit the beaches and then the bars, and then the girls, after all, what else did we have to spend our money on? Most all the girls were friendly, and I had a pretty good time. I was not looking for a girlfriend, that's for sure so things were easier for me than some of the other guys. One of my best pick-up lines was, "Want to save water? Shower with a Marine."

A lot of my buddies picked up girlfriends and suddenly, they had these expectations put on them. Too bad, buddy. Do this, do that, why didn't you call? Why don't you care? Do you love me? Oh my God, they wouldn't shut up. They were worse than a Drill Instructor!

One of the nice things was it made it much

easier to get dates because all these girls were trying to introduce me to their girlfriends. I didn't have too many lonely Friday or Saturday nights. I had a couple of girls that came close to getting me exclusive, but my brain engaged at the right times to get me away from commitments. Yes, I did have a few girls pissed at me, as well as my buddies and their girlfriends. I don't think my buddies were pissed, they just had to put up with their girlfriends nagging at them that I was an ass and took advantage of their friends and then left them. Sorry? Not my fault.

Eleanor Roosevelt said it best:

"The Marines I have seen around the world have the cleanest bodies, the filthiest minds, the highest morale, and the lowest morals of any group of animals I have ever seen. Thank God for the United States Marine Corps!" –Eleanor Roosevelt, First Lady of the U.S. 1945

Chapter 16

September–October 1977

After the three-week qualification[16], we were getting ready for our duty assignments. I was going to stay at Camp Pendleton or head to the desert at 29 Palms. The hope was I would have orders to just stay at Pendleton. I got my wish and was assigned to a troop movement detachment but didn't get a true gunship. That is a Huey decked out to provide pure fire-support. I was on a troop carrier with just one door gunner. I could switch sides but the pilot I was assigned to wanted me on his side so he could direct the fire if needed.

What do I know?

Great question, because in the end, we didn't *do* much of anything. I found out what "support" really meant. Sit around and wait till someone needs you. The other problem was being a low man on the totem pole meant that every additional duty was headed my way. We all had a lot of clean up assignments—go pick up trash, go paint something, go help move stuff, mow the parade field. Boring.

There were a lot of days at the ranges practicing with my M16 and M60. I enjoyed the free time to shoot and met Gunnery Sergeant Hardin at this point. He is a weapons expert in the unit and range officer. We got along well even if he was a Gunny. He is the

---

16   (P. 424) MOS 0331 Machine Gunner

first Gunny I met that had a neck. That didn't make things any better, it just meant we could see his neck muscles straining when he wanted to kill one of us, which was often. He showed me a few things about moving targets and helped me understand better the art of placing rounds ahead of people to make sure when the enemy got to a certain spot, there was a bullet to meet them.

We were always shooting at static targets and this was something new to learn. He allowed me to fire the M14 Sniper rifle which was the Platoon Sniper weapon. He showed me some new rifles that were coming out and we were able to fire all types of rifles and pistols. Gunny Hardin knew Gunny Garza well and they discussed me. Hardin mentioned we needed to start the paperwork to see if I could get a slot in OCS or the Academy. There wasn't anything to lose so, sure, why not sign the ton of paperwork to maybe get to college. Since I was lied to about getting to fly airplanes, maybe this was the way to meet that goal. I put the thought of college out of my head after signing the paperwork because I'm simple minded, and I figured nothing would come of it since I wasn't too bright to begin with and you had to be really smart to go to college. Hopefully after my obligation, I could think about these things.

One day late in the month we received a briefing asking for volunteers for a mission down south. That sounded interesting. So, what's down south of Pendleton? Texas? Mexico? I head on over with a few other guys to the main auditorium. It seems a lot of people are bored, and the place is filling up.

On stage, the brass shows up and along with them are some guys with sunglasses and suits. It is all pretty dramatic because there are armed guards and were told at the beginning that this is a closed briefing and should be considered secure. I guess that means secret? Who knows?

When the doors were closing, the guards stepped outside to make sure there was no unauthorized access. The suits begin by declaring, "The President is concerned about drugs pouring up from Central and South America and into the United States. We are going to help 'interdict' that flow with the help of governments of Central America. We, the United States, has been requested to provide air mobility to multinational troops as well as equipment to help battle the drug lords." Well, I guess that's why we all were sitting in this big auditorium with a few hundred soldiers, volunteers in the making and we were all ready, willing, and able, including yours truly. Our training is mission-specific so all I have to do is protect the aircraft if we receive ground fire and support any units that are on the ground.

No additional duties, extra pay, and maybe some action. I decide to sign up.

What the hell, it's what I wanted, right?

When you're that young, you know you're going to live forever! Besides, this was doing a good, positive thing for society and the United States. Since

I didn't like the drugs that are being brought up to the USA it would feel good to "stem the tide." Maybe I could get some payback for what the drugs did to my brother. When you're young, it feels so easy to tell the good guys from the bad guys, and I had drugs and anything they touched in my sights.

Another positive is that the only thing I had to worry about was myself. The logistics of getting ready for deployment simply didn't matter to me because being a Lance Corporal, I am just responsible for myself and what equipment I have to bring. This meant for me, an M16, and an M60 but that would be the armorer's job. We each had about 75lbs of personal equipment that we packed and were told we would be living out of GP Large, which is a very large tent. Not only that, but we would also have all the C-rations we could ever want.

I'm not sure how everyone was going to get there, but I was told we would be deploying to Panama with rest breaks in between, just the pilots, crew chiefs, and essential personnel, of which I was one.

Soon enough, we would be in Panama. Just one problem. We were never going to Panama. That is a ruse.

The real base of operations ended up being in Honduras. President Carter is having a lot of difficulty with all the countries down there. They are fighting each other over borders and internally each country has Soviet-led insurgents trying to take over the governments. We are told to sign paperwork that stated that talking about any operations that take place will be a federal offense, and if we do, we will serve jail time. The U.S. has been sending military aid to all these countries one way or another in the form of cash, materials, or advisors. Being just a lowly jarhead, there was no real reason to keep up on the governments, politics, or what was happening in these countries.

As far as I am concerned, I am just going to terminate the drug movement. Give me the paperwork - one thing I'm good at is signing Marine paperwork! After all, I signed up to be a pilot. Look how well that worked out for me. At least they let me hang out the side of a helicopter, right?

I began to out-process from my current unit and am comfortable with what I was going to do and am ready and willing to put my training into action.

One thing I didn't count on was having to go back to the hospital and get a series of shots. They called it POM—preparation overseas movement. I hate needles. I did not want shots. I did not like shots and now it was too late to back out. All I could think of was the flashback of Boot where men in their underwear are laying on the floor acting like worms. I didn't want to go through that again.

As I went in to get these shots, I didn't see any Corpsman, what I did see were nurses. Pretty, blond, brunette women all in the same place. I think I had a dream about this once except it was much more

149

wonderful than this nightmare was going to be. Now, I had to act like I was a stud and not afraid of a simple set of shots.

Okay, I am going to give it the best shot (no pun intended) at this as I can.

I hesitated, couldn't do it, breaking down…

A very attractive nurse came over with my first shot and I just told her, "Get that away, I've changed my mind, I can't do this." That seemed to work because she was so understanding.

She smiled at me and put her hands on my shoulder and caressed me lightly. In a seductive voice she purrs, "Roll up your sleeve, and if you're a good boy, I promise you'll get something sweet at the end to put in your mouth."

Oh God. I can't turn down this date!

I closed my eyes and felt the sharp pin go into my arm. I wanted to scream bloody murder so loud because of the pain that was being inflicted on me, but my resolve held. She gently grazed my back and kept her hand on me. This was so much different than the Gunny smile and one hundred and fifty-pound hand when I was being recruited felt. I would have followed her anywhere.

I suffered through the next two shots and the last one with some kind of air gun. Relieved that the hell I just went through was over I was ready for that phone number or address. She smiled and asked me to come over to a metal desk and she rummaged around. This was so good: my charms worked even when my eyes teared up.

What is she holding up? A sucker? I don't want a sucker...

At least not for a lollipop, but her lips looked like a tasty treat.

She led me out of the room and as our eyes met, I knew I had been suckered after all! She handed me a lemon lollipop, and I enjoyed it as best I could. Wishful thinking was all I had left. And soon enough, it would be my last hope.

We were being released from our units and forming a set of new units. Nothing that was on the "books." I'm not sure how that happens but it didn't seem like we appeared on any "real" authorized unit lists. This isn't just strange. It's scary.

When I asked what unit I was in, I was told not to worry about it, just listed as chalk 3. We were also told to pack our stuff as it would be put into storage and after our tour of duty. Our personal effects would be shipped to wherever our new orders were sending us.

We would not be coming back to the original units that we left, and they could not tell us where we would end up when this was all done.

All I have left is wishful thinking, but wishes and prayers and hand grenades are useless when you don't know what you're facing.

Chapter 17

Late October 1977

Later in life, I understood what was really on the agenda. We were fighting drug runners and drug lords but if you read the history of each of the countries, Honduras, El Salvador, Nicaragua, and Guatemala, you will see we were supporting dictatorships or trying to topple them based on the daily political arrangements. Honduras was at the center of the four at-risk countries and we had, I think, the best relationship with them of the four.

As we landed our helicopters from our journey from the states, we could see that advanced elements had already prepared the airfields and bivouac areas for us. This was a big positive that made me happy because I wouldn't have to do anything but set up my own space. It looked like we sent quite a bit of money to these governments in the hope that they would change things and do better by the population. You could see the money that was spent here in the form of equipment and people. I had read though that there was so much bribery and graft in these countries that it didn't matter what we sent; it wouldn't help. It certainly never made it down to the towns and villages we were at. Maybe when we started spending our script, it would help some of these people.

Our area of operations is someplace called Cerro Grande. Nothing there but a forested jungle area. We are south of the capital and just north of a larger city, Sabana Grande, where we could get supplies and take some time off. I wish I had more detail, but I am a worker, not a planner. When we have a mission, all I know are three things.

We are taking off

We are going someplace

We are dropping troops or laying down firepower.[17]

Our first real mission after familiarization flights in-country is to support a sweep operation that government troops are doing. Because the mission is just about an hour's flight, I am sure it still will be in Honduras. I guess we could be going to El Salvador or Nicaragua but that would have been a bit of a stretch. We mounted up and checked our systems. Once we lifted off that entailed us going over an empty zone and checking our weapons by firing them at nothing. It also gave the pilots a chance to work out some kinks and make sure the aircraft was ready for the mission.

As we approach the area, the pilot let us know that there had been ground fire on the insertion of soldiers earlier, so we needed to stay alert. The government troops were going to be driving the enemy south and west of us and we were supposed to support a blocking party that was like an anvil blocking the way. The pilot was told that there were American troops in the blocking party but not in the sweep troops. I took that to mean, be careful not to

17   (P. 424) Me (age 18) and my gear ready for action

hit the blocking party, but otherwise...

We landed in an open area and I and the other door gunner leaped out with our 16's to provide some security. When I got out of the chopper, the late summer heat wrapped around me like a thick jacket. You could see wisps steam rising out of the jungle ahead of us. We needed to wait here for a bit until the troops called us in because they were starting the engagement.

An easy way to know when it's time to leave is when the propellers started moving. That is the time to haul ass and get back into the bird.

The wait wasn't that long. After about thirty minutes on the ground, the rotors started turning and the pilots waved their hands for us to get back to the chopper. Up we went and heading for our overwatch position. The cool air and the downdraft of the rotors made things much better for me in my sweat-soaked shirt. Wearing the flak jacket didn't help much, but it was unbuttoned so I could cool off a bit more.

I couldn't see anything because of the ground cover, but we understood we would attack when the enemy had to cross some open fields. The blocking force would engage and drive them to the open fields and that was our time to come in and help terminate their existence. When word came over the radio, the pilot explained that our angle of attack will have the right side engage first and when we made our turn, I would engage.

This is going to be intense. I have never shot

at a person before. I understand that this is what all the training is about, but still, this is some scary shit.

The thoughts that run through my mind are driving me crazy. Will they all be just staring up at me? Running, hell, probably shooting at me! I suddenly don't like that idea. The joking about door-gunners lasting about three minutes wasn't so funny now. I've trained on moving targets, but from the ground, never from the air. When I shoot, it's from static positions. What if I fucked up and we get shot down?

I don't need to be thinking about this shit. I hope the pilot knows what the hell he's doing. I steal a glance upfront, he doesn't look stressed, but the copilot does!

The Chief is just grinning and mumbling to himself, "Gonna get some."

What the hell does that mean? Fuck me, I really have to do this. I don't want to see their faces, not if I have to kill them. I hope we stay high.

The chopper pilot has done this many times before and told us to stay buckled in because if we fell out, no one was coming to get us. That made your pucker factor go to zero. I double and triple checked my monkey harness. I should button up my vest because with my luck a bullet would find an open area. Now I start thinking about the chair with the belt I could strap in with.

Screw flexibility, staying in the aircraft is more important.

Unfortunately, it's too late now.[18]

As the chopper banks hard into our run, I look over the shoulder of the right-side door gunner, but I can't see anything except a mess of green. But just because I can't see what's happening doesn't mean I can't hear it.

The opposite door gunner starts shooting at something or someone. Bam Bam Bam over and over. The whole craft is shaking, and it's only an M60. The next thing I hear is "taking fire", "evasive action." Up we go, then straight down. My stomach went straight to my brain. Then it feels like we turned like a roller coaster.

The pilot hollers, "Ski, your turn." Just like another day at the office.

I'm already scared, and it's my turn? Now my breakfast is in my mouth and I am supposed to shoot? This is the last time I am going to eat before a mission! I can't see very many people on the ground in front of me. A few people are laying in the clearing and some running back the way they came. I see some blinking lights on the ground and the pilot yells at me, "Shoot the fucking blinking lights, Ski!"

That is the muzzle blast of rifles shooting up at me. Boy, do I shoot. I'm aiming but we are going a million miles an hour and bouncing up and down and skidding left and right. I don't think I'm hitting a damn thing, but at least I'm holding the trigger down and creating some kind of distraction. After the pass,

---

18 (P. 425) My Chopper and our flight

we're told to move away and hold for a few.

That was quick. Almost too quick.

The thinking is that the enemy will be pushed back through the open area again or close to it and we will get another chance to attack. I have no idea what I was shooting at. We moved so fast and were high enough that all I was able to see were outlines. I think I shot at whoever was shooting at me, but for all I know, I could have shot cats and dogs as well, if there were any out there.

There are four ships in our flight, and we have no other birds in the area providing support. My heart hammers in my chest louder than gunfire. If we make another pass, I have to do better.

But after a few minutes of hovering in place, we're called off and RTB (return to base.)

Looking out over the jungle canopy, everything looked the same, green, green, and more green. My heart ought to know we're headed back, but it won't quiet. It maintains a steady pace, a rat-a-tat-tat steadier than the guns.

I sure hope the pilot knows his way back.

###

When I hopped out of the chopper, my legs wouldn't hold me up. Somehow, I managed but was a bit wobbly. The other gunner felt the same way. The crew chief went through the aircraft and made his inspection with us. After tearing down the aircraft, we inspect for damage so maintenance can do the repairs and clean everything up. No bullet holes or damage, just brass.

Looking inside the aircraft, I thought most of the brass from our guns would fall out of the aircraft but there is a shitload on the floor. That's my job, cleaning up the brass.

My next job is tearing down the M60 and cleaning it before I turn it in. It's not a hard job, just time-consuming. There are not a lot of parts, removing the barrel group, swabbing it out and lubing it. Taking apart the receiver group that feeds the belt of bullets, next the Operating group and buffer group that have the most moving parts. You need to clean them and oil the shit out of it. This area needs to slide and fire. After that, the trigger and stock group. The mistake most newbies make is that they get the oil into the gas cylinder. That clogs up the system so it's the only area you need to be careful with. Gunny Hardin taught me to make sure it is cleaned to perfection because the next time you use it, you needed it to purr. I inspected both M60's as did the other gunner and we went to turn them in. Next stop, the After-Action Review.

I was happy to listen in to see if we did any good out in the field. Maybe another gunner kept track whether one or two of my bullets hit more than air.

Jokes aside, I also wanted learn a little more about what we were doing here. The helicopters were not as effective as the mission commander would have liked and we didn't do much killing. When we showed up, our success was in driving the enemy right back where they came from, which was the wrong direction. We pushed them back to the sweepers who were not in defensive positions and the surprised sweepers took more casualties than they should have. The enemy was able to escape the anvil that was set up for them.

I shook my head. Even if my aim had been good, the mission would have still gone to hell, but that didn't excuse my performance. I had to do better next time. Because as they then explained, there most certainly would be a next time.

Next time, instead of coming in behind the blocking force, we would work our way around and come in with the sweep teams. This way we could continue driving them where we wanted them to go and let up our fire as they were committed to the blocking force. One positive thing was that the sweep team had destroyed a base camp in the area.

After thinking about it, I had one question.

A base camp is usually military. Shouldn't it have been a drug manufacturing or storage or something else instead? I hope we didn't stir up a hornet's nest.

That was my first real-world experience in making contact with the enemy. We hadn't been hit, I don't think I hit anyone, much less killed anyone, and I learned what scared shitless was. Boot camp was easy compared to this!

The other gunner and I started our meander

back to the tent area and I could tell he needed to talk. I held out my hand and declared, "My friends call me Ski. You might as well too."

He didn't so much relax as breathe a sigh of relief that turned into unexpected enthusiasm. "I'm Lee, my first name's John, but I just go by Lee, too many Johns!"

This was his first time out as well and we both looked at each other and laughed. He was as scared shitless as me. "I won't tell anyone how you about pissed your pants if you don't tell anyone about me."

Lee announces, "No fucking way will anyone ever know, after all, we were badass, right?"

We both knew that was bullshit! Lee is one of those big guys that likes big guns. He didn't hold the M-60 free style (in just his hands), but I wouldn't put it past him if the crew chief or pilot would let him.

Lee likes to work out a lot and out here he improvised with whatever he could find. I watched him lifting ammo crates, mortar tubes, and sandbags. I liked working with him primarily because he would lift the 60 for me. I guess he figured he was impressing me, and I just thought, "What a strong guy! How can I use him to my benefit?"

We went up in the choppers with different teams practicing crew loads and how well we could work as a team. We were told what chopper to report to and then meet the pilot and crew chief. Back in the real world, we had our teams and kept together. This was way different than what we usually did. Lee had been on a few practice missions with me and the crew chief was thinking about keeping us together going forward.

An interesting side note was that I swear I saw a CH-53 out in the distance. That's a much bigger helicopter. I asked around and was told that there were some PJ's (USAF Pararescue) out for training. I sure wouldn't want that kind of training. These guys were badass. I met a couple back in the U.S. on training and they had no fear. Their job was to be dropped someplace no one wanted to be and recover or save pilots and crew. They also had a mini-gun on board the aircraft. My M60 is hot shit - the mini is like a razor cutting everything it hit. If I did fall out, these guys would be the ones to recover me or at least my body.

After a bit, the powers that be settled in on the crews that would be in each bird and it made things a bit easier—or harder if you had an asshole crew chief or pilot. I have it good on both accounts.

I didn't talk to the two pilots very much and just a little to the crew chief. He was a nice guy but kept to himself. It was me and Lee who became fast as thieves. Ink and Dink they called us. We had a couple of missions where nothing happened and had different pilots, but Lee and I were able to stay together. Ink and Dink to the rescue, the best combo in the unit.

Chapter 18

9 November 1977

It's now early November and the word comes down that the Honduran Government Intelligence has found a large production facility that is in a jungle area pretty far from our position. Lee and I head on over to the briefing tent and stand around the back with about 20 other gunners and crew chiefs. All the pilots get the good spots with chairs but what the hell, we can at least move when the bugs come in, they have to just sweat and get bit.

Some Colonel gets up near some maps and starts talking about the mission. The Honduran government is going to supply a large number of troops to a FOB (forward operating base) and we will pick them up and drop them off at a staging area. This is the first time we would be moving a large number of soldiers. As he goes through the list of units, I notice that both the CH-53—two of them—and four Cobra gunships would be reinforcing us.

The Cobra is a mean M.F. The main gun is a 20mm Cannon which is in the nose of the aircraft. Also, it can carry side pods with small 70mm unguided missiles that will ruin the enemy's day as well. The Cobra looks like a thin grasshopper nose on so it's hard to track and it is fast. Nothing can withstand its firepower, not even a tank. I'd seen one once on a live-fire range destroy some bunkers, old tanks, and some five-ton trucks. A lot of fun to watch. The whole area explodes in a beautiful choreograph scene of destruction.

The CH-53's are made by Sikorsky Aircraft. I wish I was related! The CH-53 is a big helicopter and has a minigun on the side as well as one on the back ramp. These were the P.J.'s main platform and I was very happy to see them as part of the plan. I could see a lot of pilots smile and get a bit more comfortable when they heard the CH-53's mission as a search and rescue platform.

This new mission is going to be a major operation because we are going to have foreign soldiers on our bird. In addition to this, we are going to fly at the maximum range of our fuel and are told we would refuel on the ground before our mission. I didn't like the sound of that because wherever we are going it's far away. Scuttlebutt is that we are going to Nicaragua, someplace near San Lucas which is in the northwest corner of the country. It won't be the first time Marines are there. In July 1930, Chesty Puller won his first of five Navy crosses chasing Sandino guerrillas in Nicaragua.

Might be a violation of somebody's border? I mean, I guess, we can go wherever we want, but Honduras troops in Nicaragua?

It made about as much sense as me being in the Navy, bunch of squid truck drivers moving real men to battle.

By this time I was a little curious as to what

was going on in the countries we were helping. Before this mission, I asked some of the officers about past missions, governments, and the troops we were supporting. The officers who did talk to me have some interesting views. The Gunny's I talked to told me they weren't paid to "think" and neither was I, so stay out of it. Not going to happen, I wanted no part in any "omission" of what was going on.

What I can piece together is that we are going to attack a staging area of the Sandinistas in Nicaragua. The Sandinistas are trying to overthrow Somoza's dictatorship (the President of Nicaragua) that the U.S. supports. Not drugs as we are told. The U.S. is concerned that if Nicaragua fell to the communists then El Salvador might be next, and then the godless communists' eyes would be on Honduras and Guatemala after that. This northward climb by the Soviet Union would go right up to Mexico. The Soviet Union is sponsoring insurgencies all over the world and it's believed that they are also providing advisors to the guerrillas. Better Dead than Red is the motto.

I know the CIA is involved heavily in this because almost every briefing includes the men in suits. The briefing broke up and the enlisted Jarheads were told to stick around. Lee and I quickly nabbed a seat when the pilots left. We wait, and then we wait, and then we wait some more. We aren't leaving without info. It was like watching golf on TV, real action. After about thirty minutes the suits show back up. Obviously were pretty low on the totem pole.

The suits started talking about operational security and that we needed to just do our jobs, support the ground troops, and shut up. We are not to ask the pilots any questions and our officers would brief us in more detail with whatever they deemed we needed. What a bunch of jerks. Who were we going to call or talk to? I like these guys less and less. At the end of the mini briefing/ass-chewing, they remind us about our non-discloser and we are not to talk about these missions.

Fine. Probably dead anyway with these guys in charge.

We hustle down to eat chow and sit and talk a little about the briefing and what we needed to get ready for tomorrow. Lee isn't feeling the love any more than I am with the spooks. I'd like to go over and talk to them but that nagging feeling—plus Lee telling me to not be stupid—prevent me from opening my big mouth.

We needed to get the M60's mounted and covered tomorrow as well as link up the ammo. I'm hoping for a thousand rounds for each gun but that might not happen since we will be bringing in troops. We will have to get that clarified tomorrow by the Gunny. The next thing will be to reconfigure the aircraft for the soldiers. This will give me and Lee a much smaller area to fight from.

When we put in the seats for the soldiers, they will be facing front and back. We will have a small bench seat behind them facing the side. It's a real bitch because our ammo cans will be linked and go under the seats and then up to us by a metal bridge. This will hopefully lessen the chances of the links breaking or getting jammed. Not ideal. Also, even though we will be wearing our flight helmets, it's hard to hear shit and this position doesn't let the chief talk directly to us if he needs to. With all the noise of the rotors, the headsets and mic don't always work well.

I'm also going to bring an extra flak vest to put down under my legs and ass just in case. If we're moving that many people and then going to fight with them, there is going to be a lot of metal flying around and this will give me a little extra protection.

With a full belly and our checklist done for the morning, we trundle off to the GP Large to get some rest.

I wake up to some heat and humidity and know it's going to be a scorcher of a day. Lee comes over and acts like he's going to piss on me.

When did we become friends again?

But I feel lighter knowing we are.

I give him a quick kick and hop up to get ready. Laughing, we head off to breakfast and when we're done, make sure our canteens are filled for the morning. We meet up with Gunny who has been with us on the last couple of flights. He has the maintenance monkey there and going over the chopper. He pauses and gives us a little grief about taking our time getting to the bird and goes back to talking with the monkey. We set up our mounts and double set them (a second pair just in case). We check our monkey harnesses for tears or latches that are not closing, all good. I set up my flak vest and Lee looks over and mumbles, "WTF? Where did you get the extra vest? I want one!"

I explained, "I traded it for a ride a few weeks ago, some head cook wanted a ride and I got them permission. The cost was his flak vest. Told him after this deployment was done I'd give it back."

Lee looked like he would steal my vest, so I told him I would cut his balls off if my vest was missing in the morning. That seemed to stop his gluttonous eyes from wanting my shit.

Next up, picking up the M60's. A jeep came by and picked us up and took us to the armorer. He was ready for us and we signed for our M60's, covers, and cleaning gear. We would take the cleaning kits with us so that we could make sure the guns were all oiled up before we went on mission. The Marine in the jeep drove us back and helped us unload. He stuck around, which was nice because we needed him next to go pick up ammo. He had never helped with the bungee system in mounting the M60s and wanted to learn. No problem, OJT (On the Job Training) for this guy. We were able to get things done a little quicker with him there, which was helpful. I pulled the Gunny aside and told him my concerns about the ammo and the weight. Could we bring two thousand rounds or would that be too much weight?

The Gunny remarks, "That's about one hundred and twenty pounds, should not be a problem. Link up five hundred and have a break for the next five hundred. That way if we need to kick some out, there not all linked together."

"Roger that," I respond.

Off we go to the ammo dump and get the rounds. I am pretty happy to have too much ammo. This time our new buddy doesn't want to stick around and help link up the ammo. No problem, we have armed guards out here in the flight area so we have him take us to lunch and get a break for ourselves. After lunch, we get back to the chopper and start linking the ammo.

The Gunny shows up with a crate of C-rats and smiles at us. With a wink and a nod, he says, "Just in case."

Evening comes and we go to our next mission brief. The commander of our four-man flight—he's ranked as a Major—gives the briefing. He looks very uncomfortable, shoulders tight, face even tighter, eyes tightest of all.

I wonder why?

The Major explains that we will be flying into another nation-state and destroying a drug manufacturing site that is presumed to be defended by a large contingent of enemy insurgents that will be well-armed. We are part of a 12-ship formation and if any of us goes down, the two choppers will be tasked to form a protective ring and pick up along with two Cobras providing overwatch.

If we went down in an occupied area, the Cobras would blast the area clean and CH-53 would be on the ground to pick up. I like this idea a lot. If I fell out, maybe I would be picked up! That Monkey harness would be as tight as it ever could be. If we went down, we are to stay as close to the crash site as possible for pick up. We are not going to leave anyone behind that could be paraded in front of any cameras showing American involvement.

This got me to thinking again. We were going someplace that we didn't have permission. Also, since we were picking up troops from an outside staging site, they might not have been Honduras troops at all but Somoza's people.

I hate to say it, but they all looked the same and spoke the same and acted the same, so no way I could tell them apart. The CIA may have been lying to the State Department about the operations and this is the only way it can be done.

We all head over for dinner and everyone is thinking about tomorrow's mission, somehow we forgot today, November 10, is the Marines' birthday. Two hundred and two years. Look at the spread for us. Someone went over to the city, or village and we were having steaks, potatoes, and all sorts of weird stuff. Happy Birthday, Marines! I know I said I wouldn't eat a lot before a mission, but I am not passing up on steak.

First of all because it smelled delicious.

And second of all because everything tastes good when it might be the last thing you ever eat.

I sure as hell hope this isn't my last meal.

Chapter 19

11 November 1977

Veterans Day in the U.S. is a buffet of parades and BBQs. Or as we called it in the service, a BBG: barbeque, beer, and girls. None of that for us except an early morning wake up, breakfast, and a ride out to the airfield. It is an impressive display though; better than any Veterans Day parade I've seen. There were twenty-four ships all set and ready to go. We are in the fourth chalk—each chalk is made up of four birds, so that puts us in the second wave.

We go through our preflight checks, which for me is making sure the ammo is set up, belt feeds are good and the tie-downs inside are set. All seats are in place and safe tied with cotter pins. My harness is set up, and lucky for Lee, my flak vest is on my seat where it belongs.

I take off the cover on the M60 but don't cycle any rounds through. Accidentally firing the thing would be a great way to start the mission, right?

I check in with the chief and we make our comm checks. All good. Won't hear anything when this bird lights up, but what can you do? The pilot goes through his preflight and we just listen in. Rotors are ready and he calls out to spin them up.

I'm watching the empty flights ahead of us taking off, and before you know it, its skids up for us. I verified our ammo load before we left and saw we had room for extra, but the crew chief said that space was reserved for the C-Rations.

"I've been shot down before," he said. "I'll be damned if I starve waiting for one of the rear area MFs dummies to pick me up."

Screw that. What if you get attacked? Trade rations for your life?

7.62mm was a better deal for me.

The flight is kicking along nicely. I brought my camera intending to take a couple of pictures, but the wind coming through is about 140 mph. The camera is next to worthless when I'm more intent on holding onto the damn thing than taking pictures. Still, I squeeze in I hope I get some good ones when I get this developed.

Trees, green canopy everywhere. I've heard the term "a sea of trees" but now I had the full effect. There was no way out if we went down. And the pictures would reveal that sea of mysterious green. Who knows what is in hidden beneath that beautiful canopy?

I do! Shit that will kill you and then eat you. No thanks. Better to take a picture. It'll last longer and won't risk its life just from existing.

After over an hour of flying, I see a large open area with smoke rising and tents set up. This must be our FOB.

When we land it's as if a self-contained base has been set up to take us. Most everything looks new and the fuel bladders are there as promised. We aren't going to stay long, just for the night. We refueled from the bladders, ate, and Lee and I elected to sleep in the choppers. I didn't know these people; I didn't trust them and I sure as hell wasn't going to be away from my ride out of here. We don't have to supply security because the troops that are here already had that job covered.

The sun comes up early once again and the heat has a mist rising out around us from the jungle. Lee and I uncover the M60's again and oil them up good. C-rations all around and the pilots show up fresh as daisies. Big smiles on their faces and they go and relieve themselves at the front of the aircraft. That's their ritual superstitious crap (pun intended again). The Gunny shows up and tells us to lock and load the M60's. That's not protocol, but if he orders it, we do it.

Charging handles back, round chambered and safety on. Intercom checks out all around and we're ready to load. I can see hundreds of soldiers now lining up. These guys are not in the same uniforms I've become accustomed to seeing at our base camp.

Damn, if the rumor mill is right, these are Samoza's people.

The pilots told us we were not starting until everyone was on board. Usually, we're running hot and ready to load ASAP. Feels dangerous. Not my call, but since we're not taking fire, I guess it's safe.

Here they come. It's 0600 hours and the chalks are loading up. We are getting seven soldiers plus me and Lee, the crew chief, and the two pilots. We are heavy but have to go just under 112 clicks (kilometers), or about 70 miles for civilians, we didn't have to go high so we should be okay.

Part of the mission brief is that some other units would provide ground transportation for the units we dropped, and we would not see them again.

That's another reason I don't think we're in Honduras.

The drop off points are about 10 clicks to the north of where the enemy base is plotted, so the troops had to do some organization and humping through the jungle. That will be a few hours depending on the terrain. Not too much fun to be them! It is a bit humid and warm, the rotors are spinning up creating a cooler breeze, and the air is providing the lift. Up, up, and watching the line behind us do the same.

This is what it's all about, slicks and gunships getting ready to go into the storms. We are at treetop level and just flying like a falcon, claws out, ready for the hunt. A rumor going around, but not confirmed is that some pilots had loudspeakers hooked up to a tape reel so they could play music as they fired on the enemy, psychological warfare is what I was told. That will be awesome if any ships do this.

I can barely hear the pilot tell us to check our weapons, and I see sparks flying out of the trail birds.

"Light 'em up!"

RRRRHHHHup...

The Pig (M60) is rutting into the jungle and no

misfires or problems. I report in all good and clear. Same as Lee. No clouds out today and you can see forever, that "sea of trees" once again.

We arrived at the staging area and dropped off all the soldiers. We didn't have much of a mission until things got hot in the zone so we shut down and broke out some C-rat's. The unit we dropped left about 25 soldiers to provide security but none of the Chiefs seemed to care, they made all the gunners go out and provide extra security with our 16's. I kept a close eye on the choppers, again, the signal was if we see the rotors turning, we hauled ass back.

I found myself a nice little spot in some shade as did Lee and we tried to relax. Both of us took turns going back to the chopper to get updates and try to not get too bored. During that time I asked the Chief if we could move out of the cramped gunner slot and into the main cabin since we didn't need to haul troops. Thank goodness he said yes. I changed out first and set up the new feeds on the M60 and then Lee went and did the same.

Afterward, Lee came back and confided, "Good call, Ski."

We waited for about four hours at our stations, and then Lee came back and got me. He said, "We're getting reports over the radios about some large caliber weapons being shot and the recon units engaging."

I could see the rotors starting to spin up and hauled ass to the bird. Checklist and harness all tight. I let the Chief know with a thumbs up and off we went. I could hear most of the chatter over the radio net and there were ships ahead of us I could see shooting into the area. The next thing I hear from the pilot is we have orders to light 'em up because it's our turn to provide supporting fire for the ground troops. The shit is going to hit the fan! Off we go and it's our twelve choppers coming in hot.

When we break cover and have our first look at the area, it seems to be a small city scorched out of the jungle. I'd never seen anything like it, the air is thick with smoke, tracer fire makes long ribbons of light, pointing up or down, whichever way the shooter is firing. Troops in the open shooting at other troops in uniform and people not in uniform. We are low to the ground and all I see is everyone running everywhere, having no idea who is who. RPGs (Rocket Propelled Grenades) going off and exploding with heavy percussions. Heavy machineguns blast away, tearing up the jungle and town. The noise rose over the chopper and somehow, I can hear all of this while wearing a crew helmet. It is insane!

I am looking at hell from above and we are just sitting there watching and waiting for someone to call us in. Blinking lights are stretching to hit us, but we are too far away for the rifles to be effective. The chaos is unreal, and the only way I can tell good from bad is in the direction of the tracers.

I had barely any idea of whose side any of them are on. Watching from my vantage point, I could see women grabbing kids and going to the jungle away from it all.

WTF?

We were here to shoot the enemy. Soldiers. People who signed up for war and would take our lives if we didn't take theirs. What did women and children have to do with the mission?

Soldiers shoot in their direction. People fall like dominoes, puppets that lost their strings. Kids being dragged along, dead, wounded, or just out of energy. The soldiers on the ground didn't care where they shot or who. I know I couldn't hear the screaming over the gunfire, but damned if I didn't as good as hear it anyway.

My blood boiled. I've been angry before, but never like this.

I yell on the mike, "Pull us around and over to those kids, Captain!"

But the pilot refused to get close enough. We have a mission. Saving women and children isn't part of it.

But killing them is?

What's wrong with him? This isn't right! It's both of the fucking Sins!

I don't give a fuck who those soldiers are, they can see what and who their rounds are hitting and they don't care. We can terminate them. We *should* terminate them.

But the pilot is yelling at me. "Shut the fuck up Ski, we're not getting shot down for anyone, get off the goddamn net!"

Those images are now seared into my brain, especially when the kids fell. Motherfuckers. Women and kids. Wet shit was coming out of my eyes.

Must be the high wind in my face.

"SKI! Wake up! Your side, heavy machinegun 3 o'clock. Going in hot."

A spray of bullets tears up the side of the chopper, reminding me that it isn't just the people on the ground that could die. My life is on the line, too.

"Roger." I see the heavy machinegun and its gunner surrounded by sandbags. It looks like a .30cal. The M60 won't go through the bags so I have to get an overhead shot. Another chopper is tearing it up.

Do I shoot also?

Only if his aim was true, but his angle isn't right. Mine is. Here goes!

Thunder and lightning erupt out of my hands, full auto, 650 rounds per minute dealing death and destruction. Twenty, fifty, one-hundred rounds impact. No more fire coming from that emplacement and its smoking. We're heading higher and away. "Nice shooting, Ski." I have no idea what I just did. I pulled the trigger and watched the tracers dance to the targets. Red mist exploded.

They're dead. I can't believe it. All those people gone in a spray of red mist.

"Chopper hit, going down," a voice says.

What? We're hit?

NO!

Everything looks good, no smoke from where I

sit. Then I see it. It's not us that's going down. At least then I would know what to do.

We're moving back into hell on earth when the falling Huey comes into view. It's hit and found a clearing close enough to auto rotate into a controlled descent. We're now crossing in front of the smoking chopper and dropping in front of it. Another chopper is coming alongside us covering the downed chopper completely. I can't see the bird anymore but can now smell the smoke.

Is it going to blow up and take us out also?

"Shoot Ski, shoot!"

Who is yelling at me...?

It's me. I'm screaming. Ordering myself to get my shit together and follow my training.

Soldiers are moving towards us but there not there anymore.

Did they fall?

More soldiers show up out of the smoke. I feel the power running through my hands. I'm choosing death for these people. I'm burning through ammo.

Did they fall asleep? I mean, they just went down.

But I know the truth.

I'm plowing rounds through them as fast as I can fire, but there's too many. Lee and the crew chief fly out and are plucking the guys out of the downed chopper. Blood is everywhere on the floorboards and sidewalls. I can feel them bumping into me. We're still sitting there and I'm still screaming. I wish I could quit. I know this is it, but we're not leaving yet.

More people rush towards us. I can see their faces, that's how close they are. Rounds are pinging off the metal, sparks are flying around me. I hear and feel flies buzzing past me, tugging at me trying to take me down, but they're not flies.

My head is screaming get us the FUCK out of here! My mouth keeps that to myself. The only orders on the menu are fire, kill, or rescue. There is no retreat with wounded men on the ground and the enemy still advancing.

The second chopper is lifting, and their gunners are plowing away at people on the ground, and my barrel is glowing. I'm an idiot, I'm incinerating the barrel. Never mind, better the barrel then me. I must have killed a hundred people. When will this end?

Now I can't hear anything, but I see. The world in front of me blows up. I mean, it blows the hell up. I'm about to die. About fifty to seventy-five yards away from me doesn't exist anymore except for dirt, dust, and explosions. These blasts are so strong I can feel them in my bones, it's like a heavy bass tone that vibrates my insides.

What comes flying out at me through the blasts now are not people but parts of people. I see arms, legs, and just parts. Slow-motion. I see what used to be people flying towards me in the air.

Can you even understand? It's a horror show.

Just parts and they are coming in to kill me. Some parts hit the rotor, blood splashes on me like

I'm running through a water sprinkler.

My stomach churns and threatens to fire its own rounds.

What hell just came down from the sky?

God reached down and declared, here is the angel of death, and then a Cobra flashes by and turns for another run further back. 70mm rockets from the side pods were coming out like dragon fire, the 3-barrel 20mm cannon was roaring death from above, and thank God we are finally lifting off and away from hell.

I can taste the copper sensation of blood in my mouth. Sweat is dripping into my eyes and running down my nose and face along with blood. We're moving out with two more choppers, leaving the area and going back to the staging area.

Get us away, please!

I'm stunned, speechless, shocked. I still can't hear but somehow, I have my hands in this guy's stomach. I am pushing his guts back inside him. I know him - we'd hung out a few times at the M60 school. I can't remember his name, but he is just staring at me like I'm a ghost. I'm either covered in his blood, my blood, or the enemy's blood. The Chief is working on the other guy's arm and wrapping it.

I'm yelling at the Chief, "Help me get this guy cleaned and wrapped!"

Chief just shout's, "Keep pushing his guts inside and keep the pressure on the outside!"

I can barely hear him over the rotors, but screw

it, I pull up his shirt and get a gauze packet from the first aid kit and start wrapping this guy up. Gunny tells me to leave it, but I won't. I did pretty well in combat med training and had him wrapped up, found two sticks of morphine, and shot him up. Next, I put a big M on his forehead (to let the Corpsman and doctors know he has been given morphine, so please don't overdose him) and attached both empty sticks to his utilities. I felt like a machine and knew what I was doing. This was one thing I could feel great about.

The third guy seemed to be okay, but he's just sitting there and wouldn't or couldn't help. I have no idea how I got pulled off the gun and moved to help the Chief. The second chopper picked up the other two guys and a Cobra went back and destroyed for good the chopper that was hit. Thank goodness, when we land, the Corpsmen were going to be at the landing site to pick up the wounded.

I looked over at my M60 and saw that I had ruined the barrel. It was still smoking and would never fire again. I guess when my gun locked up and ceased firing, Chief pulled me off and told me what to do to help him with the two wounded Marines.

I asked the Chief, "Why were you telling me to just push the guy's guts in?"

Chief answered, "The gut wound is fatal and that's why I worked on the other guy's arm. Save who you can."

Lee kept his M60 manned and ready because he had to shoot just in case more bad guys tried to take us out. The ride back was an hour of hell, but I stayed with my wounded buddy and held his hand and talked to him. He just stared but he was alive.

We finally landed, and the Corpsmen are standing by to pull off the two wounded. I roll out of the chopper, sat down, and puked. Not moving from that position because it was better than standing I decide to just sit there a bit.

Gunnery Sgt Davison sits down next to me and just looks at me. I never really talked to him before even though he was the crew chief. He didn't want to talk to anyone either. Gunny was infantry in 'Nam and transferred to choppers in 68. I never saw a man so alert. I think he slept with both eyes open. He was the type of guy that just showed up without you even knowing he was there. I think when he was younger he could glide through the woods without bending a blade of grass. He fit the mold, no neck, all muscles, but he did have more around the waist than most of the Gunnies I had the privilege to meet. The transfer to choppers got him out of constantly running around and his eating habits didn't change.

As we sit and try to calm down, he doesn't talk for a bit and then gives me some advice on how he handled situations like this in 'Nam.

"Ski, you gotta just lock it up."

Lock what the fuck up? How do you lock up kids and women being shot and body parts reaching out to maul you, grab you and pull you down to hell? Doesn't he realize I had my hand in someone's body, trying to keep his guts from spilling out?

He explains, "If you don't put this away, it will stay with you and haunt you for the rest of your life. Your fucking brain will lock up and you will be on drugs for the rest of your life. Is this what you want?"

I don't have an answer. I don't want that, but I also don't want *this*.

Chief goes on and confides, "Vietnam was a different kind of war, and by God, I saw things there that were about as bad as any man could ever see. It would have paralyzed me if I didn't find a way to deal with it. I needed to push the memories where I couldn't get at it very easily."

This is where he taught me his trick.

He says, "I learned to take a little piece of my brain—my memory—and put it in a box. Lock it tight. Put it away. It will always be there because you can't un-forget, but you can hide it."

He is right. It is a memory that I don't ever want to talk about or see again. It's not like a scene at the movies. How can so much shit happen in such a short time? It was only ten or fifteen minutes, but I swear it was an hour or more. It was a lifetime. My eyes keep replaying the attack on the women and kids by supposed allies. The Cobra attack, not my attack on those soldiers.

My throat is sore, and Chief tells me I was vocal, and it is the first time he heard me cursing like a Marine. Something along the lines of "Eat Shit and Die Mother Fuckers."

I believe Chief Davison saved my mind from blowing up that day. I completely learned that you have to pull up your bootstraps and get on with living. Because one thing for sure, nobody else is going to do it for you. As every Marine is taught: improvise, adapt and overcome.

How you get on with living determines whether that beast you locked up is a prisoner fighting isolation until it escapes—and you explode—or a tortured part of you that may never be whole but at least can be rehabilitated. Of course I didn't know that then, but even if I had, knowing you have to get on with living doesn't tell you how to do it. *I never talked about any of these experiences in all my years. Only from time to time, to other combat veterans when we were sharing lies. This is the first time I have ever told anyone all of this.*

We still had a job to do. Inspecting our chopper, we found we had about 20-30 holes in our aircraft, no more or less than anyone else. Some critical areas were hit, and the bird would be out of action for a few days. The maintenance jarheads showed up and washed out the floor and inside from all the blood. I didn't know there could be that much blood spewed like a fire hose inside the bird.

And of course it wasn't just blood. It was also what the blood came from. We had body parts in our chopper. How the hell did they get there? I know I could never have cleaned out the aircraft at that time.[19]

19   (P. 427) 282nd Air Assault

How any of us came out without being hit is beyond me. This is one of the times I believed in God. Not that he was on my side, but that he willed me to not die. One aircraft was lost, two wounded. I heard the M60 guy lived, was rotated stateside and I had my first credit of saving a life rather than taking one. No one teaches you how to fix a gut wound and I am very happy I didn't freeze up. They stated the mission was a success and that hopefully, we would have more just like it. I prayed to God that I never have anything like this again.

There is no way I can ever do justice and explain the sheer terror of it all. I don't think I will ever be stressed out by bullshit anymore. After this, anyone that complains about the stress they have from some bullshit crap, I'll just shoot them in the face and shout, "That's stress mother fucker!"

Fuck you. Fuck you... Fuck you!

I am so pumped and drained at the same time. It's horrible, but I just want to go kill someone, I just am so pissed about killing people that now I want to kill someone. It makes no sense and maybe a doctor can tell me why I think this way.

Women and children, how could they?

Fuck them all to hell. Veterans Day means something to me now that no one else will ever know.

So for those of you reading this, keep it just between us, okay?

Chapter 20

13 November 1977

I wake up from a deep sleep that would not let me go. Looking around gave me no idea about where I am. A dark green ceiling moves slowly with what sounds like wind. A tent, that's where I am, not in Riverside, not safe, but someplace hot, humid, and—now I remember—bloody. Blood. Everywhere.

My nightmare has me clawing through a river of blood with dismembered body parts bumping against me. Fuck, Gunny promised if I locked things up, this would not happen. My T-Shirt is soaked, as are my underwear.

Crap, did I piss myself?

Thankfully, no, just sweat. I'm not sure I even slept but it is morning, the sun is out. The sun rays are shooting through small cracks in the tent trying to give me a gift of light to hold on to. Last night is coming into focus, dinner at the mess, throwing up because of too much beer.

Why did I chug so much?

I have as good a reason as those soldiers that shot women and kids. This is to say I don't have a good reason. I just have the weight of what I did and whether I can live with it.

Someone stripped me and put me in bed because I sure as hell I didn't do it.

My heart is racing and bad shit is running

through my head.

I need to talk to Davison. I need to get out of here. I panic, and leaping out of the hooch, I look for Davison. He needs to fix me.

Someone yells, I get hit from behind, and I start kicking. Another body lands on me and puts me in a headlock, arms pinned. Was I captured? Is this a cruel joke? No, it's Lee and a couple of other Marines. They have me tied up well. I feel myself being carried back into that tent, and the smell of canvas becomes a comfort. No worries ... back in the green womb of the Corps.

A Corpsman comes over. He has a needle in his hand. Do I tell him I hate shots? No, put whatever you got in me pal, send me off someplace nice.

Lee sits next to me and starts mumbling things. Maybe he is talking and I just hear mumbles, like he's speaking another language. That's okay Lee, one day you will learn to talk like a man.

For the second time today, I get to open my eyes. I feel better, and this time Lee has my shit out like he's a butler.

I wonder why?

I know I woke up but then went back to sleep. For some reason, I am happy old reliable Lee is here and will plod with me to breakfast. Why is Lee always taking care of me? It's one of those things Marines don't have to explain. We always have each other's backs. He feels I saved his life that day. He says that I did all the heavy work and kept the bad guys from hitting him. He believes in God and states I was put on that bird for one purpose only and that was to save the lives of all of the men on both choppers. Lee also said he will never leave me alone and it is now his responsibility to make sure I come out of this alive. Fuck. That means I have to do the same. Kill me with honor, why don't you!

Chief Davison is waiting for us and waved us over to the NCO section. We never eat with the NCOs, so something must be wrong.

It is silent for a bit and the Chief looks at me. "Go get some lunch, Ski, and come back here so we can chat a bit."

Lunch? Looking around the group, I notice that it is lunch being served. What happened last night? Must have been wasted because a few hours just became missing.

Lee grabs my arm and whispers, "Let's go Zombie man before Gunny gets pissed."

I still don't know how it became lunchtime but my stomach is growling like a dog ready to kill. We take our grub and work our way back to the table. It has cleared out a bit from when we left. Not sure why, but maybe Gunny wants to talk to me alone.

Gunny looks at me while I imitate a pig. "You good, Ski? Heard you were crying for me this morning and the Doc had to give you a shot."

I have no idea what he's talking about, but I don't need to know for me to fight back. "Gunny, if I was crying for you, it was because you were dead and nobody else cared."

"That's fine, Ski, knowing you love me makes my dick hard. Besides that, let's talk about yesterday. You did well yesterday, but the action is going to stay with you for a bit. I'm going to put you in for a much-needed break."

Anything was better than these guys pressing me to talk about what had happened.

Did I get the golden ticket? Why is he being nice to me?

"I want to go over with you what others saw from the air yesterday. No one else in the air was as close to the action as you were, and a couple of other choppers providing top cover reported what was happening. Their after-action reports observed that the enemy was about 30 to 40 yards away from us, but the combination of the door gunner—which was you—and the Cobra that came in decimated the attack. The Cobra pilot wanted to know how the hell you were doing because when he passed by, he mentioned you were putting as much lead into the targets as he was."

The nightmare was creeping back. Suddenly the food wasn't tasting good and my hunger fell down a black hole.

Davison continued, "I've seen my share of shit and yesterday was pretty intense, even for this old cowboy. Did you know somewhere in all of that you ran out of ammo and linked in the next five-hundred rounds?"

I just stared at him. I don't remember anything.

I'm not going to eat anymore and Lee was finishing up his chow.

Davison finished off his talk to us with a nice ending. He said, "The company commander is giving our flight a week off from missions to regroup and get some downtime for maintenance and repairs."

Fine with me. Sleep, eat, shit, but only the one problem, no women. I barely escaped death. All I want to do now is taste a bit of life.

Chief continues with, "You're able to go into town and get some R&R (Rest and Relaxation). You just have to promise to stay out of trouble. The only way I can assure that is if you stick to me like glue."

This sounded great, but you know. I had one question.

"When can we go?"

"Tomorrow. After the Doc has checked us all out."

I'll be ready, that's for sure.

As we were getting up, Chief tells Lee to leave as he wants to talk to me alone. Lee, being the smart man he is, decides to disappear like a ghost, but he mutters he'll wait for me at the tent.

Davison sat back and has another NCO I didn't know come over.

Chief stares at me intently. "I want you to tell me in detail again what transpired yesterday from the moment we landed down at the busted chopper."

"I don't want to. I locked it up as you told me to."

Chief smiled and comments, "You didn't do a very good job, so let's open the box, talk about it, and beat the shit out of it. We will put it back in the box and lock it up again when we're done."

What is he, a psychologist?

If he didn't scare me shitless, I'd tell him I already got my therapy order from him. Lock it up and throw away the key.

I stutter, "No, I would rather just leave it alone."

Hasn't there been enough crap infecting the small reaches of my mind already?

But Chief knows something I don't, and I can hear it in his voice. He's been through this before, and as much as I want to tell him to kill his good advice like those guys killed those kids, the better part of me recognizes that I need his insight. This thing inside me can stay locked up forever, but if I don't deal with it, it will haunt me forever too. It will fester and explode and hurt the people I care about the most, and because I never stopped to heal what I experienced, I won't even be able to tell them why my anger can be so volatile.

The Chief barks at me, perhaps sensing the way to bring out my anger is with his own. "Okay, how about I beat your ass instead and put you in a box."

Hmm...I hate it when they get all logical on me.

I sit there and decide to let loose again. It was difficult for me to described what I saw and felt. I fell over it like a waterfall dropping one hundred feet. The memory poured out, but when it hit bottom, it sprayed blood everywhere once again. When I was done, I did not feel good at all and was drained like a well that gave up its last drop. Had I honestly tried to hold all of that inside me?

It would be decades later before I understood how important it was to talk about this before it broke me. If not for him, you wouldn't be holding this memoir.

The Chief looks at me with a surprising amount of relief. "You did great under fire. I'm proud of what you did."

That surprises me. No one ever comments that they are proud of me except for Mr. Williams. I always wanted to hear my father utter that, but it never came. Hoping to one day be good enough for him made me try harder in everything, but nothing was good enough, but here in the jungle, someone was proud of me.

Let's find that box and wrestle this demon back into it. Crushing the shit out of it, kicking it in the ass, off the demon went again, this time whimpering all the way. I'm feeling pretty good after this. I really am. I guess I had to talk about it, acknowledge it, face it, and then put it six feet under. Bury it forever. My Psycho(logist) Gunny knew what he was talking about.

Hey Chief, "That other NCO? Why is he listening in on us?"

Davison spits, "why, he's here to help me beat the shit out of you in case you went nuts. It happened a few times in 'Nam and it always works better when it's two against one!" *Glad I didn't go nuts!*

Chapter 21

14 November 1977

Going to sleep tonight is a little better than last night, no drumbeats of war playing on my skull. I go to sleep with visions of meeting beautiful girls and food. Lots of grilled meat!

Waking up and seeing the same tent as I did yesterday didn't put me in a bad mindset. Today is R&R. Lee has his shit in his ruck and we put our rucks outside the tent and head over for breakfast. SOS today (Shit on a Shingle or chipped beef in cream), one of my favorites along with biscuits. The cooks must want us back!

We wolf down our food and take some fruit for the trip out. The five-ton trucks are already lined up, I'm sure the drivers are just as excited to go someplace different as well. The paymaster is waiting near the trucks and this answers the question of what do we use for money. We snatched our rucks and lined up to hopefully get some good old Uncle Sam's money. I can hear some grumbling as we get closer and when I go sign for my money, I notice it's not U.S. currency but something called Lempira. What the hell is this? Were also given some script that looks like our money, but we're told the locals can exchange it for U.S. dollars.

The paymaster adds, "Use the Lempira first. Each Lempira is worth about fifty cents and fifty cents will give you a full meal in any of the villages."

Fifty cents barely gets you a hot dog back home. What paradise is this?

I think I will stay here forever. This is part of Uncle Sam's program as well, give us money to spend on the local economy and we will "win their hearts and minds." That's an old Vietnam program that didn't work either. Don't matter anyway.

Free money, I'm all in.

We all start climbing in the five-ton trucks and a new, unsettling concern hit me. We don't have any weapons. I try to tamp down my fear but it gets the best of me.

I grasp Lee by the shoulders. "If the shit hits the fan out here, what do we do?"

"We got guys with us that have 16's. If any of them go down, we get to them first."

It's a plan at least. I also have my bayonet that I'm not supposed to have, but fuck that shit. It is quite a ride in the back of the trucks. The rear and side panels are open so we could see the countryside as we drive past—thick, dense jungle. Anything could be hiding in there, even Godzilla. Probably all sorts of shit like lions tigers and bears, oh my! I can handle any of those things but don't let me near a fucking snake, I will cut its head off in a second, don't care, it's dead.

All the guys are smoking and joking about things and what we will find in the city/village. It's about an hour and a half ride and some spots are pretty rough. As we get closer to the city the road has more asphalt than dirt which smoothes out the ride. I've seen forests, and some jungle, but this was like a woven basket with very little room to go through. The look is very different than when you're flying above.

Seeing it this close makes me more worried about getting shot down in this type of terrain. Truly, no way out. I need to put this stuff out of my mind quickly and try to enjoy what's coming up rather than worrying about something that hasn't happened. We arrive in the city at 1300 hours and it looks like a ghost town. Everyone is probably on Siesta. I wouldn't know. I just heard they had Siesta's in Mexico so figured maybe it was the same in all Latin American countries.

The streets were very clean, and the people were well dressed. Some were poor but seemed to take care of themselves. It was like a small mid-western town in the United States. We stuck out like a sore thumb and felt a little self-conscious. I had no clue what we were supposed to do but we didn't have to worry. A few signs say "G.I.'s Welcome." Problem was, we weren't G.I.'s, but we weren't going to dispel a perfectly good reason for them to be a little hospitable.

Our first mission is to find a place to eat since we hadn't had any food since breakfast. We stuck our heads inside a couple of places that appeared open to see what the inside looked like. As we headed into one restaurant, I spotted a couple of young ladies that were pretty hot.

I gave them my best smile and raised my

eyebrows in a sweet hello. They smiled back and started giggling. I knew where I wanted to eat.

Then an older version of the girls came out of the backroom and scooted them along.

Damn, already on to us cowboys.

The older lady brought over these menus. I had no idea what they said but the pictures looked good, and as I looked up at her, she looked pretty good also. Okay, I've been in the jungle too long, she must be at least thirty.

A couple of guys spoke Spanish, so they translated the menu for us. Chorizo, pork, pulled pork, ground pork, pork this, pork that, rice and beans.

Rice? What the hell is rice doing out here—isn't that in Asia and Japan?

Lots of rice and beans. Steak? Yeah, steak with weird stuff in it. Bananas. Different kinds. They had these homemade flour tortillas that smelled great. I ordered the steak (Carne) wrapped in tortillas, no beans or rice, please. The drinks were varied, and some guys ordered this milky-white drink that had cinnamon and nutmeg and some other stuff.

When in Rome, right?

I tasted it—awful. What is it even made of...? Rolling it around on my tongue tells me. Rice. Disgusting.

I chose a safe option: Coca-Cola. It is much sweeter than I remembered. The Chief remarks that they liked their Cola sweeter down here, so it was mixed differently. I asked for lots of ice but didn't realize ice was a rare commodity down here. They had cold water that they kept the bottles in, so it wasn't too bad, something to get used to. We ate and paid our bill which was one Lempira.

Almost worth the rice milk.

Once again, living here might not be so bad.

The steak was very good, and it was rumored that some of the best beef we would ever eat was in this part of the world. This was probably because the beef is grass-fed.

The S-4 (supply) had booked rooms for everyone that made it out tonight, about 40 of us and we decided the next step would be to check out where we were staying. The hotel was more like a big house with rooms and we all picked out a room. Two Marines to a room, so Lee and I picked one out and relaxed a bit. Lee started to make some small talk in between farts. I think he had too many beans.

I'm not in the mood to talk, and normally that'd be what makes me and Lee perfect roommates, but I could tell he wants to talk about the last mission.

"Ski, you got to tell me more of what happened. My back was away from the action and I was dragging guys out of the chopper. I missed the Cobra attack, how did that go?"

I take a second to think. I really don't want to tell him anything, but I have to tell him enough that he'll let it go. "Wow, there are no words to describe it. The Cobra saved our asses and I hope we have them on station for all our missions." He knew there was more to the story than that, and he pressed the issue. "Ski, I know you were rocking and rolling, everyone could hear you screaming and the rounds going downrange, but damn, the explosions? That was some shit. I could feel the target on my back, and you held them back but how did the body parts get in the chopper? Fuck, the Cobra blew huge chunks of people at me is what I wanted to say but choked up. Thank God chief picks this time to show up.

Chief came around to check on us and said a small group of guys were going to just wander around and we should come along. Sounded good to me, get me the fuck away from talking about that shit again, so off we all went. This is a small town, and we can get around without a car. Since we didn't know the area, it was best to just stay near where we were sleeping.

We went to a park, which is strange because of all the vegetation that surrounded us, you would think a park was the last thing they needed. I guess there were no wild animals to eat you in the park so it was safer than going outside the town where you could get lost, and presumably be lunch for something else.

Someone had brought a chest full of beer, so we popped a couple and sat around and talked. I asked our translators if any areas had girls around, like a dance club or mall. They laughed and added, yes, but since the gringos are here, all the girls are locked up. I witnessed that earlier today, but the way I was feeling, the mamas looked just as good.

Casually I asked, "Are they afraid of us?"

"No," one of them said. "But the mothers are, and the fathers will end up killing a bunch of Americans that are supposed to be here helping their country. Killing you might create a political incident if they found the body." Then they laughed hard, but there was an undercurrent of warning. Damn, okay. They then promised to take us to a couple of bars where some girls hung out and we could get some drinks. Now that's what I'm talking about.

The translators were from the unit we were supporting and seemed like nice guys. Different types of men than what I saw on the last mission. I know I wasn't supposed to talk about anything, but the old mind was rolling along, and if these were the type of men willing to kill women and children, well, you remember what I said would happen to my anger if I didn't deal with it.

The problem for these guys was that even if I'd been ready to heal, they'd caught me too soon to when it had happened. I was a powder keg, and they were a lit match. Young "Ski" might be going to jail tonight.

In my most pleasant voice, I ask, "Were you guys on our last mission?"

"Yes, a few of us went along with your officers to help out coordination."

"Was your unit part of the action?" You could see in their eyes that I just went someplace I wasn't allowed to go. Hoping the beer would either make them talk or forget the question, I anxiously awaited the answer.

"You see," one stated, "we really didn't go with you, if you know what I mean. These people you helped, they were not as you say, 'our people.'"

Do I question from here and just play stupid?

Chief took care of that. "Ski, you have a problem with these boys?"

"Don't think so Chief."

"Then let's just drink and be happy, boy. You're just going down a rabbit hole you don't want to visit. Pack it in."

Chief was right, I needed to let it go for now, and I didn't think these guys were involved. At least that's what I told myself so that I didn't lose control. But the closer I looked, the more certain I felt. The soldiers I talked to here spoke differently, dressed differently, and didn't act as aggressive. Besides, I wanted to meet some girls, and pissing them off would not help tonight's mission.

Two of the translators were our age and asked if we were ready to take off. You bet we were (at least Lee and I). They led about ten of us, no Non-Coms, to a nice sized bar. It was packed. I guess there isn't a whole lot to do in the evening around here but drink. Looks like most of the troops got here before us so I assumed it was a safe place.

There were quite a few girls out as well and they are pretty good lookers, even the heavy ones seemed to look good. I guess being out in the jungle for a month plus made every woman look good.

Food was sitting out on some of the tables and

we realized that we were more hungry than thirsty. Trying to be smart, I knew what alcohol did to me on an empty stomach, being stupid would be bad, especially since Chief wasn't around to take care of us. The food here was more appetizers and I wanted real food like lunch was.

I elbowed my way over to one of the translators. "Is there someplace close we can get some dinner?"

"Yes, just a block over are a few restaurants that have great food," he states.

"Can you let our Chief know we took off to eat when you see him?"

"I can do that for you, be careful Gringo, the people are nice, but they like money also."

What does he a mean? A warning that we could be assaulted? Cheated. We'll find out soon enough. I grab Lee and out we go, on our way to find some more local food. We skip outside and I smell that smell. Real steak being grilled. That's what I wanted so we followed the smell to a restaurant that had this great big grill. We amble on in and a few heads turn, but then went back to eating. Since steak is on the menu, I figured we can point our way through this and be okay.

A nice older lady comes over and points us to an empty table that holds about six. That's fine. I'll probably eat enough for six, so it works for me. Minding our business, some nice people come over and ask in English if they can help us.

Next thing you know, another couple joins us

and the table is full. I'm hoping the custom isn't that we pay for everyone.

We make some small talk about the town and the local things available to do. I glance around and see a couple of young ladies come in and are pointed over to where we are. They sashay this beautiful walk in these too-tight jeans and give a hug and kiss to one of the couples. Some Spanish is spoken and chairs are pulled up for them. I, of course, stand as my father taught me, and they gave me a nice smile. Sucks to be you, Lee, they know who the gentleman is here.

Everyone around the table wanted to hear the Yankees talk and learn a little more about us. Fine by me, stare at me, and I will stare right back...at the ladies.

Time to put on the Marco charm.

We put in our orders with some help, and when the food arrived, everyone left but the two charming ladies. We asked them to stay and if they wanted something, to please order. They said thank you but had eaten already. If it was all right, we could get them some drinks. Yes, please guzzle, lots of alcohol, are we lucky or what? I have no clue what they ordered, but if it pleased them, it made me happy. I always make my ladies happy.

Our steaks came and they were great and big. I liked the seasoning and asked how it was done. Salt and pepper in the right mix along with some other spices. Okay. Keep it a secret, that's why I will be back. We made some small talk as best as the four of us could. They were students and going to school that was like a high school, college mix. They called it University, but I knew it wasn't like our Universities.

Lissane is seventeen and Maria just turned eighteen. Both have long black straight hair down below the shoulders. Their hair moved like a clear stream going over rocks. Polished. Brown eyes and little curvy bodies. So perfect and then reality hit. I immediately thought about how jail would look here. Even though I was eighteen, I didn't know the law down here. How do I bring this up without sounding stupid? I decided to let Lee be the ignorant one and ask, but how do I get him to do this?

"Lee, are we allowed to talk to beautiful young ladies here?"

"I don't know, Ski, why wouldn't we?"

"Maybe there is an age thing, you know?"

The young ladies picked up on this pretty quick and opened up that we could talk to any of them without a problem. "Besides, what's the harm in talking?" they asked.

We finished our meals and asked where they would like to go. We had some time on our hands and would like to see their town. Giggling, they were happy to take us out and show us "their town." Off we went to a small bar and had a few beers or birras as the girls called them, and talked about what they did and what they liked to do. Lissane warmed up to me, and I was able to sneak in a couple of kisses.

This was going much better than expected for

me. Maria kept looking at Lee but for all his talk, he was being really shy. How sweet, I will never let him live this down! Hoping we were going to get lucky, I suggested we take a stroll someplace where we could sit privately. I should have kept my mouth shut. The girls explained that they needed to get home and it would be best if we said goodnight.

All right, I'll salvage this. "Can we walk you home then so we make sure you're safe?"

That made them laugh and Maria states, "We live with our parents and if they saw us with a couple of white boys, they wouldn't understand. But, if you want to meet us for breakfast, we would love to show us around some more."

Be still my heart, you bet we would.

They wrote down an address and said they would see us around 10:00 am. That was late for breakfast, but that sure didn't matter to us. Luckily we weren't too far from our hotel, so finding our way back wasn't a problem. The problem was Lee being so shy he lost his voice with Maria and now here he is, talking shit the whole way back about how suave he was tonight. The bed looked so lonely when I arrived and I thought how much happier it would have been with more company than just me. Maybe another night. I hope I have some better dreams than I've been having.

Well, sleeping didn't work out as I hoped. I just fucking laid awake all night. I wish it was because of the girls, but it wasn't. I couldn't get the body parts

208

flying at me out of my mind. Watching kids drop and dragged with a red streak of paint behind them on the ground, women yelling and crying over broken little bodies. Men I needed to shoot, but I was unable to pull the trigger on. The Sin of Omission my pilot committed and the evil those so-called allies engaged in.

Sleep came at some time, but waking came too quick. I was being smothered by something on my face. Opening my eyes, all I saw was Lee was dumping shit on me and telling me to get up.

"Is there a fucking fire? Leave me alone, asshole."

More things fly at me, boots, shirt, dirty underwear.

"Quit, fine, I'm up. Where're the showers?"

It's beginning to dawn on me that I'm the only one wasting time talking.

No showers. Snatching a washcloth and scrubbing warm water over me satisfied my urge to at least get some of the sweat and grime off my body. A quick shave because I needed to look good for Lissane today, the shave will finish off the look I needed. Like most guys, I checked out my ripped body and made sure to tell Lee, "You want this, don't you?"

We both laughed as he just flipped me the bird. As we left the hotel, a couple of Jarheads were going to stick around so we asked them to let Chief know where we were going in case we didn't come back.

We struck off on our new adventure in trying to find the address we had been given by the two lovely ladies. Winding our way through the hard-packed dirt streets we arrived at our destination a bit early. Our anticipation of seeing these goddesses gave way to a different kind of hunger, food. We missed breakfast and now we're paying for it because obnoxious sounds are coming from our midsections. What to do? A dilemma for sure.

If we eat and they catch us, we look like pigs, if we starve, our stomachs might make us sound like pigs.

A Jewish pig, great.

I am making a command decision, we wait, but I quickly nip in an open stall vendor to get some candy bars. Chocolate, dark chocolate, the best kind. It notes something about 80% cacao, that must be good. I take a big bite and, shit, this tastes awful. I feel bad about spitting it out, but it tastes just like cocoa powder without sugar. Worse than rice milk. I'll just down the water we brought along.

We resign ourselves to sitting outside, waiting as usual for women, and taking in the scenery that was moving by. These people had more horses than cars. I felt like maybe I was out west in the late 1800s.

The girls, Lissane and Maria, finally showed up looking great. I like long, straight, silky hair and they both have that look a mile long. Short skirts instead of the jeans they wore last night, long tanned legs ending with sandals on their small feet. Open button-down shirts showing off their beautiful assets. And the smiles, wow. I could wake up to that every morning. This will definitely turn out to be a great day.

The girls helped us order breakfast after hearing the grizzly's growling in our stomachs. They ordered for me, eggs and some sort of puffy tortilla stuffed with cheese. They tried to order pork, and now I had to explain why I couldn't eat it. I should have commented that I was allergic but no, stupid me, I have to go on about my religion. I tried to explain that I was Jewish and couldn't eat pork because it was against my religious beliefs. They thought that was stupid. Fine, I just want to be with them so I didn't get into any debate that I know I would have lost. Maybe winning the fight would have happened, but it wasn't worth losing the war by having either of them leave.

Everyone else had pork and something, probably to prove a point. After breakfast, we amble along through the town and the girls show us points of interest that are part of their upbringing. Grocery stores, a small mall, lots of outdoor markets, and a small movie theater. Too bad we couldn't go see a movie, didn't need to understand the language on the screen as far as I'm concerned. Unfortunately, we had to be back at the pickup area by 1400 hours and it was getting near noon.

I glanced around and noticed a strange occurrence, places started shutting down. My spider-sense started picking up because this didn't seem normal. What I thought was happening was one of those moments when the local population knew something bad was going to happen and they were clearing the streets and business.

The girls could tell I was getting nervous and my body language was screaming RUN. Lee was a little on edge, probably because he could see me tensing up. Maria asked me what was wrong, I explained to her that I noticed the shops were closing up and the street was becoming empty.

"Is there something we should know?"

"No, why would they stay open when they needed to go home and eat and relax?"

Huh? I guess this isn't a tourist area.

It made some kind of sense.

Maria said, "Everyone will open back up around 2:00 pm to 3:00 pm. It was just the way it is."

She went on to explain work usually ended around 7:00 pm and then people relaxed and enjoyed dinner and friends. I was still a little worried and decided that I should learn a little more about the countries I might be going to in the future to meet people and possibly kill them.

The girls wanted to spend some time talking to us, learn new words, and hear about North America. It was interesting because we think of America as, well, America. They don't view it that way. To them, we are North Americans. After all, we are all Americans, just South, Central, or North. I never thought of it that way. They thought it was strange we were so presumptive to think otherwise. I guess we are the "Ugly Americans." Always good to learn something new.

Time ran so fast it got away from us and ultimately it was time for us to leave and get back to the pickup area. We were able to give the girls a nice kiss goodbye and succeeded in getting their address so we could maybe meet them again. Unfortunately, we couldn't tell them when we might be back. First of all, because we had no clue when we would. Second of all, because we had no clue *whether* we would. And I don't mean whether we wanted to. Wants don't mean much if a bullet limits your options.

Besides, they didn't have phones or anything, and we didn't either for that matter. I asked what we should do if we showed up unannounced? They said to just leave a note of where we would be, and they would find us. That's the best we could do.

Wandering back to the hotel, we talked about how lucky we were to meet such gorgeous girls in such a short time. I hoped we could meet up with them again, and that went double for Lee.

Arriving at the hotel, we snatched our overnight bags and went outside to wait with everyone else. That's the Corps for you, hurry up and wait. The five-tons were there but we didn't want to load up until we had to.

I decided to look for the Chief and let him know everything was good but didn't see him. I asked around and was told that a couple of officers had to go get him out of the local holding area. He got a little shit faced and decided that some people were looking at him wrong. I know the feeling! So, he did what every Marine would do, he made them pay. I'm sure he will tell us later, and if not, I'll be like a little kid and stutters please one-hundred times.

We loaded up and drove back onto the jungle road. It was as uneventful as the drive to the town was and the jungle stayed right where we left it, green, dark, mysterious, and deadly. Chief eventually did show up the next day. He looked like shit which for some reason, which made me feel good. Problem was that he decided to make sure we all felt like shit too because he laid out a lot of extra duties. Not good. I couldn't get him to comment on what happened, but I did hear through scuttlebutt that a little extra money had to change hands before the police released him.

As promised, two days R and R and another five to take time to clean, repair, fix, and get ourselves back into our heads to get ready to fight again.

How do you get your head on straight after the last combat mission you might ask? You really don't. The R and R helps you understand that there is a real world that doesn't involve killing, and life can be great no matter where you live if it's given a chance.

I guess the 'real' getting back into your head is the vulture that circles over you when you get back to put you into the 'combat' mindset rather than what you might think of as getting your head on straight. You need to forget all the good stuff and focus back on how to best support and kill if needed.

A couple of other flights went out while we were gone and there were some small engagements reported. We must have stirred up a hornet's nest wherever the last mission was located. We noticed extra security posted around our base area was a bit tighter. I'm glad we didn't rely on just the Honduras Army but put our own guys out at the wire as well. It made for extra duty, but I didn't mind feeling a little more secure. The new intel suggested there might be some sort of retaliation coming for us.

Chapter 22

November–December 1977

We sat on the perimeter defense several nights. You would think since I was M60 qualified, that's what I would be behind the fence. Nope, the decision was to have the choppers ready for liftoff just in case we were attacked. When I got the word to return to the airfield, I would be ready to rock and roll with the M60 because it would be mounted and ready.

Of course when the Marines have a full menu of artillery available for shooters, why stop with the M60? Chief knew I was pretty handy with a rifle because he had seen my scores on the range. The Honduras unit had some M14 rifles available and he knew that had a longer reach than the '16. He picked a couple of '14's up and gave one to me.

He told me, "Ski, get up a little higher on the ridgeline in front of us and provide overwatch. You should be able to see most of the perimeter from there." He also warned me, not to engage unless there is firing on the perimeter, no need to give away your position unless you see some troop movement and the troops below will be surprised. "Also, make sure you have a clear shot but to be ready to high tail it out to the chopper."

We had plenty of Honduran troops protecting us, they seemed to be a well-run unit and hardcore. Nothing like the troops we supported in the last mission. I don't think these guys ran from anything. The military treated them very well, or at least better than they would be back on the farm. Lee's job was down below my area in helping coordinate lines of fire with that unit and us above. We are directed to coordinate fire support with adjacent units if things became hot so that he can safely come up to my position.

We were expected to rotate out in December just before the holidays, and no one wanted to die. We had a few rain showers come through, different days, so the stickiness went right through your clothes and on to your body. Some days we could cut through the air with a knife. With this weather, maybe the Sandinistas would give us a break, or whoever are their allies in this part of the world.

I had overheard some of the CIA guys talking about current missions and one of them was called Operation Condor. This was some really nasty business if you believed what they said. I stayed quiet because it seemed pretty spooky at the time and I wasn't cleared—I did not need to know. What I overheard is that the Honduran government has this special battalion, 316 or something, that went out and made people disappear. All the countries around us are like little Nazis and the problem is that the U.S. supports them. On the other side are units just as sadistic and awful, but they are supported by the Soviet Union.

Politics, damned if you do, damned if you

don't. More Sins in the offering.

We had a normal week with rotations on and off the line and waiting for more missions to come down. It appeared that everything was winding down for the holidays, which was welcome. I was hoping to get back into town to meet up with at least one of the girls. If I can give them my address in the U.S., maybe if they get a chance to visit, I would be on that list. Always need a distraction and girls are the best kinds.

The third week of November proved to be a bad week for all of us. Intel said there were troop movements to the east of us and it wasn't friendly forces. There was a lot of jungle out there, so unless we had a good fix on them, our mortars would do no good.

One of my drills always yelled the six P's and it sticks with me now. Prior Planning Precludes Piss Poor Performance. Just so, we made sure they were zeroed in on the open areas and into the jungle from where opposing forces might come from, anticipate, and plan.

The soldiers did some burning of the jungle a few weeks before to clear the area, and that helped our line of sights as well. The soldiers in front of us numbered between 300 to 400 so it was a sizable defensive force that would be hard for anyone to get through it. The town south of us was far enough away that they probably wouldn't even know something was going on.

On the evening of 22 November, we heard a

few traps go off in the jungle. Someone is trying to get close to the base and is having a bad night for sure. One positive is that our guys know this area well and can booby trap the trails as well as any cutouts that could be taken.

I ask our Captain if our allies are going to set up some ambush sites, and if they were, I would like to go out with them. Maybe get some payback for those kids that were murdered.

I am told no, too many wild animals to worry about, didn't need any dead Americans, and it is better to let the drug runners worry about not getting eaten versus us. It made sense to me, but I still have some animosity towards these folks.

It's hard to see into the jungle because of the wetness. The reason is that the steam coming off the jungle floor is like a mist that envelopes everything it caresses. As the evening ended and night crept into the area, we started sending up flares every five minutes just to make sure all was good, and that no one is poking around. The flares give off a white reflective glow that is eerie. Shifting shadows look like animals moving in for the kill. Next thing you know, tracer rounds are going into the forest, I'm watching intently for rounds coming out of the forest but don't see any. Maybe they don't have tracers. No intel on that.

Flares are launched again and nothing. A few sporadic shots go out and everyone is on edge. Davison comes up to me and brings a couple of guys I don't know, Frank and Samuel, not Sam, but Samuel.

Davison said, "You all are going to bed down together the next few nights so cozy up and settle in."

Frank is a small Italian guy that has a lot of nervous energy, whereas Samuel is about the same build as me but has a very calm and quiet manner about him. More of scholar verses a fighter. And black as night. I don't want him next to me in a firefight because no one would see him when we fired and all the incoming rounds would be directed at the young white boy with a dark tan.

As the flares came down again, the shadows of the jungle moved back and forth, but not in a calming fashion. The sensation was like there were evil things slowly crawling out to find you and take your soul. We made it through the night, and we had a shift of one on while two slept. That gave us all the time we needed to make sure we could function during the day. A few patrols went out during the day and as the patrols slog through the steam, they were swallowed up by the jungle.

The next night, the 23rd, started no different than any of the others. We had our fill of C-Rations and Samuel and Frank were setting up our position and making sure we had connecting fire with the teams on either side. Remembering something from Gunny Hardin— "if the enemy is in range, so are you"— I made sure we had cover as best we could and some concealment.

Down below Lee and a couple of other

Americans were setting up as well. I could see Lee and he knew where I was positioned. We make it a habit to know where each of us sits so we can cover each other if needed.

As we settled in, the flares are again going off about every ten minutes. The jungle moved and swayed and gave a false impression of peace. The mist would swirl around with each breath the jungle took and you just knew that something wicked this way comes. We have been getting warnings and the day patrols reported that they were finding traps set along the trails. Bad news, they weren't our booby traps. The bastards were trying to get us now.

Our troops did some recon by fire, which means we shoot into the area hoping someone shoots back and gives away their position. We didn't get any return fire from the jungle.

Uh-oh.

We weren't supposed to see the enemy, but when you do recon by fire, usually the opposition gets pissed and will fire a few rounds back to mess with you. If you don't get these things, and you get traps laid out against you, then you are dealing with a different animal.

I'm sorry, the idea we are dealing with some drug runners little army didn't make sense and is probably not true. Someone out there meant business, and if they knew our strength and are coming anyway, they have to be sizable in numbers. You don't attack unless you have 3-1 odds which meant there were 900 to 1200 enemy combatants out there. You just don't hide them this well if they are a bunch of druggies. We did send up choppers for recon, but unless they were cooking a meal, you couldn't see shit.

Pop, pop, pop went the flares. Shifting shadows and mist. Then darkness. I could sense the coming attack the way you sense a dangerous animal stirring from sleep. Only 1000 yards ahead of me, it sniffs for my scent in the humid darkness. Baloom, crunch, boom.

Incoming mortars start hitting the area, these are small caliber, not the 81mm. We still didn't see anything, and I felt like we have a target on our backs this time. When you sit in a static position like we are, there is nothing you can do when you can't see your enemy. We had placed ourselves into a position to be hunted. There was no other way. If you follow a panther into the thicket, you step within reach of his razor-sharp claws. Our enemy is no panther; instead, they are the deadliest creatures in the world, humans driven by anger and blood lust.

These mortar drops seemed to be more random verses having any positions locked in which is good. The shots were falling short of our positions which meant the enemy is afraid of getting their mortar squads too close. Someone on their side made a mistake because we can range them now even if we can't see them. They were at their max range otherwise they would have adjusted closer when their recon units would have had them adjust fire. Sucks to be the guys up front getting ready to assault our position. They thought we would be softened up.

Now I hear some larger mortars going outbound. The whistle is away and then the loud boom farther into the forest. Some commander is smart back in our rear area, they have figured the same thing I have and decided on counter-battery fire, except ours are bigger and range farther. You can see the bloom and the explosion, the white flash, and then the red heat smoldering out. Fireworks at night, except hitting the ground at the end. Maybe we hit something, maybe not, but the return fire ended, and we continued to send flares up. The shadows were dancing now because of the fires behind the open area adding to the desolate scene.

There, now I see soldiers moving out of the mist and running towards our positions. A few soldiers turn into several groups which becomes an ocean of bodies. The M60's open up and I know we had at least two 50s out there. I didn't know we had M79s but I started hearing the kerplunk of the shot and the 40mm explosion. Bodies are dropping and going to meet their Jesus while the men killing them worshiped the same Jesus. Strong Catholics meeting each other on the field of battle, or not, maybe godless communists if I'm right. If they have a God, it's not the one I serve.

Long shadows are made of the running men until they meet their shadows on the ground. Some pause and return fire, others drop to do the same or drop dying. I'm trying to look for soldiers who are in charge. Leaders pushing their men forward. It's hard to see because of the light moving in and out, bodies dropping and rolling through the mist that's following them. Samuel and Frank were taking shots where they could, as were the small groups we had up on the ridge. I waited for targets that needed to be hit rather than random runners. These poor guys were getting blasted and I started thinking...

Did we bring enough ammo?

I finally see someone out about 100 hundred or so yards away. He is kneeling and talking to someone. That person runs off and another takes his place. He must be directing traffic and if I can get him, that might fracture the assault in this area. I line up my sights and try to relax.

What did Garza mention about the trigger pull? Just like stateside, make it a surprise. Let your breath out as you squeeze.

I let all my air out and test the trigger pressure—the damn trigger is on safe. I'm an idiot. I change the safety to off and make sure the selector is on single shot, iron sites locked in on the center of mass. Let my breath out slowly and boom! The rifle rocks me back and a 7.62mm bullet is on its way, pulling again and boom. The man is hit with the first round, taking it in the shoulder and the second round on the hip. He is down and moving back to the jungle.

Lining up and I hit a guy in the leg trying to help him. I fire about five more rounds into the area because I can't see anything with the mist embracing him and pulling him maybe to safety or death.

I'm scanning for more targets when Davison comes up and yells that there's a breach down below near Lee. I had tunnel vision with my guy and lost what was happening around me. I needed a spotter, not more people firing. Looking down, I see that some areas are being overrun and it is now hand to hand. I'm talking forty or so yards away.

Davison already has the other two guys sending rounds into the area and I can see a stream of the enemy moving towards the breach. I start shooting like everyone else into bodies, didn't care who they were this time. The bodies are pitching forward or back depending on the angle. I'm changing Mags, went through 20 pretty quick, and start up again. I catch a glimpse of Lee and he is trying to move back. I see him get hit and down he goes.

No, no, no.

We don't get hit. Never me. Never my guys. Never us.

But that's not true. It's never been true, and it definitely won't be any closer to true if I just sit here in horror.

I have to find the shooter, but it could be anyone. Davison directs me to a group moving towards Lee, about eight guys taking cover and then advancing. I change mags so I know I'm full. Breath, relax, Sgt. Hardin, CSM Klinger, Sgt Garza are all talking to me.

"Good stock weld, breath deep and let out slow,

aim for the center of mass and squeeze."

Crack, down goes one, crack, down goes two, crack, down goes three.

Crack. Crack. Crack!

They stop moving and are looking up. Crack, down goes four. Flares are streaming down and new ones up. Its daylight with long shadows, crack goes five. They are dragging men back, Gunny is yelling at me to shoot them. I can't. It's not right; they are leaving the field of battle. My Dad is talking to me now. "Let them be, Marco. They're done." That's fucking creepy. My Dad's talking to me in the middle of a firefight.

Lee is moving again, but not real fast. There is hand to hand fighting, but it looks like we stemmed the tide. They hit us hard but not hard enough. It wasn't as coordinated as it should have been. They did things okay on the initial assault but fell apart after about five minutes into it.

Shit, five minutes. As often as I've seen nothing happen in five minutes, I've now seen enough to fill a lifetime.

I've got to go get Lee. I always have his back because he has mine. I tell Davison, "Here, take the '14 and cover me, let me have the .45!" It's too cumbersome to run down there with the '14 and then to try to drag Lee up here.

Chief hands me his .45 and growls, "It's full, will talk when you get back."

I say a prayer of thanks that he gets it. This has

to happen, and it has to happen now.

Off I go. One eye on the ground which keeps shifting with the changing light and one ahead of me tracking Lee. I figure I'm going to shatter a leg or at the least twist an ankle running like I am, but I don't have a choice.

As I look up again, I see a new problem, I thought the enemy was retreating, and they were. A new leader must have emerged and is pushing soldiers forward again. More shapes are moving out of the trees.

Please God, send in the Cobras.

Wait, they're not night capable. Shit.

Mortars are opening up on them again and the ground reverberated as if we were having an earthquake. I fall a few times but can get to Lee. He had to sit and catch his breath. I look him over and can only find some blood on his shoulder.

I ask him, "Where did you get shot, dipshit?"

He points at his shoulder and flips me off. He must be okay then, or at least in good enough spirits that he'll make it until a medic can patch him up.

I look at the area and see that he is lucky that the bullet only grazed him on the top of his shoulder. Cut it, but not like a hole. He got lucky, but as I look around us, I wonder how much longer before that luck runs out.

We are not in a good position; it is bad because this is a natural draw up the ridge. If I were the enemy this is where I would assault. I can see that the enemy is getting very close and are moving through the breach again. We didn't have enough men here to hold, and I hope the guys that are running this are moving people over to knock it back. Lee didn't have his '16 but has an old carbine with him.

"Where the fuck is your '16? We need the firepower," I say.

He pointed and said, "Out there, want to get it shithead? I used up all the ammo I had and seized this carbine from some asshole that didn't need it anymore."

We and the soldiers with us did not use the old M1 carbine. Son of a bitch, that means Lee was close enough to touch someone who was trying to kill him. Too close. It is a lightweight weapon but very effective in close quarters of which we were in now. We need to get the fuck out of here, now. I am not fighting hand to hand, not my job. Still, we had other Americans out there and I wanted to clear them through as well.

I ask Lee, "Where are the other Jarheads? They still out there?"

Lee yells, "They bugged out the minute rounds started to fly, I left right after them. They went up a different draw and I just got unlucky."

Chesty Puller once said: ***We're surrounded. That simplifies the problem.***

Our problem is now simplified. We now had to decide. It was a tough choice, if we stayed, we might have to go hand to hand and Lee wouldn't be much help. If we moved, then our odds of being shot were pretty high. I knew Davison with the other two were up on the ridgeline watching us and would give us protective fire. Would that be enough? It almost certainly would have to be.

Then I see new bodies coming in from the west. Our reinforcements.

Shit yeah!

I decide to move but the enemy has other ideas. A new wave is coming in and that spurred the ones that were near us to get up and rush us. It is chaos. I lost sight of Lee in just a few seconds. I had pushed him back into a rock outcropping in the draw, fired my .45 point-blank into some guys head. One minute he was there, the next he was at my feet without a head.

I wipe my face, disgusted before I realize what happened. The .45 is one mean son of a bitch. Shit blew all over me.

I swear I'm going to throw up. Another guy is rushing me and shooting at me. He's about 10 yards away, I have no idea how many rounds I shot, but his stomach opens up. I don't have a spare magazine and I don't know how many rounds I have. I pull out my knife and have it in my left hand with the .45 in my right. Weird, right? I shoot a rifle left-handed and a pistol right-handed. Go figure. Why does that come into my brain at this time?

Somehow, over the sound of constant fire, I hear myself screaming again.

RPG's are going into the area, flares are

lighting up the sky, mortars are pounding the ground, tracers flying everywhere. I know what our guys look like only because of the uniforms, otherwise, they all look Hispanic.

My body cringes into itself as tightly as it can. I want to look like I'm one inch tall, I don't want anyone to see me and just let me quit and slide out of here. I don't want to be here, and my Dad should have got me out.

I'm backing up and trying to get near where I last pushed Lee when two guys come right out of the mist and are next to me before any of us realize our lives will be decided now in less than a second.

They have to be as surprised as me, but they have rifles and couldn't bring them around as fast as I could shoot the .45. Two more rounds point-blank into the first guy, maybe more, I just keep pulling the trigger. Blood fucking everywhere on me and him. It is horrible, I can see this guy's eyes just go glassy as the second guy runs into me.

The .45 puts out no more rounds and don't ask me how, but my knife just slid into this guy like he was butter. He comes down on top of me and is clutching at me. We are the same size, but he has a knife sticking in him, I don't, and I kept taking it out and pushing it back in. My hand is covered in gore and slick with blood. I am not losing that knife. Over and over I kept twisting it.

Finally, he ceases moving and I push him off me.

All I could think about is his hot breath in my face and him screaming. And me screaming.

This is too much. Too much. I have to stop, and yet I can't stop. If I stop, I die. If I die, everyone else dies.

Lee, where is he?

I can't get up; my legs won't work. I start to crawl, and I hear Lee yelling.

"Drop, drop, drop!"

Not a problem. I dropped from crawling to just laying there. Over my head, I hear the loud burst of automatic fire. Lee just fucked up someone's day, and it wasn't mine!

I am spent and done. Lee grabs me and hauls my ass up and points up the draw. We're both alive and ready to climb out of this nightmare. Something is crashing down the draw.

Lee bellows his carbine is spent. I'm ready with my knife and we move into the shadows of the outcropping. I don't know if I can take anyone on again, but there's still fighting going on, and I'll be damned if we sit here waiting to die.

Flares light up the area, but it seems less intense. I'm sweating and my chest is heaving for air. There is no way someone can't hear me breathing. I sound like a freight train going uphill. Lee is drenched and his eyes are huge and white. Starbursts are going off along with the flares and a guy flies past me. Another one moves past but they're in uniform, American uniforms, the good guys.

I get ready to step out to yell at them when another guy comes by real slow and breathing harder than me. I reach out and snag him, he screams and spins, but he is too close to use his rifle.

I'm yelling "I'm Ski!"

He backs off—and Lee and I start to laugh uncontrollably. Its Davison, he came to the rescue. He is still pissed about something but stops being angry when he sees us. I don't know why but the two of us can't stop laughing. I think it was because we were either so happy to see them or it was better than crying. I know I was crying anyway, call it tears of joy.

Davison calls back Samuel and Frank and sets up a little perimeter for us. It was bad. The scent, the sight, even the taste. I was caked in dirt and gore and blood. I did not want to see myself. I ripped off my shirt and my t-shirt right there. I used it to wipe my face and try to clean up some. Every part of me was sticky. I wanted to just wash these people off of me.

It's now about midnight and even though the fighting is about an hour's worth, it feels like days.

Davison bellows, "We need to get back up the ridge and get the choppers ready in case they come again."

I said, "How can they? We must have killed thousands."

He just shook his head and led us up the ravine and onto the ridge. I notice he has the .45 and my knife.

"Chief," I say. "The 45's empty."

233

He smiled. "Not anymore."

We got back up and Davison told Samuel and Frank to keep an eye on me—see if I could sleep. He needs to get Lee to the aid station, and he will be back to check on me. I got my M-14, laid it into the shooter's position, and went prone myself. I tell them there is no way I'm sleeping, so they can sleep if they want to.

But soon after, my eyes close to an inescapable darkness, and my only defense is a prayer that whatever closed them doesn't keep me from opening them again.

When my eyes open, it's because someone is shaking my shoulder. Bright sunlight is overhead and the heat is back on my skin. I have a blanket half over me, and my boots are off. Where the fuck am I? Still on the ridge and it's past noon. The Gunny just showed up and hands me some chow, announced I had slept enough, and it is time to get cleaned up.

I have no idea what I look like, but I know it isn't good.

I have no idea what I *feel* like, but I know that isn't good either.

Samuel smiles and coos, "You look like shit."
So much for the philosopher.

I smiled back and answer, "You smell like shit so fuck off."

Davison lets me go back to the rear area by myself for once and I stumbled to the showers. Lee is all patched up and had his shower and was waiting for me. "You hanging around again to see me naked, Lee? You love seeing what a real man looks like, don't you?"

He just smiled and answers, "Yup."

I threw away the pants and underwear, have no clue where the T-shirt and utility top went, nor my cover. I stand under that shower and watch the red and brown roll off my body. It seems like it will never end. I scrub and scrub but can't get it all off.

I gather more soap. I increase the pressure. I rub my skin raw. I feel violated and can't get the stench off. I can still taste the copper in my mouth from the blood and feel the hot breath still on my face. The hell was still sitting there, like a vulture waiting for its meal.

I never thought to bring anything to the shower with me. Nude and in the sunshine with no clothes. Luckily, Lee had figured that one out and had utilities for me. No underwear, but at least I am covered up. A few older guys from 'Nam mentioned not to wear underwear, they chaffed after a bit and then rotted out. No need for them they stated. I like having them along with clean, dry socks. It's a wonder about the things you think about after having a day of horror and mind-numbing pain to your brain.

Davison shows up and said he needs a few minutes to talk to me before we go to headquarters. Sure, like I have somewhere else to go. He leads me under some trees and we sit down.

I'm a little nervous, hands are shaking and my body, even exhausted, feels tense. So I talk first. "What's up?

"Ski, I told you to shoot those guys that were running off and you shouted no. Why the fuck didn't you listen to me?"

"It wasn't right, their backs were to me."

"Who the fuck do you think came back to kill you and Lee down there? It was the three fucks you let live. You shoot them in the back before they shoot you in yours. You got me?"

This stunned me. That wasn't fair that they would come back and try to kill me.

Maybe Dad was wrong. What if they had killed Lee and I knew it was the same people?

I have to think about this one. Fortunately, Davison is happy to push me in that direction.

"I know this is hard for a shit for brains motherfucker who can't find his asshole from a hole in the ground. I want to know that I can rely on you going forward because what you did back there was fucking stupid. Lucky it all worked out well otherwise your ass would be dead, understand? And I wouldn't have had to kill you, those sorry ass drug-induced fucked up bastards would have done it for me."

He is really pissed and I don't know what to answer. "Okay, Ski, I've said my piece, so never fuck up again. Next..." As awash as his expression had been with naked rage, now he smiles with pride. "Where the fuck did you learn to shoot like that? You

236

took down five guys inside of ten seconds. All perfect shots, I watched you like a machine blow the fuckers head off their shoulders."

I don't remember hitting them in the head, but thought I hit them in the chest. I don't comment on anything, just stared at Chief.

"You are wasting your time here sonny boy, you are not a door gunner even though you're good at it. When we rotate back, I am going to get you to a school to shoot. From now on you stick next to me with a '14, you are my fucking personal protection, understand?"

I feel like a walking zombie after that ass-chewing. It was like, here you are the biggest fuck up I ever met...along with you are a fucking stud that will never leave my side.

The Chief now smiles and remarks, "Damn if you ain't fucked up in the head." He laughs and grasps me and leads me off to the battalion headquarters where we get to do an after-action briefing on our area. The Captain or whatever from the Honduras Army listens to the Chief and then, since I was the closest on the ground, the Captain wants to know what I saw from my position. I explained where I saw the enemy, where the breach occurred the fighting that took place, and me not knowing what else happened because I went to get Lee.

The Captain said, "Did you see any of my men run? Did they stand and fight or what?"

Asshole wants to cover his ass.

Not going to give him any more information than what he ordered.

"Your men were badass. They fucked up the enemy pretty damn well and saved our asses at the end when the breach was sealed up."

If not for my training I wouldn't have noticed, but he puffed up a bit acting like he was up there with them.

I added, "They stood toe to toe with the enemy and fought them off. I didn't see anyone run except towards the sound of fighting."

Which was true, every word. The Captain was an asshole, but his men really had done a good job. We were alive because of them. They weren't Marines but they could be in my platoon any time. It's part of what makes us Marines stick together no matter how much we fight with each other off the field. We've saved each other's lives more times than we can count. Eventually, we stop counting and accept we all owe each other a debt that can never be repaid.

The Captain was pleased with what I said and told me I still looked like shit and should get cleaned up. He also said, "Were you the guy up on the ridge they're talking about that killed all those soldiers?"

"There were lots of guys on the ridge doing their job." I wanted to add, "If you were around you would know."

And there had been all sorts of guys ready to stand their ground. The Latin guys have some sort of Latino macho image to uphold, I guess. Me, if I could have hidden under a rock or snuck away, I would have, but they didn't give me or Lee a choice.

Of course Davison is the closest I'll get to an old Rabbi when he decides he needs to talk to me again. We get outside and he points to a rock and spits. "Sit."

So, I sit. I know what he wants and the drill. I've got no problems with this and go through this again and relive last night. That was some serious shit like it wasn't me out there, it was someone else I knew. No way that happened to me.

He smiled and asked if I had the box? I told him I had a brand new one made this morning and would lock it up and put it next to the old one. I figured I had lots of room but was hoping it would never be needed. Gunny told me that it, unfortunately, fills up faster than we know but to just keep making space, if not, then I would probably blow my brains out or someone else's. I looked at him hard and knew that just wasn't going to happen. Two things Chief, "Women and kids weren't being shot so that's not a problem, I can handle this time better than before, and two, I needed to live because I had a brother that needs me." What was unsaid was that I still had to work out this "shooting people in the back" thing. I'm sure one day, back in the World, I will have time to talk all this out, but until then I just got to keep moving forward. I think if there is a next time, I will have no problems shooting people in the back knowing what I understand now. Not only what I do now might haunt me but also what I fail to do might kill me.

Chapter 23

December 1977

We had sporadic firing the next few days and the Honduras soldiers did a lot of patrolling. There was a lot of picking up and burying bodies. Thankfully I didn't have to participate in those additional duties. The farther into the forest our allies went, the less we saw of any POW's or body bags. They just cremated the bodies on site.

A shudder went through me at the similarity to pictures I'd seen of concentration camps in Germany. A cloud of smoke rising from somewhere in that dense green canopy and hoping the rising ash never came near you. The feeling was creepy, the smell worse, but it had to be done for sanitary reasons. You don't get to understand combat, you just survive or become ash.

I did hike around some and what I saw disturbed me. The bodies were wearing uniforms, or parts of uniforms. I didn't recognize any of the uniforms, but they had insignia on them, which to me represented a standing army of some sort. These guys were lunatics to just run out in front of us knowing we had the advantage, so maybe they were drugged up as the Chief said.

We fired up the choppers a few times and went up to do some Recon and try to find targets of opportunity but never found anything. Seems we did kick their asses, a lot dead and even more captured.

I watched the POW's being lined up but had no clue where they were taken. I asked but was informed that there were no POW's, there was no war, just drug lords and their Army. Being smarter than the average bear, I decided that it would be best for me to leave that one alone. I have enough ethical problems to wrestle with right now.

This was also the first time I started dreaming again. I had no dreams since basic wiped my memories. These were not "good dreams." I would wake up in the middle of the night being chased by shadows. I now would dream of eyes watching me, and they were of the eyes of people I killed. Nothing earth shattering that would make me scream or wake others up, just would wake up, look around, and go back to sleep. I didn't admit to them except to the Gunny, and like he tried to tell me, box it up otherwise it would eat me alive. Need to tighten down that box! I think Gunny had his share of dreams and trying to help all of us was stressing him, so I tried to not overburden him too much. We talked a little, he smiled and said, "You good?" I replied, 'Roger that'. This wasn't going to go away overnight, but ain't shit I can do about it now.

We enjoyed Thanksgiving as only Americans can, and the rest of the troops we supported just looked at us as crazy Gringo's. After a week and a half of clean up and work, we were given another 2 days' leave into town. As usual, they rotated us through, so we were still mission capable. I was pretty excited and Lee and I both knew exactly where we were headed, right into town, with directions to someone's house.

Last visit we had purchased some civilian clothes with the girls. It was fun letting them pick out what they wanted us to wear. Our journey over to the town was no different than the last time, more jungle, wild animals waiting to eat you, rough roads, and then our hotel. We quickly ran and checked in, then hit the room to change out of our uniforms.

Looking dapper, we made our way over to the housing area the girls gave us directions for. This definitely was not the poor side of town. Mansions lined the streets with about three hundred feet between them, manicured lawns, and stately drives. The house we arrive at looks like an old colonial mansion, tan stucco, with a wrought iron fence around the grounds.

After I use this big brass knocker on the door, an elderly lady answers. She smiles and uses her hand to gesture us inside the house. That's weird, is this some type of alien sci-fi movie where we are going to be killed? Hopefully, they are just very hospitable people.

A young man shows up, in his mid-20's and using good English. "Buenas tardes, how can I help you?"

"Well...you see..." I stammer. "A few weeks ago we met some young ladies in town. They asked us to come by the next time we were able, so, here we are. I'm Mark, and this is John."

"Welcome, I am Roberto and unfortunately,

senor, my sister Lissane and my cousin Maria are on holiday at the capital. I assume that they are who you wish to see?" With a smile, he adds, "They will be gone until mid-December."

No...

How are we going to get to Tegucigalpa, the Capital? And then how do we find them in a city of 250,000 people? This sucks.

Roberto, perhaps used to seeing this yet again with us Americans falling for the locals, continues with infinite patience. "They had talked about these two boys they met in town, they will be so disappointed to have missed you. I am sure they will be happy to see you next time."

I am not sure if that was true, but he seemed genuine. There wasn't much we could do so I told him, "Let them know we came over to say goodbye, we might be leaving soon and don't have any idea if we will be able to come by again."

He wished us well and a safe journey. Talk about a letdown, you get all pumped up, and then the disappointment about kills you. We had been in the shit and decided we deserved some fun, so after we left the house, we went to one of the bars we had been at before.

We did *not* get drunk. At least I don't think we got drunk. Truth is, I don't remember except waking up sick a few times and being in the hotel. I'm guessing we schlepped back, and someone took pity on us and got us to our room. Interesting to note, it was a weekday this time around, but the lifestyle was no different than a weekend. I think every day is Saturday in this town.

We slept in late, then went to have lunch but had forgotten everything is closed. We had to starve till about 1400 hours. I drank a lot of water because my mouth had somehow filled with cotton and smelled like something crawled up in it and died.

I can't wait to get some food in me.

We found a place that served hamburgers of all things. It was great and the bread was fantastic. No buns but sliced bread with some herbs embedded in it. It was good to not have to think at all. I wish the hotel was like the ones in the U.S. where there was a pool, girls, and food. Although it wasn't bad after what we just went through. I just miss home more than I thought possible.

Lee is going to ship out before everyone else since he had forgotten to duck and has his wound. I give him shit about it because I ducked when he yelled drop, but he didn't have the good sense to at least run low when he got shot. Ungrateful bastard croaked back that he should have nicked me just for the fuck of it.

It wasn't exactly a last meal, but it felt like it. He was leaving, I was staying, and for all people talk about real friendships lasting forever, this was going to get a lot harder without him there to lean on.

Chapter 24

23 December 1977

Sometimes lady luck stays on your side. After handing our stuff over to the next group coming in, we were shipped off to the airport. No excitement, no fanfare, and no parades. I'm not sure how the helicopters got back, but I have a feeling we just left them for the next group.

We loaded our crew-served weapons and carried our rifles with us. First time I flew with a rifle on a 707. Of course, the Gunny's made sure all our weapons were unloaded. That's all we needed was Private Joe Snuffy fucking up everyone's day and shooting a couple of rounds through the aircraft.

Just when it seemed our luck was running out after all, the ladies of Pan-Am graced us with their presence. Now there was a welcome sight. Almost enough to make me forget the two girls me and Lee would probably never see again.

The first stop was Miami where we were not allowed to get off the aircraft. Some of the guys were transitioning somewhere else and they were allowed to leave with their equipment. The airline kept the air conditioning going while they refueled. Probably some sort of safety violation, but they didn't want a bunch of Jarheads getting off the plane with M16s and running around because we were pissed.

Instead of going on to Pendleton, we went

north. I never had asked when we were leaving where I was going to end up. That proves how messed up I was. I knew I was a control freak but now I didn't care. My personality was changing and instead of needing to know 'everything', I could give a fuck. Maybe I needed to see a Doc. I assumed my gear would be following me and catch up at some point. The Marine Corps would tell you what you needed but I hoped my civilian clothes would show up. A good little memory of the ladies I met. I'm sure all my shorts and sandals would do me a world of good if I ended up in Quantico in the winter. And if not? The Marines would issue me new ones.

Next stop, Dulles. It was nice and cold in Washington, D.C. This was not what we expected. From the jungle and hot to the cold of the north. This time heaters were on the plane and on the buses that picked us up. Off we went and were dropped off at the barracks in Quantico.

Never thought I would consider the barracks five-star accommodations!

Flushing toilets and hot showers on demand. And heaters. Why is it so cold? We had to go outside, which was stupid, but we had to get some safety briefings about keeping it wrapped and watching for muggers.

That would be something. Some poor mugger pulls a knife or gun on one of us? Shit, bad day for him.

Now we had jackets on, gloves and green

beanies to keep our head warm. Instead of steam from our mouth because of heat, it is frost because of cold. I decided hot was better and I didn't like the cold.

We spent the next day processing our equipment and getting ready for orders to the fleet. Lee had come in ahead of us and was on leave back home to Irvine, California. I had his address and promised to look him up. Samuel and Frank were here, and Davison was on his way somewhere else. I don't know where because he lived off post, and once we were back in the "world," we didn't have (and didn't want) much contact.

We went out to the machines a few times to practice loading and unloading, just busy work cleaning up a lot of ash and trash. We didn't mind. The calm before the storm never lasts, so you enjoy it while it's there. Finally, orders came down for us.

Lee hadn't come back yet, but he was on his way to 29 Palms, California with a chopper unit there. Samuel was going to Ft. Benning, Georgia to be Airborne qualified. He wanted to get to Force Recon and needed badges. Frank was going to a new chopper unit in Kaneohe Bay, Hawaii. We all figured he hit pay dirt. Davison came around and congratulated everyone and checked up on me.

We did get to have his final talk and he comments, "Ski, you're a hell of a fighter. I put you in for some awards and sent it up the chain, but like everything else, don't count on them."

"No one going to admit I was there?"

He nods, pleased at my answer. "That's right, because as far as the rest of the world is concerned, we never were there."

"That's fine. Medals are okay, but having your body and all your friends in one piece at the end of the day is better."

He nods again, the closest he'll come to acknowledging what happened. "I still have some good news for you, I contacted a couple of other Gunnies—Hardin and Garza—and talked to them about you."

I was surprised and asked, "You know them?"

He frowns like I'm a kid asking why crayons taste like wax. "Are they Marines?"

"Yes."

"Then I know them. It's a brotherhood, son, you know that. They are in your files with your evaluation paperwork at personnel and I talked to them about getting you ahead in the food chain."

I had a little chuckle. "Food chain?" I could choose to be an apex predator, take out everyone in my way on the way, but even sharks eventually get eaten.

He went on, "Imagine my surprise that others thought your good for nothing ass was worth at least a dime. All that Mickey Mouse bullshit you spout caught some others by surprise as well. Looks like you have a good shot at one of the Academies and ROTC. Somehow I was convinced to write a letter on your behalf, and you know I hate writing anything. That and the Captain's recommendation are going up to the S-1(Personnel) and into your jacket."

This is getting real. I never gave much thought about going to school but just maybe. But wait, there's more...as the sales commercial goes.

Chief states, "Your sorry ass isn't going out to the fleet. I watched you kill five men like it was nothing. Steel balls my friend. You are going to be a professional assassin. I put in some calls along with your other buddies in San Diego, you are staying here and getting orders. Don't thank me yet, you might end up hating me."

As though sensing I was about to thank him anyway, Davison shuts me up by revealing a secret. "I'm looking at retiring. I've pissed off enough people in my twenty years and probably won't see E-8. I'm okay with this because I'm alive." Then he put his hand on my shoulder and said, "Ski, I know I was hard on you that night I told you to kill those bastards, but never forget, a fool is someone who believes in fighting fair. Always cheat, always win. The only unfair fight is the one you lose." And then, he left, and I received my new orders.

Chapter 25

Late December 1977

I took a week off after getting my assignment and went home to Riverside. Of course, my first thoughts were about the wonderful girls that must have turned into ladies while I was gone. I set up a few phone calls and dates for the week. It feels good being home. I forgot what clean sheets smell like, not military canvas and wool. Walking on grass and either not getting yelled at or watching your step for a land mine. I find myself still looking in the trees, even if they are olive and palm trees for snipers but smile when I clear my head. It's hot, but no humidity to sweat up a towel. I don't have to run anywhere, guess where cover might be or possible ambush points are. I am free!

Next up is to visit Mr. Williams and the crew at the Drive-In. Need to make sure I can get some free passes to see some movies while I'm here and to check-in as well. Mom and Dad are doing well, and David loves his new room.

I can tell he's worried I might kick him out. He went from upset about me leaving to worried that I might come back. What a great brother.

I just want to really squeeze him, but the little shit will probably think I'm trying to kill him and tell Dad. I forgot how much I really love him. I can't tell him what I went through, he has enough to deal with already in his life, I will just tell him the fun things and how I fucked up. He likes hearing those stories of me messing up!

My Fiat is still looking and working good for a car that's been sitting there gathering dust. But surprise, my Dad confesses that he is using the car to get to work and back.

Hmm...

I've told some whoppers for excuses in my time. Maybe that's why I see right through his. I guess he is reliving his youth. Besides, who doesn't like a convertible?

After making my calls, setting up dates, and visiting some friends in the first few days, I can relax. I have not told a soul about anything that I've done. I remember I signed paperwork to that effect. I do want to talk to someone though. The question is who? CSM Klinger comes to mind. I think I can trust him and he will understand the things I went through.

I give a call over to the JR ROTC Battalion and get him on the phone. Sarge is just as I remember him, gruff and easy-going at the same time.

"Ski, get the hell down here and tell me what you've been up to."

"On my way Sarge!"

I drive on over to my old High School, Polytechnic, and stride on over to the building the unit is in. Sarge is in his usual place behind the desk and he does look a little more, shall we say, comfortable.

"How's it hanging, Ski?"

"Pretty good Sergeant Major, thanks for

having me over."

"Tell me what's up with Uncle Sam's Misguided Children."

"The same as I left, American by birth, Marine by choice."

He had a good laugh at that and told me all was good. He said, "I would rather have had you join the Army, but seeing as how they don't let people dumber than rocks enlist, I figure you did your best."

I chuckled. Glad to be back.

Sarge and I spent the next few hours together and he listened very well. He was surprised at the intensity of what I went through, he mentioned most people go into the military and never have a fight in their life. He also let me know that I had some good Gunnies looking after me and I did him proud.

Then came the part I'd been dreading but needing all along.

We talked a little about some of the dreams I was starting to have at home. They were a little darker, and instead of running away, I started fighting. Sometimes the bed would be torn up in the morning and wet from sweat, I wouldn't remember much except moving around a lot.

He said not to worry, with time they would go away. His were very infrequent now and told me lots of guys had them. There was a name for it in WW2 called shell shocked or battle fatigue, and now the term Post Traumatic Stress Disorder.

As far as I'm concerned, it's not a disorder.

As I understand the condition, it better fits the term "syndrome" because it's an injury, not a disorder. Though I suppose they may be describing the disorder that comes from the injury.

A lot of guys turned to drugs, so Sarge told me to be careful and if it got out of hand, to go to the VA. He wasn't sure about how he felt regarding my next assignment but wished me luck and told me to keep in contact.

As he left without me asking to keep talking, I felt him taking away the possibility for something I didn't even know I needed. Every time I stepped onto the field, I wasn't just facing enemy soldiers. I took shots at the enemy I'd carried with me all this time but always stayed just out of sight. Every shot I fired brought it into closer view. I'd hoped Sarge would help me narrow my scope on this thing. Maybe I could finally focus on it for a clear shot. Instead, we parted ways and all I had were the literal enemies that would shoot back.

Looking back, I really didn't expect to see any combat, just train for it because of my commitment to Israel, if it ever came to it. I was able to do things very few had and survived by training and luck. I don't know if anything can top this life experience and I really don't need it to. I expected my next assignment would be to continue to hone my skills as a marksman and prepare me for something I hope never happens. War.

Emboldened by how happy my parents

were with me being home for the holidays, I able reconnected with Tamese. Seems she didn't forget about me and wasn't dating anyone. We had some long talks over the next couple of days and I knew I had blown it with her, but thankfully, she helped me enjoy the last few days at home. It was great just getting to catch up on the news, go to the movies and eating out with her.

Dealing with my friends was another subject. They were stressed over simple things and magnified little problems like they were under mortar fire. But they were just complaining about their boss at work, being rejected by a girl, how boring this time of year felt. I couldn't relate anymore.

I'm in a different world where each decision can end a life, maybe mine. Their decisions made no impact on life or death. Tim and Pat were still at Stater Brother's stocking shelves, Bob is going to Cal Poly, and studying engineering. Gary is at Riverside Community College doing nothing.

I tried talking a bit to my Dad. I didn't know how much I could really tell him, or what he wanted to hear. I could tell he was happy I was home, because he gave me an uncharacteristic hug and said he was happy to see me. I think he could tell I had been in the shit but left it alone. Probably better that way for both of us.

I had a few sleepless nights and some nasty dreams but always woke up fine. I've been gone eight months in January and I didn't belong anymore.

Time to get back to my home, a Marine Corps rifle company, where I can be comfortable with men who know what fear is and have stared it down.

With any luck, I might finally figure out what I'm trying to stare down.

Chapter 26

January–April 1978

It's off to Sniper school in Quantico. I told my parents and David goodbye, loaded up at LAX and flew off to Quantico. I have to go through some initial testing and am assigned to a school billet. The process works like this, the Marines have schools across the states for sniper training, and after completion, you receive your secondary MOS, 8541.

After Vietnam, a formal school is established in which specialized training from lessons learned in combat would be taught. The instructors are the best of the "best" in the Corps and are dedicated to the long rifle, long shots. To get into this training class, you have to have a good background and demonstrated ability either in competition or combat. Otherwise, you need to go to the standard sniper schools and then, if qualified, could try for admission.

I'm jazzed but hadn't shot for distance in a long time. It doesn't leave you, but it gets rusty. Understand, you need to put thousands of rounds downrange to get good, and then thousands more to become a real expert. My class would start in mid-February and go 11 weeks if I qualified. If not, my other class would start in late February and go for 10 weeks. Since I had the letters and combat experience, I am going to try for the elite class first.

Since getting back to the Corps, the dreams

and worries have disappeared. I don't know why but I think being back with people I know I can trust and have my back, make life a lot better. I never gave it much thought, but I knew this training would be more surgical in killing made the ethical dilemma easier. Rather than having to worry about stray shots killing kids, I would be much more responsible in my killing. Also, I could make the decision on putting someone down that was out to kill anyone they came across, no matter if they were allies or not.

During the lull in qualification, I was allowed to go to the ranges and practice over and over in my spare time. There is a group of us, and we had time between stupid details to practice. The range officers were pretty good and gave us the time we all needed. Our practice distance is set for 300, then 500, then 600 yards, of which three were static and two moved. At 700 yards, you had to hit three static and two stop and go. At 800 yards, there are two statics and two pop ups. Then at 900 and 1000 yards, there are five static.

I kill it at 300 and 500 yards, a little tougher but in the black at 600. 700 yards about half the time, and good luck on the 900 and 1000 yards. I can hit in the black one out of five. Practice, practice, practice.

Before I know it, my time has come to take the qualification test. I don't think I'm ready, but I can't push it out anymore.

It is a pleasant day, about 50 degrees so no problem for the rounds being impacted by the heat. No wind so that eliminated trajectory drift. We're able to shoot some practice rounds getting the barrel warm and that will help to add consistency to the shot groups. We have to shoot at a marker with our spotter, then we will trade places, and he will shoot, while you are the spotter, then move to the next position and repeat. If your spotter gets it wrong, you pay the price.

Here we go. In position, I snuggle up nice with the M40A1 and pull the trigger...

What a rifle![20]

At 300 and 500 yards I put the rounds anywhere I want, all in the black. At 600 yards and moving, still in the black but not a good shot pattern. Five rounds into each target. 700, three in the black but all on the target area. 900, two in the black, 1000 one in the black. My best shooting. My partner did a little better.

Then we get the results. I failed. He failed. We suck.

Before our hearts hit the ground harder than a grenade, however, we get the good news. Since we hit the target at 1000, we have another chance.

The next day of qualification, the weather is equally as nice, except a little cooler. I am calm and relaxed. I mean, what are they going to do, send me someplace to get shot at? Fine.

I get a different partner today, some guy named Dan Higgins. He likes to talk and seems wound up like one of those toys you spin up with a key and let

20   (P. 427) Chuck Mawhinney shooting the M40A1, confirmed kills, 103

go. I just hope he is a better spotter than he appears.

We begin. I relax, get into a good position and fire. Then I trade, become a spotter, trade, fire, repeat. I hit all black till 900 yards. Three in black, 1000 yards, one in black. Not going to make it. Damn. I shot better than Danny, and he joked about it being my fault for not gauging the wind at 900 and 1000 yards. I insisted he made the shot wrong because there was no wind, but he didn't listen. He missed all at the long ranges.

The range officer who was the OIC from the Elite school came down to give us our scores and talk with us. He is a Captain ready to be a Major. His name is Jack Cuddy. To top it off he brings his buddy down, the NCOIC of the school, Carlos Hathcock. OMG, I had heard of him. CSM Klinger talked about him and here he is, in the flesh. He could kill you with one shot out to a mile! He didn't look like he is mean or anything. I heard the Marines did give him a hard time, though, since he is a loner and the Marines didn't like loners.

There were about 25 of us who didn't make it. We're told that we can hang around for the standard sniper school and when we're done, depending on how we scored, we can try for a spot again. If not, if we didn't have assignments yet, we can leave for the fleet, or be assigned back to our originating units.

I have no assignment or originating units and wasn't ready to give up. I decided to stick around for the normal sniper school. Dan does the same and we decide to partner up. The old idea is to go to a dance with an ugly friend that way all the girls want to be with you. I am the better shooter so everyone will be impressed with me! Danny is an ugly friend! He is a big, huge target of an ugly friend, which makes things even better. I wish that is how it would go, but no, it will be hard to impress any of these guys at the elite school.

Back to ash and trash details while we waited for school. I move over to the training battalion barracks and get situated. No one yelling, pushing, early wakeups, etc. School starts and it is normal class work. Angles, deflections, hides, wind, line of sights, weapons, etc. A lot of bookwork.

Next is fieldwork, look at where you want to shoot, go to that place, look back at it and see where you want to set up your hide. Concealment is different than cover. We rarely have cover (protection) so rely on concealment.

Then the work of shooting over and over and over. We shoot different weapons at different ranges, getting us familiar with each so that we can make an intelligent choice of what weapon we want to use. I want to be a sniper, not a designated marksman or an accessory no one knew what to do with, which means I need the M40. I want the M40. That was what they are using at the elite school that is what I shot at my qualification.[21]

I get my wish and am assigned a loaner M40. If I make it, the Corps will build me my own. We have

---

21 (P. 428) My Qualification Certificate on the M40A1

various trainers come through, and some are from the elite school because they need to also learn how to train other snipers. Almost all the elite guys are former 'Nam vets who elected to stay in the Marines and civilian shooters who joined the Corps to hone their craft and try the ultimate hunt. These guys were National Competitors on the competition circuit. No wonder it's hard. Any other place I would have been at the top, not here.

We keep in shape, that is the first requirement because our job was not to stay and fight, it is to shoot and run like hell! I guess not run like hell because if we did, we are going to probably lose that race. Nice and slow is the rule of the day. We have to go long distances and be able to shoot quickly. We need to improvise while on the move and understand how to not to engage as well. They do not want dead snipers but live snipers who can abort a mission and leave without anyone knowing we were there.

I continually concentrate on the long shots and finally start hitting consistently at 900 and even hit the black up to 1,200 yards. I know I am being watched and have a good shot at getting into the main school. My reviews are positive, and I finally start meeting instructors from the main school. All the guys that are going through the main school all know each other or have high recommendations from other shooters. All I have are some jarheads that fought with me or are range operators who like me. I am allowed to go to some practices as well with the really good shooters. They intimidated me. Where I killed it at 500, these guys acted the same way at 1000. Maybe with more practice, I can get there. For today, I'm humbled by how good I am but how great I'm yet to be.

The elite school graduated the class I was hoping to be in, and the next one is up for selection. The main instructor of my school told me I need a little more field time and I will not be in the next class.

Field time? What do they think I did the last two years?

I get a little emotional and have to be led aside before my big mouth gets ahead of my brain again. These are not the people to get mad at, they make the decisions. It's explained to me that almost all the shooters in the class were veterans of combat as snipers. They have all gone to scout sniper school before this class or are world-class competitors.

So where do I fit in?

I guess he had a point. When someone puts in the time to explain things and put it into the proper perspective, it makes you feel good that they care. Contrast that against my dad, who was more likely to tell me to pound sand.

I have forgotten about my spotter, Danny. I guess he calls me "his" spotter also... Okay. Point taken. He is offered the same thing as I am: a little more training.

When we go to the OIC, it is explained that we can get some real-world training to make us better.

The previous class has a few Gunnies who are going to take volunteers to certain areas to get more practice. This way we can be further evaluated and for our wellbeing, see if we could handle the difficult stress a sniper has both physically and mentally. I think that is fair. One interesting note is that my dark dreams disappeared. Seems that going back and preparing for combat relieved stress more than sitting around thinking about it.

I heard of guys never leaving the Marines because they couldn't cope in the real world, killing was all they knew and when they got out, they went to work for international security companies providing protection in hostile areas. It was either that or kill themselves, and quite a few have. I never saw that as an option. Better to point the barrel at an enemy who deserved it.

Anyways, the Marines know my background and I didn't crack or go off the rails, as far as physical, I don't think I can get in better shape than what I currently am. What I didn't know is there are scout sniper schools all over the Corps. It is a volunteer position and only in 1977 is when the formal USMC Sniper School is put together. We are no less a sniper than the formal school in training, but we are not the absolute elite.

I am close, but no banana. But it gives me a clear shot at my next goal.

To get to the level I need to be at, I have to get real experience. To get that real experience, I receive orders for a temporary duty assignment to Beirut Lebanon. Our embassy there is under heavy protection and has been attacked a few times. We have intelligence that all our embassies in the Middle East are targets for militants that thought we support the Jews too much.

Our mission is to augment the embassy Marines as well as the units that are sent in to help protect the area. We are to coordinate with Army units that also are present. I will not do any of the coordination, but a Captain will be assigned along with three NCOs to the TDY (temporary duty) unit and we will have a minimum of 16 shooters. Each school would provide volunteers and get On the Job Training (OJT).

It could be perfect.

I know how to pack: light. I know what to do with my mouth: keep it shut. I know how to shoot: point and fire.

I want this.

We graduate in early May, and three of us go from Quantico to the Middle East.[22] I can't believe it; I have to go through POM again! Shots! This time I will not believe any nurses. No matter how cute they look, they lie.

This time, there are no nurses, just Corpsman. I make it through and only receive one shot. They'd never miss a chance to jab someone, so I guess the other shots are still okay. I didn't even get a sucker this time.

---

22   (P. 428) My Graduation Cert MOS 8541 Sniper

Chapter 27

5 May 1978

The loadmaster gives us our briefing on the aircraft. "Once we land, we can come under fire, if we do, we may just continue rolling down the airfield and leave. Once we land, un-ass the aircraft as fast as possible and run, don't mosey on to the waiting busses."

Some dummy from behind me chimed up. "What about our gear?"

He continued, "If we have time, we will roll the pallets out onto the tarmac and they will be picked up after we leave. If we're not able to, then when we come back again, will try and drop them off."

This sounds like some fucked up shit.

We can hear the pitch in the engines and propellers as the aircraft starts to drop. It's like an "E" ticket at Disneyland's Matterhorn. The C-130 drops like a rock and stops on a dime. We run, all 65 to 70 of us to the waiting buses. No one wants to die just off the airplane. The buses load us up quickly and rumble off. Looking down I notice that steel plates were welded on the bottom of the busses in different spots. Armored buses, that's messed up.

Now I'm really in the middle of it.

We arrive and transfer through the wire hoping to arrive at barracks that are in a building. No, these are Quonset huts, similar to boot, but they are better than GP Large tents as far as I'm concerned.

The steel won't be much help with bullets or mortars, but they're better than the tents would be. But as I look out the window, I see we're moving past the huts and now I see the tents.

Damnit, we were told huts, not tents.

The Gunny on our bus tells us, "Children, don't worry, tents are temporary until we get you separated into billets."

That makes me feel a little better, hope it's just a couple of days.

Danny and I decided that on our first day after landing is to go to the beach and get ourselves a tan, be waited on by the exotic women of the Middle East, and find ourselves wrapped up in their enjoyable pleasures for the night. At least that is the fantasy we all talked about on the plane. The reality was the assignment of cots, where the chow hall was (in a real building), where our weapons were stored and a mission brief later that evening.

Before the mission brief, we went to the briefing tent and each team is paired up with a Sgt. who has been in country a little while and will help us get acclimated. There will be three teams going out day and night and were told that we could see action at any time. I'm glad I wasn't going out. It will be much better hearing from other guys about their impression of what we're facing.

This Gunny's name is Ornelas. He doesn't talk much, just grunts and tells us to behave like good little boys and he would see us at the evening briefing.

Remembering Davison, this guy is the same mold, leave him alone and he will give us our space. That's fine. Danny and I are still a team and will just roam around the area to see what's what.

There isn't much to look at and we're told we can't go outside the wire unless it's something sponsored by the MWR (Morale, Welfare, Recreation) which probably isn't going to happen anytime soon. There is a war out there and our only real friends are the Israelis who had recently invaded. Well then, so much for women. Darkness is coming in but we can still make out the beach, and what a wonderful beach it is, well, if you lose all the barbed wire, and possible mines in the ground. What to do for fun? I guess we can play some games, I know a few guys brought some along. Danny and I get to our tent and the game of Risk is laid out. It's a game of world domination and has about six guys yelling and laughing while they played. The tape decks are playing and everyone is listening to a lot of music: Pink Floyd, Led Zeppelin, Kansas, BTO, Alice Cooper...there are so many. It's almost good—at least until someone later plays the songs from the '60s and Vietnam.

After dinner, we head on over to the evening briefing. The reports had very little activity other than a lot of people shooting at each other. The teams went over the routes they took, impressions of ambush sites, and the shock of buildings just blown apart. This had been a real, live city that was destroyed by its people.

We listened to the next set of mission briefs and are told we (Danny and me) would not be going out until the eighth. That is a good sign, giving us time to acclimate and get a better feel of the surroundings and history. As we pack it in and start to fall asleep, I try to keep the demons at bay. This is a different war here and I should be fine.

Chapter 28

6 May 1978

The next morning is a very pleasant and routine. No bad dreams and the smell of breakfast on the wind. After eating, we are going to roam around the area where we can ask questions and learn as much of the history as possible. Know your enemy, as they say.

Through our make-believe headsets, our fictional tour guide's voice announces, "Welcome to the Riviera of the Middle East." This is beautiful Beirut, Lebanon."[23]

I am told this is where all the rich people went on vacation in the 1950s and '60s. Beautiful beaches, Grand Hotels, gorgeous women, and money to burn. You could have fooled me. I suspect even though most people in the U.S. would consider me poor, I am probably richer than most of the people in Beirut. The city now looks like pictures I had seen of German cities after the allied bombings in WWII. Buildings with bullet holes, sides caved in from tank rounds, light ribbons of smoke wafting up into the sky and rubble everywhere. Kids are in the street begging for food or trying to steal what they could. There are all sorts of nasty looking individuals carrying weapons around and you can feel the sadness of women with their heads bent down, probably remembering better

---

23   (P. 429) Beirut, 1978. SeaCobra providing overwatch

days and now desperately trying to find needed items for their families. God forbid they look any man in the eye because then they may be labeled harlots.

It's normal to see AK-47's to M-16's, along with people carrying paper bags and pushing carts. Occasionally, you will even see someone with an RPG (Ruchnoi Protivotankovye Granatamyot, in Russian), better known as Rocket Propelled Grenade. This is a nasty weapon that would ruin anyone's day for sure. The beaches north of us had concertina wire around different areas and we were told some sections were even mined. It doesn't look like human life is too valued around here, but I guarantee you, I value mine.

Growing up in Southern California, I should have realized how cool the weather can be near the ocean. I expected one-hundred-plus degrees, but being this close to the ocean, along with the light breeze, kept it cooler than the interior landmass. The temperature today is about 80 degrees, no humidity to speak of, and no noticeable ground effect. When I said ground effect, it was from a shooter's point of view. You look at a target, aka a warm body, and try to analyze what will change the trajectory of the bullet. That's ground effect—wind, humidity, and rising heat. I like this weather better than Central America, where your shirt sticks to you like glue and every time you breathe.

I now have a better understanding of what the school meant by OJT here in this rocky piece of earth. We would now get practice. Real practice. Not target boards but real people. As Dorothy in the *Wizard of Oz* says, "We're not in Kansas anymore!"

One of the new restrictions that came out after Vietnam, the powers that be handed down rules of engagement that concerned me. They might keep me from doing what I am trained to do—kill people. Jimmy Carter being president didn't help since he is a pacifist, diplomacy in his mind always worked better than the sharp end of a spear. This might not be a big deal anyway since we did pretty much what we wanted to in Central America. It might be because the C.I.A. was running things down in Central America and poor Jimmy didn't know anything about it. Probably one of those "Omissions" the military is great with.

Just having been here four days, I felt this place has to be worse than Honduras or Guatemala. At least the Central American states had food, shelter, and some respect for each other. The people in Honduras were nice, clean, and smiled at you. For the most part, they weren't trying to kill you and put your head on a spike as a warning to others. Not like the good citizens of Beirut are trying to do.

In Honduras, you can talk to the people, even the women, and not have too much fear of dying over that. Maybe the Central American governments are corrupt, but the people have a more normal life in the cities and outlying villages. The drug-running was bad, but the population wasn't the users, it was being exported primarily to the U.S.

Our briefing in Honduras regarding the local

population was to be careful and polite, treat the locals as best as possible because we were guests. Understand that the men and women will tell you straight up what to avoid doing, but in general, everyone was happy to have us there.

By contrast, the Beirut briefing was short and sweet. "Stay the fuck away from everyone. They all will kill you for a dime. No one wants you here and if a woman even smiles at you, beat feet because death is around the corner."

Nice place, right? These poor people, you either had money or you were very poor. The war became a conflict of rich vs. poor, and about a dozen religions fighting holy wars against each other. They all think they're right and everyone who didn't believe their way must die. No one could trust anyone.

The mission briefing educates me on how the city is laid out. It's split in half with The Israelis and a proxy government on one side, and the Syria government on the other side. The space between them is a no-man's land of rubble, dirt, and the ongoing tension in the air of hatred.

The previous year, some rag head bastards assassinated the ambassador from the United States and the U.S. decided to increase the number of soldiers here on the ground. Everyone was trying to exert power over the others and Israel had no problem kicking the shit out of anyone who got in her way. In this part of the Middle East a fairly new organization, about ten years old, called the PLO

(Palestine Liberation Organization), is being run by some monkey called Yasser Arafat. They caused a lot of the chaos that was happening. The PLO wanted the Christians to break ties with the Israelis and were also trying to keep the Syrians from brokering peace with the Israelis as Egypt had just done in April. Their mandate is to assassinate anyone who tries to make peace with Israel. They were probably responsible for a RPG attack against the U.S. Embassy that happened a couple of months ago as well. Bunch of shitheads trying to kill all the Jews.

Reportedly this group was formed for the sole purpose of killing Jews and returning to Israel, what they called Palestine. They were responsible for the Munich Olympic killings of the Israeli athletes in 1974. It is also rumored that the Israeli Mossad killed Abu Hassan, right in Beirut! He had been one of the PLO who planned that attack in Munich. This past January, a car bomb had been detonated by a remote control that killed him and a few others. This just proves that if you fuck with the Israelis, your life is forfeit. This city is not for the faint of heart.

Being Jewish, and assigned here with a long rifle, I'm curious why the Marines never asked me if I wanted to be deployed amongst people that hate my religion. It's not so much that they hate me as that the easiest way to wipe out a religion is to wipe out the people who practice it. And listen, just because I'm no Jimmy Carter doesn't mean I *want* to kill anyone. But if you threaten me, my family, my friends, my religion? Maybe the Marines already knew and were comfortable with it.

Well, I hope they are comfortable with it, because if I get the chance to take out the PLO, I know I will. Some people deserved dying, and I can think of no better group than the PLO. If they had no clue about my feelings and religion, too bad for the Corps. The only conflict I could see is if the Corps told me NOT to kill one of the PLO soldiers I had in the reticle in my scope on my sniper rifle. More than likely I would have to ask for forgiveness or claim ignorance because I know what bad is.

We reported to the Company Commander we would support in the coming days. He is an older man, about thirty-two and looks forty. I don't think he likes it here or the people here. For his first words, he says, "Everyone outside the fucking wire, as far as I'm concerned, is a bad guy. All they want to do is kill each other and Americans."

I don't know if I have a problem with this, but I'm trying to follow the advice of wiser people than me.

If I listen to Davison's last words, then the advice is easy. "Fuck 'em all! Let God sort it out."

If I listen to my father, it's deceptively simple but impossible to master. "Do the right thing, no matter what."

One of our guys, or me, might die because I don't kill. Nineteen years old and told that everything is okay to shoot, situational ethics is going to mind fuck me. Omission, Commission, shit. Well then, I hope they are all PLO, this would make the ethics portion easy.

We are here to back up the troops that have to work out in the open and keep a watchful eye out for anything out of the ordinary. I have no idea what is normal, so it happens to be good we have a Sergeant with us. He is our next stop. Asking around, I'm told that he is at the Mess. Where else would these NCO's be? I've learned they are no better than us lower enlistees when they want to hide: the mess hall is the place to be.

Finding him there, we pick us some grub and sit next to him.

He looks over at us and just grunts. "Afternoon, Gunny, can we talk a bit?"

"About what?"

"What's normal here?"

"Nothing's normal here, now leave me the fuck alone."

Typical Non-Com. I am not impressed. Here we are, risking our necks and wanting some intel and getting the run around from one of our own. He had better change his mind or I will clip him for fun if he's not careful. We finish our meal and tell him that we'll see him tonight. He just grunts again. Maybe he's one of those ROAD people, Retired On Active Duty.

There are no ranges here to practice at or to zero our rifles. It was a good thing that we took care of most of that back stateside. We, trained snipers, are always checking heat, humidity, distance, and wind. My rifle was already zeroed for three hundred yards. When you zero your rifle, you shoot at a target that is a certain set distance away and set the sights on your weapon so you can consistently hit a target at that range. The best way to imagine this is that a football field is one hundred yards from one goalpost to another, so, three football fields. Over that distance, I can put a bullet in a man, anywhere I want to.

We each picked out what type of weapon we want. My weapon of choice is the new Remington M40A1 and it is sweet. Five rounds of 7.62mm locked and loaded with a 10× Unertl fixed-power scope. The rifle has one of the new fiberglass stocks, not wood. I liked the wood, but this had to be more rugged to handle an urban setting. It looks like it will do just fine. The armorer had finally finished making it in Quantico for me and handed it off before I left sniper school. Some modifications are made from the civilian rifle (Remington 700) and hence, need to be custom designed for us. As I said, the wooden stock was replaced by the fiberglass one and changed out the scope from the Redfield to the Unertl. The sling swivel and buttpad were replaced as well. The rifle can hit out to 1000 yards, easy--even 2000 yards in the right hands. It can, but I wasn't that good because I qualified as a platoon sniper, not a distance sniper.

This deployment will be my chance to make it back to the elite school. Didn't matter, I can rock anything out to 500 yards and still good at 650 to 700.

I don't much have to worry about here! Everything is 300 to 500 yards away. It is a city and urban warfare engagement area with some open areas to our east. Hard to believe it, but Northeast from our position, forests are out there, the Cedars of Lebanon I had read about in my Bible. I had to wait for evil to come out of the jungle on my last missions, but now my nightmares are going to come from dead cities.

Chapter 29

7 May 1978

We wander around some more and use our scopes to look at landmarks and areas we were briefed on. Tomorrow we will be going out and my nervousness is creeping back in like a snake hiding in the rocks, just waiting to strike. I am covering as much as I can with the maps and orienting the locations of action that have been reported over the last two days. Danny doesn't seem to give a shit. He just keeps talking about how he's going to "get some."

Shit.

I talked to him a little about combat, but it fell on deaf ears. Until you look at the worm at the bottom of the tequila bottle, you have no idea what you're about to swallow. He is no different. I hope he doesn't fold under pressure. I've seen big guys fold and small guys be the heroes. You just never know until the shit hits the fan and bullets start flying.

Our afternoon briefing gave us our mission parameters and ROE (rules of engagement). We will have an evening brief to go over any new intel, but it will be a short meeting because we will be leaving early. We are going to have a routine mission to cover an area where some fire had been taken from sporadically in the last few months. The thought is to cover that area every day now that we are here in the hopes that the rag heads would try again.

You can guess who has a bunch of questions like they teach us at Quantico.

"Excuse me, Sir," I say. "Have we sent out patrols to check on potential concealed or covered areas the enemy might be using?"

"No."

"Do we have any intel about who the shooters might be?"

"Nope."

"How about if security teams are covering them?"

"Nope."

This is embarrassing. Okay. I can see that there is a problem going to happen with my mouth. This is when the Captain—specifically *our* Captain—remarks, "All good questions Corporal, let's get on with the mission brief and will get some answers to those questions later."

"Sir, yes Sir." I guess I made my point known.

Sgt. Ornelas looks over at me and winks. As he gets closer to me, he whispers, "You're not as stupid as you look."

I took it as a compliment, thank you very much.

We left the briefing and went to get our chow. Danny for some reason was a little upset with me. He can't understand why I had to open my mouth. Our mission is to remain in the background and be seen and not heard. This coming from someone who had verbal diarrhea. I told him that is what we are supposed to do, that is our training, but we should get as much information as possible, so we don't die, and he knows it. The last thing I would die from is a Sin of Omission!

As my hero General George S. Patton said, "We're not here to die for our country, we are here to make the other poor dumb bastard die for his!"

We are an expensive weapon that needs to be used correctly, not as sandbag filler. Danny's biggest complaint is what if we fuck up? Won't that look bad?

I said, "Yeah, as in death would be better? We're supposed to know when things won't go well and get the fuck out. What do you think these guys are doing? No wonder they're getting shot at. Let's go get a good night's sleep and I'll see you in the morning, deal?"

"Sure Ski, whatever. Just be right, okay?"

Chapter 30

8 May 1978

It's black. Nighttime and flares are going off like crazy. I'm on my hands and knees and slipping around like a fish out of water. I bring my hand up to wipe my brow—and I notice blood. There is a body under me and a knife handle sticking out of him.

Holy shit.

As I get up and turn around, about fifteen soldiers are coming at me with weapons. I have to fight them off!

But they're already on me. They grab me, they pull at me, and I'm screaming. I raise my fists...

"Wake up man! Stop screaming, I got you." I look up and Danny is holding me down. He whispers, "We're good, just take your time."

Breathing hard, I look around and see I'm not back in the jungle. The early morning is warm, and the tent is open on both sides to let in some of the cool breezes that come through. The light from the bulbs in the tent makes the shadows dance like flares of my dream. The smell of the city is different than the humid foliage of the jungle, and the breeze brings in smoke from the shelling that took place last night.

Laying here three quarters naked with a sleeping bag half on and a big black man practically laying on top of me makes me self-conscious enough to bring me out of the dream.

I'm in pretty good shape, not the body type of a hulk, but more of a lean runner with a swimmer's upper build and tan. My hair is cut razor short and a stubble of morning hair is on my face. Danny is the opposite: he is a large muscular hulk with dark skin and a shaved head that had a sheen to it. Thank God I didn't hit him. One smack with that hand and I would be asleep again.

Looks like the dreams are back.

The brief we had last night didn't cover all the bases, and the Captain telling us he would get answers turned out not to be true. Too many Omissions. In addition to our minds working overtime, we had to contend with something else I didn't expect: all the noise from the city. The jungle had no noise, and if it did, it was more like lulling you to a quiet death.

In the city, the noise said I am coming to kill you *now*. These rag heads liked to shoot at each other a lot. Boom boom crump! All night long. It doesn't help when you dream the shit, they got to make it real. Funny how no matter where you went, humanity is trying to destroy itself the same way everywhere. Thank goodness I could close my eyes and sleep just about anywhere. I just have to contend with fucked up dreams.

Like it or not, we're getting ready for our first mission in Beirut. The city is a war-torn struggle of buildings just trying to stand upright after its population tried to destroy the shit out of it. The rubble is everywhere and each morning you see government workers go out with equipment to clear the streets, of both cement and bodies. I am working hard to get used to a different kind of heat than we had at Quantico or even in Central America.

After putting on my utilities (combat fatigues), Danny and I worked our way over to the mess hall to get some chow. The path is clear, and we had walls erected all over the place to provide cover and to conceal us from the people we were helping. Why? Because those people were taking potshots just to fuck with us.

The food here is okay, not as good as back in the world but better than what is available in-country, at least that's what we're told. As Danny and I scamper over to the mess, we can at least smell a little of America coming our way. The aroma this early in the morning makes our stomachs growl like two hungry bears in anticipation. Scrambled eggs (not reconstituted), mushrooms, tomatoes, bread, and milk for me. Add bacon for Danny and we are fixed. Imagine - bacon in a Muslim country! Who would have figured that? I seriously thought about covering my bullets in bacon grease rather than machine oil to mess up the rag heads' trip to paradise.

We planned to get out early, during the early light, and set up in our hide so we could just check out the lay of the land without being seen. Hopefully, our trek out would prove to be as uneventful as it had been for everyone else these last few days. Starting our workday, we go and draw all our equipment.

Rifles, ammo, packs, scopes, water, C-Rations, and bug juice.

I had to laugh. Bug juice is what we call insect repellent in the military. Now we are ready for our little dance in the park.

We pull ourselves over the rocky outcroppings, making sure we don't get caught on the sharp edges of concrete or rebar. This whole area was at one time a group of houses that are now smoking ruins. We start to work our way across some open areas that were either leveled to help protect our line of sight or were a park area where kids probably played in.

I'm sure if were seen, we will have some rounds shot in our direction. Since it is still dark, with just a sliver of light showing that lessened the probability. The camel jockeys though, never let a good shooting go to waste, so we still had to use good technique and look for cover and concealment. The smell of the open sewers mixed in with the smoldering buildings brought us back to the reality of the stench of humanity that existed here. The safety and smells of our little America base camp were gone.

Our first hide is about a mile away from our base area. Something interesting I had to learn about was that our maps were shown in klicks, meaning kilometers. We were, by map, 1.6 klicks away. By shooting range, we are 1760 yards away. Confusing as shit until your mind could wrap around it. We had to constantly change from metric to U.S. Standard.

Our hide is set up on a berm, in the cement

rubble that had been a housing area or apartment building at one time. I could see the personal things that people left behind; a pan, magazines, a doll, some other knickknacks that belong on a shelf. You wonder what might have been going through the owner's minds as their life was being blown away like so many leaves on a fall day because someone didn't like another person's view of politics or religion. We didn't dare handle anything, especially toys. We worried about traps that might have been set. Best to just leave things alone. These people had no ethics. Not that it was wrong for them to try to outsmart us— but it was evil to put it in a toy a kid was just as likely to find.

Why on earth would you purposely hurt a kid in the hopes you killed an adult?

We had a long wait time before people started showing up for their daily routine. Tick tock, like a clock that just ground forward without an end. One of the things they teach is patience at the school. If you move, it's slow. You become part of the area you're in, unnoticed. A ghost. You could watch the shadow change on the rocks, that's how slow things went. It is just another day in paradise. As the morning moved on, we noticed a change in the number of bodies out there. Still people, mainly men, but much less.

We keyed in on some knucklehead 300 hundred yards out. He would stop, kneel, and then get back up. I had no idea why he decided to do that, and neither did anyone else. Then he started moving rocks and putting them in a pile above a pile of debris that already existed. That is not normal in anyone's book. That locked him in as a person of interest.

Is he building up a hide? Probably thinking he's John Wayne. Wants to take some easy shots at us. No one told me this would be amateur hour.

I didn't see a rifle, though, so that couldn't be it. It doesn't matter, easy as pie for me to get a headshot if needed. Maybe this is this guy's apartment we are set up in, and he is building a new one! I'm not going to go out and ask him though. Our briefing said that there are diaper heads in the area taking potshots at us and running to ground. Maybe this will turn out to be one of them. The ragheads became successful at disrupting our day-to-day operations because of the constant shooting, but like the seasons, all that is about to change.

1245 hours: 8 May 1978

As I said, here I am in the center of nowhere in Beirut. Clear skies, and there's a nice beach (except for the razor wire) about three miles over and northwest of my position. There happened to be enough humidity to make it warmer than the temperature showed, but the water in the air is not going to affect any shot.

We are still watching the Arab that is about 300 yards out but getting closer. My spotter kept getting excited about the raghead that kept bobbing his head up and down as if he is trying to find something.

You've seen those little toys on the dashes of cars? I think they're called bobbleheads. That's what this guy is doing. Funny as shit.

I didn't want to be in any hurry at this point to kill someone, especially since I wasn't sure I wanted to do it this way. Well, I did but didn't. Hard to explain. I just hoped it all worked itself out as C.A. had. I am tired of boxes becoming unlocked that I had locked up and put in the very secret far reaches of my head, but without my Gunny here to help me process those things, I've got no better choice than to leave them locked inside and screaming to escape. I just have to scream loud enough that no one else can hear them.

I didn't see any gun or rifle as the guy moved around. It is hard to see the surrounding area from my scope because I am focusing on one small spot in front of me. That's why we used a spotter, Danny is next to me, and he has a larger scope for spotting. Danny is just getting jazzed up because this is our first real Tango (target). He kept up a running dialogue of what this guy happened to be doing, diarrhea of the mouth. I needed him to calm down and not do a play by play of every little thing this goat herder is doing.

He probably just wanted his turn behind the rifle scope, and I had the spot for the next hour. Our rotation is one hour on and off one, switching roles-spotter, and sniper. Now Danny decided to start talking faster, and I couldn't understand him because he put on the strong Alabama accent. He is like a woman you might be with at a football game. All you

293

just wanted to do was watch football. All she wants to do is yak yak yak yak yak.

Finally, the Sgt. must have sensed a touchdown within reach, because he told him, "Shut the fuck up!" That is a bold and brave move seeing how much bigger Danny is.

My spotter's name is Lance Corporal Danny Higgins. We came over together from Quantico after the sniper school. He had his rifle—a setup M14 now called an M70 for the sniper version - that had been built in the late 1960s and converted in 1977. I don't know why he brought it. It's a solid rifle but nowhere near as good as the M40.

"Why the M-14?

"Mind my own business."

"Don't be like that."

"Make the long shots and don't worry about the close ones," he said, determined to indeed be like that.

The M-14 had a 20 round 7.62mm magazine and taped up so he could do a combat change and make it a 40-round clip by flipping it over. He promised he would keep everyone away from us if it came to it. Semi-auto or Full auto would scare the shit out of anyone. This thing could punch through walls if needed. Well, there were plenty of walls to punch through here.

If the enemy can just see Danny pissed, they'll back off. He towered over most guys because he is about 6'3", blocks out the sun on a hot day and built of solid muscle. He looks like chiseled granite. Danny is about 230 lbs and liked to lift. He told me he had been raised in Mobile, Alabama and this is his first time, besides boot and Quantico, that he had gone anywhere outside of Alabama.

His claim to fame was hunting and being able to put meat on the table for his family. He had been shooting since he attained the age of six years old, and for now the Corps is his home away from home. He would be putting meat on the table, just a different kind of meat. I am glad he liked me.

His explanation as to why we got along is that most white guys wouldn't have him as a buddy, but seeing how I am Jewish, and he never met a Jew before, I must not be white. Whatever works for you big guy! He did ask me one day where I hid my horns. Instead of getting upset, I decided to let him think they might really exist so I never told him. I just figured not knowing would scare him! I would have liked to have had him on the M-60 with me in Central America.

Sergeant Ornelas is our babysitter. He is from Mexico and joined the Army to get citizenship. I can't imagine Mexico was that bad, but it must have been to make him join the Corps during Vietnam. He explained that his family had no money and the United States is the Promised Land. If he could get in, he would be rich. He came here as an illegal but heard that if you joined the military—Army or Marines— that would be a path to citizenship.

He made it into the service and now is sending money to his parents, for the past ten years, in Mexico. His wife is in the U.S. and happened to be a citizen already. He has two kids, a boy, and a girl, and is happy that they get the privilege of being citizens as well. He just wants to make it through this and retire and be with his kids.

Gunny has the standard-issue M-16A1, 30 round mag of 5.56mm. It's a nice and light weapon but isn't in our TOE (table of organizational equipment) for snipers. It isn't as powerful as the M-14 but could rock and roll faster than the M-14. Danny and I also have the old 1911 .45cal if needed. You can lay betting odds that if we had to use those then we were in deep shit. Keeping us safe and providing rear security and instruction is Sgt. Ornelas's job.

The Sergeant looks like a standard-issue Sergeant. He stands about 5'10" and is built like a brick. I think when you put on Sergeant stripes, they change your face to look like a bulldog as well. That would be him and every other Sergeant I seemed to meet.

As I said, Danny and I came up from Quantico together and competed a lot. Just FYI, I am the better shot. One nice thing is he didn't dispute it. I resided at the top of the class at Quantico, but still not good enough for the elite school. I think Sgt Ornelas's real job is in making sure us two idiots didn't get ourselves snatched and grabbed or shot up. The ragheads would have paid good money to anyone that could do that.

The last thing we needed to happen is to have our two bodies dragged through the streets and everyone yelling 'Allah Akbar!" The sand monkeys tended to do that kind of stuff if they captured someone. They hadn't been able to pick up any U.S. military that way and hopefully, they never would.

The Sgt. had been here a few months and knew the routine. He had been in the shit in 'Nam so we knew to pay attention to what he said. All of our instructors had been to 'Nam and they were bat shit crazy, so we figured that anyone that had been in the shit had to be some sort of crazy.

Chapter 31

1300 hours: 8 May 1978

It is getting warmer sitting in our hide and we couldn't do anything at this point to cool down except by drinking some tepid water. As we were watching our bobblehead another two diaper heads pop up over by the broken cement debris. *Where the hell did the other two come from?* Buildings in the background, torched-out cars in the front, and people are now way too close to us. We had watched all the paths but never saw them. Hopefully, that is something we can check out later.

Shit... What are they doing?

Then I notice a bigger problem.

What in the hell is wrong with my hands?

Suddenly, they're sweating.

Why are they shaking?

The camel jockeys are pointing at something... I follow the arm he has up, but I don't want to lose my sight picture. Danny follows his gestures as well and sees that they are pointing at a couple of Army guys smoking and joking. I can't see the Army guys, too far away for me. Danny utters they are perfect targets right up against the wall they should be behind. Our base camp was about a mile away, these Army guys were about 650 yards away from us, working outside the wire but out in the open.

Fucking Army, Marines are so much smarter

when it comes to this. These Army guys ought to know better!

We've all been to the same briefings and were told to keep undercover, no need to make yourself a scarecrow and draw fire. I'm now locked on with my scope on one dung burner, I don't see anything like a gun or rifle. Sarge tells Danny to pull his head out and scope the three. Danny got tunnel vision and was watching the Army guys. *Dumbass. Maybe I'll call him that later when I can run away from him.*

It's about a 300-hundred-yard shot, maybe a little closer. *Why are these men doing this now? Fuck them.*

Danny pats my shoulder. "Ski looks like the last guy has a long gun. Not sure, so take a look."

"Roger that."

Slowly moving the rifle and scope to the left to try to track the last man we see, I have to move slow otherwise the sight picture will be lost, the point where the bullet will enter his body and terminate his life. He is in my sights. The heat from the cement blocks sends a mirage of shimmer in front of my position. My whole environment is calling to me and letting me make the calculations needed to deliver death. Something in the shadow by the guy's leg is sliding over the rocks like a small snake. Hard to tell, might be a pipe bomb, homemade grenade or worse, a scope. Another oversight, no intel on if the Arabs have scopes to make the long shots effectively. Now we know they might.

"Danny, I don't see a rifle, but it looks like a scope. Too dark to see in the shadow of the rocks. Lock-on that for me and watch, okay?"

"Shit Ski, can't see it either, what about you Sarge?"

Gunny Ornelas is the third team member keeping us out of trouble. Reminding me which one of us isn't a sniper, he whispers, "You shitbirds are the experts. Move Danny, let me look."

Danny responds, "Never mind old man, your eyes suck anyway."

No rifle yet. The temperature feels like it's one hundred degrees even though I know it's not. Sweat drips off of my nose and onto the stock of my rifle. Close your eyes, breathe, relax; open your eyes...wait for Danny. The Deadly Sin of Omission, the Arabs could be pointing the long rifle at me and I wouldn't know that they could hit me. We don't know what weapon they are shooting with, if they have scopes, what their egress area is. The list goes on. As ever, I have to make do with what I have.

Danny is so close to me our bodies are practically touching. I can feel Danny tense, he sees something. He whispers, "Hey Ski, the Ahab in the front has a rifle. It looks like he is putting a scope on. They must have passed it up to him."

Damn, I'm tracking the wrong guy and need to shift to the first target. I move the barrel slowly. Got him.

"We've taken incoming from that area a few

days ago, I say light them up Ski." That's all the permission needed from the Gunny.

Target acquired, I see the rifle and it looks like he is getting ready to line up a shot...

Talk about flashbacks.

My focus is on the target, and forgetting everything around me, my mind runs back in time. It's a Springfield 1903 .30-6 from WW1. It has a clip with 5 rounds and is a bolt action. This weapon from when I was fourteen years old is the exact rifle I learned to shoot with. The one that had been almost as tall as me. Fantastic rifle, also good in the right hands out to one thousand yards.

This rifle is plenty effective to take a shot at our guys accurately at this distance.

Who are these people? Why would they shoot at us when we're here trying to help them?

The positive aspect of being a sniper instead of a leg (regular infantry) is that you have a lot of time to think the negative. You have a lot of time to think.

Why am I thinking? Shut up brain!

I tell myself to breathe deeply. My throat is already closing, and a film of sweat has coated my skin.

Stick with what you know! You've practiced this a thousand times.

Train the way you will fight; you will fight the way you train.

The crosshairs are on the side of his head. Air is now filling my lungs.

Breathe, let it out, relax, pull slowly. Let it be a surprise. Pull, slowly pull the trigger—

Chapter 32

1325 hours: 8 May 1978

BOOM!

My shoulders crack from the impact, and a sea of red fills my vision. It's only the training that keeps me free of a moment's terror that the blood might be my own.

I find the next target but can't see shit. Danny is yelling, Sarge is yelling at Danny to shut up, and I continue to look for more targets finding none. My mind registered a red mist that still hangs in the air in front of my eyes. At night, with flares, things look much different. Here in broad daylight, this has a different look. Not as bad as the Cobra, but more personal.

I did this on purpose.

But he hadn't been attacking me. I hadn't killed him in self-defense. I'd killed him to prevent him from ever trying to kill me, or kill people I am here to protect. At what point did that turn from preemptive defense to outright murder?

"Danny!" I shout, the training kicking me into action again while my mind runs in circles. "Where's the next target!"

"You hit the guy, Ski, fucked him up."

"Where is the next target?"

"You hit the stock and got him in the shoulder. He's still there being dragged away, shoot his buddies!"

"I can't find them. Lead me, give me some points." I see the rifle on the rocks and it looks like it's smashed up. Only me, a hit, and a miss. Guess it's not one shot, one kill. Close but no banana for me. I hope I don't get some other nickname for this.

Ornelas is yelling, "Keep looking, watch for them coming back for the rifle."

Something is nagging me in the back of my mind but I just can't place it. Too much input and excitement. This is not how it's supposed to be. What am I missing?

Sarge is still yelling at Danny to keep looking. I keep scanning the area as well. There is no movement from that area.

Should we look beyond? What about security teams?

Shit!

"Danny, Sarge! Move, move, move!"

The rest of my training kicks in. Shoot—and scoot. How could I forget something that's drilled into our brains for weeks on end?

It doesn't sound right—rookies run as fast as they can—but what we need to do is make no sudden movements- that's what the eye is trained to see. Slowly back away from the area you took your shot and move to the alternate location, again slow as to not catch the eye of a tracker. The quick part is right after the shot, if no new targets are out there, move it. If you haven't been seen, no problem, but if you have, get the fuck out, and don't worry about stealth. You've been seen so unseen yourself!

Sgt. Ornelas wasn't a trained sniper, but he should have told us to "shoot and scoot." That brings home the next point, trust your training, and do it. Don't rely on others to do it for you.

I tell Danny again, "We need to move now!"

His eyes light up in recognition. He looks around and yells, "Fuck yeah!"

We start backing away with our gear and Sgt. Ornelas wants to know what the fuck we're doing.

I said, "Trying not to get killed, You?" I think he wanted to hit me. I have a smart mouth and one day it will get me into too much trouble, but he won't do shit out here.

He looked at us both and said, "Yeah, you're right, let's get to the alternate now."

It took us about 10 minutes of crawling and constant checking, but we made it to another rock pile. This one had a better view and we could see the 1903 rifle had been picked up while we were changing locations. Brave dudes, if we had another team out here, the Ahabs would be dead. My first real long-range shot, a hit, and miss. I had credit for a kill in Honduras but this one counted in my new job as a sniper. Not a kill, but a confirmed hit and he won't be doing any shooting for a while, if ever. I felt satisfied that I did my job, made the hit, and lived.

I did wonder about CSM Klinger's words coming back, stating that snipers were cowards or murderers.

What do the Army guys they targeted think?

I'm betting they'll be happy to hear that the shot they heard may have saved their lives. I'm equally sure that after their platoon sergeant gets done with them, they will probably wish they were shot instead.

Danny takes over the next "hide," and we stayed uneventful for the rest of the day. People were moving around doing normal business, and all avoided the area we shot into. No other threats popped up other than the normal ragheads carrying rifles. It was unauthorized to just shoot the bad guys because they were carrying weapons. Only if we had good reason to believe they were going to shoot us or people we were protecting. If they started shooting at each other, we had to stay out of it.

The only other time we could shoot was in support of the IDF (Israeli Defensive Force), and even then, only if they requested it. There was no time they needed us in the past because they were very badass by themselves and usually had a lot more firepower than we had. The ability to call in aircraft and tanks, and just across the border, another 10,000 troops if needed negated most any help we could provide.

As evening approached, we took our time as a snake would, slowly moving along the ground to keep up with the sunlight. No sudden moves to catch the eye. After getting back to the perimeter, we did our after-action review with the current company commander and our commander. We went over all the positions, areas covered, and actions taken along with results. He would pass them on to the battalion with his report.

I'm glad we don't have the night duty schedule. I'm exhausted from what happened today. I felt like I had run about 10 miles in full gear. I have always been calm but feel a little jacked up right now.

One of the things we're taught is to control our emotions and heart rate. We can't let either one of those go. Too much adrenaline will mess up your shot, and good luck when you start to come down from that kind of high. Like I said, I'm careful about drugs, even the ones my own body makes. Give me a little bit of anger or outrage and I'm as intoxicated as those morons who smoke grass and try to shoot.

That's why we practice trying to relax through anything stressful. This helps us deal with what's happening now as well as something that might occur in the immediate future. I need to practice a little more. Danny is normally wired nonstop, so there's no hope for him. He was ready though, have to give him that.

Once he calmed down, he had the 14 up and ready, full auto-selected until we got to the next position. I don't usually like being a spotter but after today, being a spotter would be a welcome relief. I'm trying to not think about the guy I shot, but now, after its done, it's starting to crowd my mind.

What about his family, friends, parents? Yes, he's a bad guy, possibly. Or he was just doing his job like we are.

Would I have shot him if he was just taking pictures?

I need to get clarification on that.

When I was a door gunner, I never had these thoughts. Well, maybe I did, but not enough to stick in my memory. So why are they creeping in now?

Probably need to see the Chaplain or doc.

I will save the poor me crap for some other day when I have time to talk to someone. Right now, I needed sleep! Our gear was moved while we were out to the Quonset hut, no more tent. No privacy but better protection all the way around. They were supposed to be temporary but like everything in the Corps, temp became permanent. Sgt. Ornelas told us to disappear and he would see us tomorrow, so, dropped our stuff, turned in our rifles but kept our side arms. It was nice we were able to keep the .45's, none of the jarheads except MP's and officers had them.

When we went to the Mess (why do they call it a Mess? Cause we eat messily?) That night, and we drew a little bit of a crowd. I just wanted to eat, and boy did the food smell good! Were always getting hand me down equipment from the Army, like were not worth the extra because we're going to die anyway, but food-wise, I think we ate better than the Army. I know we ate better than the Air Force unless they went out. Their cooks weren't shit, they never got to practice.

I let Danny do the talking because he enjoyed the attention and was good at it. I don't remember half the things he said happening, but he told a better story than I would, and I can tell a story! To hear him talk, we terminated about one hundred attackers from breaching the wire and killing everyone.

Danny declares, "Ski only had a five-round clip so he could only help so much, but I had the M14 and burned through four clips."

Funny, Danny never shot anything today, but that's a lie I don't need to shoot down. I'm just going to enjoy the food and listen to a great story. As long as I grunt at the right times, Danny won't hurt me later on.

Chapter 33

Mid-May 1978

Every soldier will tell you the same thing: war is minutes, hours, days of impossible boredom broken up by endless stretches of sheer panic.

We are in the Dog days of almost summer. Not much action for me but we have been out on plenty of hides. Set up, scan, move, repeat. Some of the teams had contacts in other areas in the city. A few kills were registered and I think the gomers were getting wise to us having some real assassins lying in wait like a scorpion ready to strike. We had two choices, we could become complacent or hone our skills. We were getting better at moving, selection, and recon so I would surmise that we were honing our skills.

A new pattern was starting to develop as well. There were reports of white guys going out with some bad guy shooters, and it appeared the bad guys were starting to put out security. Someone was being naughty and teaching them basic sniper skills now. Danny and a couple of other big guys set up a range for everyone to use. The range was only 300 hundred yards but it was the normal range for our operations anyway, so we could start training like we fought out here.

Some of the embassy staff came out and we taught them how to shoot the '14 and all sorts of pistols. A few of the sunglass guys came out as well and tried their hand with some rifles they had. There were twelve of us with the M40's and not one of us was willing to let anyone shoot them. We had good reasons for it! We didn't want some REMF messing up our sights, or jamming the thing by accident. I was very tempted a few times by some of the younger secretaries, but I was able to get by showing them how to shoot the .45cal. holding on to their sweet bodies for just a little while made the duty a bit more bearable.

I tried to get more than a couple out for an evening stroll, but there are too many officers and diplomats around that had better prospects of advancement than me.

Danny just laughed at me and said, "Give up, Ski, you lost your stroke."

Chapter 34

June 1978

Today I am going out on a patrol. Most snipers think that's a waste of their talent, but I have a good reason. I need information.

A single recon will give me insight into who was shooting at us and other areas that might be hides against us. I asked about going out with them and said I could be used as a designated marksman. If the shit hit, at least I could use the M-16 in single-shot and pop off a few bad guys. My Captain approved the request and I was introduced to the patrol as a marksman. My main job was to scope out possible ambush sites and hides. Our patrol started at 1000 hrs, we were always trying to vary the times so we didn't have habits that the bad guys could count on.

I went to the armory and drew an M-16 with a box of one hundred rounds. Next stop, the range to zero in the weapon to about 50 yards. I checked the handgrip out of habit—whether Mattel was to blame or not for the gun jamming all the time, their embossed label was a red flag to get a new gun.

I'm glad they had deflectors because shooting left-handed, the ejecting rounds would go right inside my shirt and burn the shit out of me. Well, I am almost ready. Back to the building and get all my web gear plus my helmet. Haven't worn that thing in God know how long. It feels like a hundred pounds stuck

315

on my head. Another reason not to be infantry.

I picked up six mags of twenty rounds of 5.56mm and ready to rock and roll. Placing myself in the middle of the formation gave me the option of quick reaction to the front or rear as well as being able to talk to the patrol leader about different sections I needed to take a closer look at.

Once we went out of the gates and were outside of the perimeter, things look much different. Even though we are only fifty yards away, the smells, sounds, and people look and act differently. More like real people rather than just targets. Out here on the street, I feel like the target. Everyone sees me.

Wow, I forgot what that feels like. I don't like it!

My head is on a swivel and my eyes are constantly looking for ambush and hide sites. Everyone else is just bebopping along and acting like they were back in their hometown, a day out in the sunshine. Not me, I am shitting bricks. Our mission is to patrol the peripheral area that borders our area and the embassy area. Since we might rely on the Israelis for help, we all needed to coordinate and see chokepoints, rally areas, and possible sniper hides (bad guy ones). Interestingly, life looks like it would in a normal town—if your town is a burnt-out hulk, but a hollowed out husk at least resembles what it used to be. There are restaurants and cafes, retail stores, and outdoor markets.

I am trying to keep my situational awareness

up along with trying to calm down and enjoy a little of the scenery. So much for that vaunted training to control one's emotions. One of the things normal grunts are not taught is looking at people to see what they might be doing instead of what it appears they are doing. Jarheads were just taught how to put maximum firepower to eliminate any threat. Police called this type of urban training "threat assessment."

The guys who came back from 'Nam were pretty good at it, but their problem was that for them, everyone was a threat. Just shout "boo" and they would shoot. Some of them are pretty messed up. Other soldiers who were good at reading others usually were kids who grew up in abusive homes-- they watch body language pretty close because they grew up anticipating getting hit. The last set is usually guys who were former police that joined up or guys who grew up in really tough neighborhoods.

Most of the Jarheads are making jokes and acting like this was nothing. I guess when you are the biggest and most well-armed group of guys going down the street, you get a little confident. I'd seen ambushes, been shot at, and had been in the shit before so I took nothing for granted.

Weaving along the streets, it was interesting to see how much western influence had been here. You have women in burqas and women in short dresses. Others covered and more not. Radical Islam was creeping in but hasn't taken a strong toehold yet. We are stared at a bit, but most of the people ignored us.

We are just another armed gang in their little country.

I keep my eyes up and ears glued to what is going on. God gave me two ears and one mouth and that's why I was listening twice as much today. Watching hands and gestures or people moving too quickly. The sniper school didn't teach these things either. Snipers watch to see who is giving orders, directing troops, or acting like they know what they are doing. Anyone with a radio. Anyone who looked like us, snipers. These are the people we look to target.

That works when you're in a hide or in a firefight that has the enemy coming at you. It doesn't work in terrain like this. Here, there are no leaders, just people that may or may not be looking for an opportunity to kill you.

None of the streets are empty. They're all crowded with people, which is a good sign. If you're on patrol and the street that is normally full but now empty, it's not someplace you wanted to go - no matter how much firepower you thought you had. Fanatics want to die killing you. They have some perverse religious command that said if they died a martyr, then they would have seventy-two virgins in their heaven. That is a hard thing to beat until you stop to think about it. I can barely handle one woman at a time. I'd rather run straight at a sniper than try to handle seventy-two virgins.

Why am I good at threat assessment? When I moved to the U.S., I got into a lot of fights as a kid. I didn't start them but finished quite a few. Learned how to watch for a fist coming out of nowhere to hit the fat new kid that spoke broken English. Later, at the Drive-In, you had to watch people coming in the exit and decide if you need help kicking them out or not. Very unpleasant if you guessed wrong.

Like I said, all good, everyone normal, no one hustling too fast or running. Kids are good. Parents won't let them out if they know something was coming. Just keeping my head moving like a sprinkler. The patrol leader—there are fourteen of us on this patrol—has us stagger the street so if one side or the other is hit, we can maneuver easier than if we all are on the same side.

I turn to look at my backside occasionally. Not knowing these guys or how they will react when the shooting starts makes me a little uncomfortable. I hope they know that if the shit hits the fan, I'm just another rifle trying to stay alive. Once things get sorted out, I can hit my targets a few more times than the average, but when you're talking ten to fifty feet, not yards, there is no such thing as a sniper. You aim, you shoot, you kill. Precision is a luxury, so get the fuck out of the way.

The two main distractions for me on this patrol are the kids and the women. The kids show no fear—neither do the men, but the kids are curious and want chocolate or food. The men just stared. I watched them close when we are near them. The kids will reach out and touch you, so the distraction comes when they create a movement and take your eyes away from where you should be looking. Maybe I am paranoid, but it served me well before.

Now, the ladies. I am more worried about the ones covered up. I believe they deserve decency and modesty and whatever else a person likes, but how am I supposed to tell if they have something under the robes? A bomb? A rifle? Heavier guns? No way to know. Then I see the women with short skirts, low tops. Well they're not hiding anything, but even if they don't mean us harm, my wandering eye means they could prove to be fatal distraction.

I have no idea what the name of the streets were called. Most don't have any names on them. They are known for what is on the street, one with a café- Duncan Donuts, the rich area- Broadway, tourist ally- 42nd Street, etc. Some have names but the script was Arabic or French and mean nothing to me. We give them names like we were back in our cities. On this patrol, we are going back through the perimeter area that my team fired on the bad guys a few weeks ago. This gets me excited because I might be able to find out what route they took to leave unnoticed.

One of the few times in my life, I asked if I could take point (lead the column). The patrol leader said sure but would put his point out with me. He didn't trust me any more than I trusted his guys. It would be good to have two of us watching out for traps or a potential ambush. The point man usually is the first person killed if the ambush party isn't smart. The enemy should let the point go by so they can trap the main body. The second person killed was tail-end Charlie. I like the front middle because that area has the most reaction time.[24]

Up I go to the front and look around to see where my bad guys came from and left. I keep working us towards the area that the shooter was shot and disappeared. Danny only saw one person for a bit and then, like moles, two more show up. One of them is a shooter.

My gun is ready and so is my aim. I nick the guy—like I said, precision is a luxury out here—and they all disappeared quickly down some rabbit hole. That's not normal, trained snipers, yes, but these guys, usually, you can track them moving out, not always getting a shot, but you can track them.

When we get to the spot, I ask for a halt and search. The patrol leader used this as a training opportunity and fanned out his soldiers with eight providing security to the four corners and the rest searching through the area. I found the brown stains on the rocks which were dried blood. There is a lot of it, so I knew I hit something vital. I looked at the area to see where they trailed off and followed the blood trail. I hear a shout out and the patrol leader motioned me over to an area about 50 feet away.

There it is.

A hole in the rocks that goes into a tunnel that reaches underground. These guys are groundhogs, that's how they did it! Sgt Ornelas said they had taken

---

24   (P. 430) Beirut war zone, 1978

incoming from this area a few times, but I never asked if they ever sent out a patrol. Son of a gun, they never did.

I wonder why?

Well, I sure will ask, even if it pisses someone off. That's what I seem to do best. Logically, if you were getting shot at from a specific area, you would try to determine why. Someone who repeats a pattern in a combat area is someone making a mistake. That's what you should watch for. This had the potential beginnings of a trap we could set. During this patrol and others, I was able to see patterns in the trail system they used in different areas. I couldn't be sure if it was combatants that were using the trail or civilians, but it was good to know for future target areas.

I just have to convince the patrol leader not to destroy the tunnel right now.

"We continue as if we didn't find it," I say.

"Sounds good to me," he says.

He didn't care. He didn't want to spend the time getting a team in here to destroy it and now, if things went sideways, he could always blame me. The fire team providing security was called back in and we continued to the base camp.

After we returned, I went with the patrol leader to the Company Commander, who in turn, took us to the Battalion S-3. Along the way, the patrol leader left so it was just a lowly enlisted guy with a Captain. A Marine Captain is as close to God as I have had the opportunity to be near most times. We tried to stay away from any officer above Captain because most of them didn't have time for us or would just find stupid things for us to do. That's why we gave our NCO's any information and they dealt with the brass.

I wanted to let Ornelas deal with this, but since it was my idea, I had to run it up the chain real fast. A lucky break for me, I'm in front of this Major because the Lt. Col. couldn't be bothered. My Captain heard I was back and came to listen in on the briefing. They all sat down while I stood and explained what we found and what the plan I was developing looked like. I could tell he didn't care either. Since the Major liked dealing in large numbers and moving companies around and I was talking about 3 or 4 guys, both enemy and ours, it meant nothing to him.

His ears picked up, however, when I explained that this was a route for a PLO sniper team to do some damage to our most important officers in the front units. I hit a button because he thought he was one of those important officers. Explaining the mission of a sniper to him and what the enemy sniper's role probably was earned me the okay to continue.

Targeting leadership and communications would be the primary mission. I explained that when a VIP visited the area, and if the enemy had intelligence about the visit, I would bet a sniper team would be there to greet him one day. Now I had his attention and he told the two Captains and brought in the S2 (another Captain from Intelligence) to get back the units and come up with a plan. My Captain liked me a bit more as we strode back because he would be able to show his tactical abilities to the Major, and maybe the Colonel. When we talked, he asked some pretty good questions. He was pleased that we would come up with a plan that would blow the shit out of the Arabs before any of his guys got whacked—including him.

The three Captains got together and talked for a bit, then asked me to come over with the NCOIC. I explained what I saw and how we might set up an ambush to accomplish this type of mission. After that, I was dismissed. Okay. Going back with my teammates, we talked and did our own informal after-action review.

That evening we had a detachment meeting with me as the briefer. I explained in detail, all the routes into and out of the area as well the city choke points and the tunnel system. The big question was asked, how well did we coordinate with the Israelis? I forgot; we never saw them.

Then I remembered that one of the reasons we went out was to do a joint operation. Not us as the detachment, but the battalion as a team. My answer was exactly that. I never saw anyone from the IDF and I don't think they were there because I would have spotted them. This is a question that was never answered, what happened to the Israelis? Did they leave us out to dry or were they running a parallel operation and only higher headquarters coordinated?

The Israelis didn't miss much, and I tried to not miss anything either. These patrols would bring back good intel for us, but only when one of us accompanied the patrol. We were able to determine enemy sniper hides, trails for egress, and potential build up sites to house a larger amount of troops. We couldn't share any intel with the Israelis nor did they with us.

Nothing much happened after that for a couple of days. We continued our movements and doing our overwatch for whatever company was on the perimeter that day. A few shots were exchanged from time to time, but not by me. Patrols went out almost every day, and every once in a while, they would ask for one of us, but I believe they just needed a warm body. A couple of companies had some shootouts with some Arabs at the end of the week, but it was more like thirty guys getting pissed off about something and shooting the shit in the company's direction. The company returning fire with an overwhelming rate of fire shut them down quickly. There were four confirmed kills by our guys with no U.S. killed or wounded.

Chapter 35

Mid-June 1978

Two weeks after we found the tunnel—and that area was watched like a hawk thanks to our Captain who made it a priority—a few suits showed up during one of the debriefings. They wore dark jackets and white shirts and had on the cool sunglasses. I'd seen this type before and I didn't like them one bit. They screamed CIA. Most of the CIA were rich kids out playing spy and telling us Jarheads or Grunts to go out and get killed to test some dumb ass theory they had about an area.

Let me walk you through one of those conversations. If you've heard one, you've heard them all.

I'd say, "Tell us what to expect"

They would state, "That's classified."

"So why are you sending us?

"We can't tell you."

And off we would go with no idea where or why we were doing whatever it was. These people represented the Sins extremely well! The CIA guys that refused to admit they were CIA guys wanted to hear about "my" tunnel.

"Wasn't mine," I told them. "I didn't dig it." Again, my mouth, but they asked for it.

The Captain just said, "Ski, pull your head out and tell them what they need."

I didn't need a formal order to stop being a smartass, but it helped.

"Sir, yes sir."

I explained what I knew, told them we didn't go into the tunnel since no one was qualified EOD and it was probably rigged. Explained that the Captain had a watch on it and my thoughts on using it. That appeared to satisfied them. Then, in a breach of CIA protocol, they were *nice*. So nice that a part of me wondered if I'd gotten caught in a grenade blast and was hallucinating on my way to death. It just didn't seem possible.

The CIA guys explained that a team (secret squirrels) did pick up a guy that went to a local clinic to get a shoulder wound taken care of over a month ago. The Doctor was on the CIA payroll and he had been told to watch for someone who was shot in the shoulder or neck area. It was my guy they picked up.

My ears perked up. I hated the CIA, sure, but I liked anyone who had heard about me. And tracking a guy I'd shot was the best part of me to see.

The lamb eater was PLO and heaven forbid, a real live sniper. The PLO was out for blood and not hunting any of the important officers. He was hunting for a Senator doing whatever senators do in a warzone. Well that's information that should never get to the enemy. Of course they made him a target.

The deal was the suits now wanted to spread the news that another high-value VIP was going to be visiting so that they wanted to track and see if that news got out. They were not interested in shooting or killing another enemy team, they were more interested in finding a potential leak, and the only way they could do that was to set up the leak.

The hope was that the opposition would send out a team to make the kill. The opportunity for us was our team would know when the fake VIP would be in the crosshairs and we could either take them out or capture them. The Captain explained to the suits that we were not the capturing type so either we killed them or someone else would have to do the mission.

Oo-Rah!

Thank you, Captain, please use us for what we trained for.

We were dismissed and the Captain and NCOIC told us they would brief us later if there was a mission set for us. It appeared that the CIA/not the CIA decided to go with my/their plan. My plan if it didn't work, and their plan if it did.

A couple of days later we were briefed that the fake VIP mission would happen, and plans were put into place to make it work. The time frame would be during our Fourth of July celebrations and the word was out to all the senior people, but only a few knew the exact placement and timing.

The old joke goes, "Do they have a fourth of July here in Beirut? No? Sure, they do! Everyone has a fourth of July, it's just a day."

We celebrate our Independence Day on the

fourth of July. Everyone else in the world just thinks it's another day. Well, maybe the British don't. Also, in two weeks we would have our made-up day for the VIP. We will see if the word gets out and our tunnel boys will show up for some "live fire."

The CIA boys came back to our unit and explained that the word was leaked to certain individuals they had their eyes on. It wasn't any U.S. people, but loose lips sink ships, and nothing loosens lips faster than money or a mistress. God help you if it's both.

Didn't matter to us, just fix it, and let's move on. Our Captain said since it was my idea, I would get the honors of missing Fourth of July dinner. Steak, baked potato, corn, bread, and beer. Also, I could pick two outstanding individuals to share in my "opportunity to excel" moment. If we were to accomplish our mission sooner rather than later, a meal would be waiting for us.

Danny was looking away from me, and a new friend, Johnny "J." Jones, was shuffling away. Now Johnny Jones was a tall, lanky guy who didn't have that Marine look. He had a lopsided smile and easy-going manner.

"Goddamn you're tall," I said.

"You flirting with me?" Johnny Jones said.

"Just thinking you'll get the best view standing in front of me."

"View of what?"

"The shooters. You'll get first shot at them. Of

course they'll get first shot at you too. Get it?"

Everyone started laughing and pushed them in my direction. As they were pushed towards me, I grinned and said, "Better pick your next friend more carefully. After all, misery loves company."

Chapter 36

Late June–early July 1978

All the patrolling would now pay off. We had most of the information we needed on the area and expected enemy sniper hides. We sat around and planned our hides, making sure we had a couple of other alternatives as well. My experience started to catch up with me, I was becoming good at this stuff. Even though it was boring as hell, I was able to get a better understanding of what real snipers did for a living. Long hours of nothing—then 30 seconds of adrenaline—and then hours of silent retreat. If you can call us finished with the mission along with heavy casualties on their side a retreat.

"I want our new motto to be 'silent, but deadly'."

Our Captain raised his eyebrows. "Like a bad fart?"

He had me there. "Yes, sir."

"Sikorski, the Corps has a rule that you don't fix what isn't broken. Our motto is simple:

'You can run, but you will only die tired.' "

The message was clear. I'd have to leave my mark with my gunfire, not my motto.

I only had the one-shot so far, then some stress when we were out on some patrols, but this next event would be something big. In looking and planning, I found some obvious hide sites for us, so I made sure we crossed those off our list. If a real team is coming to kill us, they will have the same training as us, so we have to be better. We needed to be unexpected.

The team we would confront would probably have some security out to watch out for those areas. The way you try to set up your position is to look at it from the target point of view. Where would they think the bad guys would be (us)? What areas were unlikely spots to find us?

If these guys are pros, they would have another one or two teams watching for us and be ready to provide counter-fire. They knew one of their guys was hit in the location so all they could hope for is we didn't discover their hide. The hide hadn't been used in over a month and a half, so no fire from that location would give them a sense of security that we just forgot about it.

Up until now, the company has been lazy going out on patrols, but me being all new and bright-eyed and bushy-tailed, I force them to do things they normally didn't do, like recon! Since the hide was found, the patrols went out of their way to avoid that location. I finally located the first hide I wanted to use on the map. I found it on my recon with the patrol I was with previously.

As I looked over the terrain from the enemy's vantage point, I was able to pick out our hide as an excellent spot. It was a low spot and it would be easier for the enemy to hit us from the side or front, but it was behind the hide they would use so it would be completely unexpected. It wouldn't give us much security if another team was out there, but I was looking to the side and front and counting on them not looking behind their hide. Our retreat route, a little in the open, would be difficult if we did hit an enemy team. I had a plan for this that would take their attention off from the rear if we had to shoot.

I plan to ask for two squads of Marines to split up and take two positions. We need a front and side position to work together to obscure each other's locations. When they hear any shot, they are to engage in the general location of where we think the enemy is going to be. The two fire teams will be four or five hundred yards away, but if they can distract the enemy, the enemy might not know where the original shot or shots came from. If there are security teams with them, hopefully, they will engage the fireteams. With this plan in place, we have some good positions marked out for primary and alternates.

We have scheduled our briefing with our new buddies, the CIA in the morning. This gives us a chance to have the rest of the detachment look over our plans and critique them for possible problems. During our detachment briefing we tune-up small areas, but I never ask, so they never tell me who the target is going to be.

Going to take some brass balls to wade out there and know you're going to get shot.

3 July 1978

Today is the day before the action. Tonight, we receive our final briefings. Fire teams are getting equipment ready, and we are doing the same. 1100 hrs rolls around and we move over to the spook's nest. Operational charts are up, radios going and quiet chatter throughout the room. We begin our preliminary briefing, which is normally an ordered affair, but my heart speeds up a fraction when no one mentions a word through the briefing. No complaints— you should keep those to yourself anyway—but also no questions.

Do they not care? They have their mission and we have ours?

I don't trust them. Well, I'm ready with my questions.

"Gentlemen (since they are civilians), who is playing the VIP? I would like to meet him and ask him a few questions."

The answer comes with a shit-eating smirk. "Andrew."

Andrew is a mannequin that will be dressed up in a suit. Two bodyguards will be "traipsing him" around the area using a set of sticks.

"We've done this before so it's not unusual."

Damn good answer as I thought about it.

"What about the bodyguards?" I ask. "These guys will be possible targets also."

"Not your problem, Corporal, they have body

armor and will take cover at the first shot."

It does seem we have two plans after all. Let that be a lesson to me that just because I'm not aware of something doesn't mean it doesn't exist. But still, these guys could have said something sooner.

As the briefing goes on, ours is like a sideshow to the CIA. The real plan is to ferret out a mole in the organization. They have had several breaches in security and have an idea of who is behind it. This will cement someone's feet into the river for sure. At least they let us hear their plans, but it means little to us. They have just one mission if a bullet is shot, and that is to round up a couple of individuals and sweat them. That brought up another question I failed to ask.

"After the shots are fired, what if we get into trouble out there. Do you have an extraction plan for us?"

"No. I'm sure your company will come out and support you. Not our problem."

I don't show my displeasure, but my life and everyone carrying fire with me is putting themselves at risk. That's one sin I don't intend to confront today. "Okay, looks like we're not going out unless we know you can pull some strings and get hot support for us." I pause long enough to let that sit. "That would mean pulling out the stops and have heavy weapons and helo extraction."

He assesses me for a second. "You telling us or asking us, Corporal?"

Thank God my Captain chimes in. "I'm telling you. My men are staying here unless we know you can pull them quickly. We may not need it, but if this mission is critical for the enemy, they may have teams everywhere."

"Will work on it and let you know. Otherwise, just keep your planning as it is, Captain."

Fuck me, I almost told these guys to shove it up their ass. I'm sure the Captain will give me an ass-chewing also for my mouth. At least I won't die out there by myself if things go to shit. I have my buddies who must love me by now! I give a little wink and a smile at them and get the bird back in response, at least their smiling also.

It becomes late in the day and our final briefing is ready. The CIA promises to bring in mortars. The army will direct heavy machine guns. Two helicopters, a Huey, and a Cobra would be on standby. If we pop yellow smoke, the cavalry would come running and the area would be lit up.

As far as I was concerned, that was all we needed. A Cobra for me, yeah baby, that bitch can sing.

The CIA stated that in order to alert the VIP to come out, we need to radio them. Uh oh. I just figured the VIP would stroll around and get shot. Then I would shoot. Nope. Their signal to come out would be when we identified movement in the area. Okay, not wanting to look stupid, I just wrote down, "bring a PRC-77. (a man portable VHF FM combat-net radio transceiver)" I didn't plan on bringing one, but it was doable. I told them we would have the squelch off and we're not going to use the prick except to tell them to start the decoy action.

We couldn't go rehearse the plan in case there were spotters out there already watching. I felt we should go out to our hide around 0330, BMNT (before morning nautical twilight). Getting out early would help us avoid detection and allow us to potentially see the enemy moving into their hides. I asked for a starlight scope that I knew we had on hand. Johnny was going to be the pack mule and carry the stuff. The scope is an AN/PVS-2 that comes in a field box. What it does is take the ambient light and collects it so you can see things out a very long way. Everything is green when you look through it, and if you see someone they will be almost as clear as day, except green.

With the case and tripod, it was about 10 lbs. That doesn't sound like much but when you're humping the gear we had; it's just another thing too much. I felt we needed it though in case bad guys were doing the same thing.

I approved of the plan with one exception: one of the suits is going with us. I wasn't too happy about that because I had no clue if this guy knew what the hell he was doing and if he screwed up and got shot, who was going to get blamed and who was going to drag the body back? The Captain told me to just shut it and do what I was told. I looked at the suit and made sure he understood not to fuck this up. He was a dead man if any of us got hit because of him. He just smiled and said not to worry.

(Turns out he is an Army Reserve Infantry Lt. Colonel, in the CIA. Oops. That'll teach me not to make so many assumptions.)

That night we collected up all our gear, piled it up where it would be ready in the morning. The suit came by to check on us and he was wearing a tiger pattern utility. That's different, made me happy because he looked important and pretty so if the bad guys did track us, he would be the first target, big huge Danny would be second, and tall, goofy Jones would be next. Little me would be digging a hole and popping yellow smoke! I loved it when a plan comes together.

Chapter 37

4 July 1978

This whole thing is turning into quite a production. The two squads were moving into position. Lookouts kept watch all night but reported no movement beyond the perimeter. A roving patrol also reported no contact.

Fair enough. They'll show themselves as soon as we take action.

It's about 0315 and our morning routine is finished, gear up, and inspected. Comms working and tiger suit is ready on time. Out we go, beyond the perimeter. We begin by hiking for a bit because we used the ridgeline in front as cover. Once we have to move perpendicular it becomes a little harder.

At this point, we are sometimes shuffling, crawling, or crab walking. Our first hide is in front of us and it's about 0400. This took a little more time than I expected. As planned, Danny and I go on to the second hide and set it up while Tigerman and Johnny set up the first. The plan is to take out the shooter and his team, then move to the second hide and deal with any security teams.

We move cautiously back after setting up the hide and came up on Johnny, who not only had the Starlight all set up and working, he was scanning the area and reporting to us his search pattern. Since we are behind the possible shooters it is easier to check things out. Doesn't look like we're going to find anything just yet, and it's getting lighter. We have a filter for the starlight, which made it a very capable scope in the daylight. I told the suit to install it on the scope while Danny and I used our scopes and Johnny used the day scope to watch our backs.

The preprogrammed time for the VIP isn't until 1230 hours unless we caught movement before then. The idea is to rush the sniper team if possible because they wouldn't want to miss their shot by having the VIP leave the area. I felt the suit did well so far and asked him how he was doing by holding my thumb up, then down.

Which one?

He gave me a thumbs-up, so all is good. I am relieved so far because his movement this morning is like a professional, and he is taking orders instead of telling me to pound sand. This man isn't going to screw things up.

I wish that made two of us.

Today I find out what I always knew: I am pretty much a control freak. The more responsibility I'm given, the more control I needed to have. This is a whole new level.

All other missions there was nothing for me to do but be part of a machine. But now I have my first command—if you want to call it that—and I am knee-deep in the manure, involved with the slightest detail and not trusting anyone. Glad this is a small team. If not, I probably would have been fragged—killed by friendly forces—already.

I start questioning the hide site, then the equipment. Why did we bring so much gear? When the shit hits and we need to move it, then what? It was like we are camping and brought a house with us! Then I worried about our egress route, and what if the two fire teams saw us and thought we we're the bad guys. How fast will they shoot us up?

Now that my head is spinning like crazy and is ready to pop off my shoulders, the suit hits me and points at the watch. It's 1100 hours. The suit finally has enough of me and my either talking or muttering.

He leans in and whispers, "Let's talk now."

"No. Can't you see were in the middle of a mission?" I whisper back.

He is calm. "The other two can cover for a few and it's important."

"Fine."

Maybe he has some secret squirrel information I need. We backed off into a gully about ten yards away.

He asks, "What's wrong?"

"Nothing."

"Then why the fuck are you talking to yourself?"

"I am?"

"Yep."

Okay, I sit back and think about it. "I'm just a little worried about everything."

He then said, "We can talk when we get back, but you have done one of the best mission planning sessions I have seen."

Maybe he saw my shoulders rise or my head stick up straighter. This was the good stuff I'd long been denied, and I guess he could see its effect on me.

He added, "You covered all the bases and then some. Most officers would not have done half the job you did. You should think about doing something better after this. I can't believe this is your first planning mission."

Either he figures I can't be a good sniper, hence a different job, or he thinks I'm lucky to have at least half a brain, since most Marines have only a quarter. It doesn't matter right now, we have to get back and do the job. Okay. I need to just get this right, I'm not a worrier, I just want to make sure everything and everyone will be okay. Like a good dad.

We don't have to wait long after our talk because Danny spots some movement in the general area we're covering. I tell him to keep an eye on the tango he sees and told the suit to keep scanning ahead with the starlight scope. I show Tigerman the map and point out the other areas he needs to cover in case I am right and security teams are in those areas. Danny counts out four tangos with his fingers and points to where they are setting up shop. These fools have their backs to us.

Perfect.

The suit whispers, "I need to get on the 'prick' and call in the sighting. Let's see if we can get these guys excited and make a mistake."

The prick is the PRC-77, the radio I didn't want

to take. I just hope he keeps radio comms quick and not talk forever, voices travel far in the early morning.

He also needed to confirm with his buddies that they needed to go round up the leaky folks. I hope they allow us to follow through on the mission. The CIA could just have easily aborted since they had their answer.

My next thought is to let Danny take the shot. While hitting these guys in the back might be our only option, it'll weigh on me to take the shot myself.

But then Davison's words came back to me.

Don't be a fool. You will save lives.

I tried not to think too hard about it because these shooters are here for one purpose, and that is to assassinate what they think is a high ranking American.

We still have some time and these guys didn't seem like a Pro team the way they moved around and talked. They didn't even set up security and cover. This is why we and the Israelis can kick their asses in a fair fight. Of course with our training, it's far from a fair fight. We are the best of the best anywhere in the world.

The suit proved his worth a few minutes later. Real close to where I thought other hides would be set up, he finds not one but two security or sniper teams. He patted me on the back and asks, "How did you know?"

I said quietly, "That's where I would have set them up, but also, they would have covered the far side, where we have our alternate, and the rear, where we are now."

These guys are not doing that, they are just looking forward most of the time. Maybe I am wrong because we don't know which is the shooting team and which ones are the security teams yet. I stick with my gut feeling. I told Johnny to put away the starlight and get everything ready to move. Next, I tell the suit to provide rear security for us while Johnny cleaned up the area for movement. Then we wait.

It's 1130 hours and the CIA told my suit we would move up the VIP to 1145 hours. I am now used to waiting and by what all the enemy teams were doing, I finger the team in front is the shooting team. None of the other teams have what looks like a sniper rifle, just AK's. That left me with determining who I thought the shooter would be. They all had weapons, AK-47's, and one long gun I couldn't identify. They set it up on a tripod, and each took turns looking through the scope.

No problem identifying their intent.

I practiced squeezing off shots each time they took turns. I finally identified the shooter: he is clean-cut, wearing robes but didn't look at all Middle Eastern. He looks like he is showing the others how to do something. I motion the suit to come over and look.

He takes a look and quickly stares at me. Then he takes a deep breath. "Don't shoot no matter what. I will be right back."

Fuck. I could hear him talking on the prick and am worried that the sound will travel. I was getting ready to trade with Danny to tell the suit to quiet down, but he came back. "What the fuck is going on? Something wrong?"

He whispered, "Nope, all's fine and take out the mother." He added, "That rifle, it's a Dragunov sniper rifle, 7.62mm with 10 rounds in the clip. Effective up to 600m or 660 yards. That's our boy."

A Dragunov? This was interesting news. The Dragunov is a very controlled Soviet weapon.

We could have started sooner, but when I fired, I wanted the bad guys all looking forward, their attention drawn to the fake VIP.

Okay!

I start my routine, which I now had down pretty well. Sweating and shaking hands are long gone. The fast heartbeat is slowed down. No adrenaline, just calm, deep breaths getting good oxygen into my lungs. Not focusing on the target, just relaxing until Danny gives me the signal. He knows my routine as well as I do.

Danny taps twice on my shoulder, which indicates the VIP has stepped out. We can shoot any time now. I lose awareness of anything around me. I see only what is ahead of me. I see only my target. Defense is not my duty. My job is to fire. Fire. Fire. I trust my teammates to do their jobs so I can do mine.

I can hear my heartbeat, and as though I willed it to slow down, the gentle thunder stretches out into enough time for me to see the target's movement before they even move. Before I even realize it, I have sighted in on the tango and the crosshairs are in the center of his back. Unlike the last time I shot, I have become a predator, a hawk, an eagle.

I am glad for that hardness. I have learned to kill without remorse. I can hear nothing.

The next word is from Danny. "Shoot," he says.

No hesitation. *CRACK*. And it is done.

Chapter 38

1152 hours: 4 July 1978

Crack! Hit, his head is gone.

Shift, target acquired.

Crack! Second target down, middle of the back.

Shift, target acquired.

Crack! ...Hit...but he spins.

There are no more open shots, and in that brief lull, my awareness comes back to what's around me.

I hear firing coming from the base camp. Must be the fire teams. I forgot about them. The next thing is Danny pulling me back by my belt and dragging me into the ravine.

I don't want to go; I want to kill. I am in the zone and acquiring targets. Danny snaps the hold of death I am delivering. All I see is red: this is everything I've trained for. I lose my mental clarity of mission and only see Arabs, people who want to kill Jews. I am delivering retribution; I am the right hand of God. Damnit, Danny stops my whole purpose in life. What the fuck am I doing? Calm down and get back to reality, Danny basically lifts me up and sets me down. Shit that was awesome!

Time to move. Good thing everything was gathered up beforehand, right?

It sounds dumb, but for the life of me, I can't remember where the next hide is. I had been there, set it up, but right now, I'm drawing a blank. Danny is leading, then Johnny followed up by me and then the suit. We can stand in some spots, crawl in others, and hopefully, the distraction from the fire teams is working. This place is not what I expected. It's got no sand, it's rocky and dirty and hard and hot. We move well and don't raise up to give away our position, but it's tough going.

As we get to the hide, Johnny moves up around Danny to poke his head in and look around. I didn't like it, but Johnny is more expendable than Danny, so he took "point" once we get to a threat area. He comes back with the all clear and we move into the new position.

This takes all of seven minutes and the fire teams are still shooting. The suit calls on the prick and gets an update, the idiot ragheads are still in place shooting at the base camp. They had very little chance of hitting anything!

This time we have two shooting positions, so the suit takes up my spotting side and Johnny spots for Danny. The M-14 is going to get some work. We bump fists and hiss, "Get some!"

I look for the two shooters that were left in the original hide, and Danny is going for the close-in security team. Hopefully, we both will get targets and then will be able to hit the far team before they know where the shots are coming from.

The suit whispers, "One guy is still up in the original hide trying to drag someone away."

Probably the white guy, right?

It was the white guy.

I finally find him moving around and he is going to be a hard target. He is a little farther away, about 400 yards and like I mentioned, dragging someone below the berm I can't see. I line up, relax, get a good spot weld and sight picture. He is using some kind of rhythm to move, up, side, slide, down, up, side, slide, down, up, BOOM!

"Target down!" the suit yells.

I didn't wait and told the suit to track far side security.

He acquires them and shouts four more but not shooting but ducking and looking our way now. Probably because Danny and his loud ass M14 is tearing it up on the other site. I glance over and it isn't Danny near me, it is someone relaxed, concentrating, making adjustments, and firing. He is like a machine. He has 20 rounds in each mag and he is using them to his best advantage. Johnny has the next three magazines all set for his reload.

This is the first real-time shooting I've been able to watch. No more of the smiling, talking, hyperactive-on-speed kid but a real professional. It scared me a bit because what did he think of me? What did I look like? I had very little emotion at this point, but it wasn't because I'd somehow stopped feeling. Keeping those emotions deep—where they couldn't make me stumble my way into death—is as necessary as breathing.

I am back to tracking the far side. The camel

jocks spot Danny and a few rounds come our way. This guy I was tracking on the far side had to be huge, 6'5", or 6" and was unbelievably standing up and shooting our way. He has his AK on full auto and the rounds are headed our way but way off. It will be lucky for him if he even comes close.

The suit makes sure I have the right target as we talk. We both verified there is only one shooter. Relax, breathe, pull, and let it be a surprise. Center of chest, largest mass, target not moving.

BOOM!

The suit smiles. "Good kill."

I know, I watched the hole blow through him. Three confirmed KIA, two probables. Danny is on fire, Boom, Boom, Boom. He would not quit.

Myself? I pack it in. My fear is the ragheads will get an RPG up, and even though we are past its effective range, it can still hit us and do some real damage. The effective range was 300 yards but would fly for 1000 and then blow up. Once the RPG blew up, anything around it to about 20 feet was dead unless they were under cover of some type. We didn't see any RPGs when we tracked them but that doesn't mean they don't have them. They are cheap and the ragheads have a lot of them. My turn to hit Danny on the back and tell him to disengage.

Only my training saves me from stepping back and showing weakness. He drops back down and gives me a look that declares he is a sociopath. I knew he had a conscious so he wasn't a psychopath, thank

God or he probably would have killed me.

Just like the part of me I keep locked down until this is over, I know the real Danny is still inside him. I just have to penetrate the spell.

"RPG!" I shout.

That did it, no problem.

Danny blinks and shakes his head, the spell broken.

"Time to scoot," I say, and thankfully Danny cares enough about RPGs to follow my instruction. Two things he hated more than hell and bad women: snakes and RPG's.[25]

We backed off the hide and as we were working our way over to our third hide, we heard the bang and whoosh sound. We all ducked and waited. No way anyone could have seen us. Bam! The area we were in exploded hugely, and then a second huge explosion in the same area! We were far away but there is a lot of dirt being moved. I think we would have been fine if we were still there because the minute we heard the shot, we would have been down into the ditch. Don't get me wrong, it would have sucked, probably wouldn't hear for a bit but we had picked a good hide spot.

We moved to our third location and set up to see if any of the targets were still wanting to play. Poor Johnny, in he goes first. He did look back at us this time, like, really? I don't want to...but he's 100% Marine, off he went. He gets back with the all-clear. We move into this hide and it is far away from the

---

25 (P. 431) Lebanese Militia with a RPG posing

shooters, about 800-850 yards. I won't see them that's for sure. We set up anyway in case some of them wanted to check out our hide number two to see if they got us and drag some body's home. We could hit that area effectively if we had to. The suit gets on the prick and calls off the fire teams and tells them where we are (they had the positions pre-planned on their maps) and that we are coming in.

"Wait one," comes the response from the prick.

Really?

No...it is time to get back to Mama... I want that steak, and more to the point, protection.

We keep watching the area and waiting. I can see that my utilities are soaked through as are Danny's and Johnny's.

A funny thought hit me just then. They both had "nny" at the end of their names. Well, it is funny to me. With so much chaos around me, any coincidence feels like it could be part of a real pattern.

They both looked like hell and aged to about 35 years old, so, I told them.

They smiled and said, "Look in the mirror: you look about 40 - close to what Ornelas looks like."

"Fuck you both," I voice with a smile.

We bust out the canteens to make sure we hydrate and take some salt pills that the Doc gave us. Time to eat our Fourth of July lunch. Hitting the jackpot, my C-Rat has a fruit cocktail, cinnamon nut roll, and turkey loaf. Top that off with peanut butter and hard crackers. I pull my dog tag chain out that has my P-38 attached and open up my scrumptious meal. No way we were using the heat tab, so we ate everything cold. Danny is pissed, he drew chopped ham and eggs—H.E.'s (High Explosives)—because of the bloating and gas they cause. The others did the same and we had a little break. It had been about 10 hours with just water and some fruit we brought out which made the C-Rats almost look good. Always better to eat when you're hungry, it makes the food so much better tasting.

The suit is now yelling in the prick.

That's okay, we're far enough from anyone he won't be heard. Someone pissed him off.

I hear him say, "We're not doing that. Kiss my ass. Screw you. I don't care or give a damn." Then, "Put him on the line." Then, "You get your fucking ass out here to recover the bodies, we're not doing it." Then he breaks contact, looks at me, smiles, and announces, "Let's go get you that steak."

Here we are, waiting to see if the Zeb's (Hebrew for dick) would send a team to pick up their bodies and some REMF decides we need to go pick up the tangos we shot. Idiots. Just like that, the suit becomes my best friend. I can tell you now, none of us would have gone back for anybody except for a U.S. Marine, and maybe the suit. The suit said that there would be questions but to just shut up and don't talk, he said that to all of us. Fine by me! They wanted to play who got the biggest Zeb. That's fine - it wasn't going to be me! This was a good mission. We played it through as we set it up and it went down as planned. A very rare event in the military.[26]

As we came back in under the wire, we were met and escorted to a building where we did the debrief. Usually, we could turn in our weapons and get cleaned up beforehand, but that wasn't going to happen this time. The suits all seemed to be worked up and stressed. Have no idea why, their plan worked great (always give them credit, makes them think you're smart).

We stacked our gear and put our weapons aside, our Captain had Mayfield, (our armorer) come pick them up and told him to clean them. That was cool, but I still would go clean my M40 later. The Captain asked me to lead the brief this afternoon. I went through each step but was paused at the beginning of the first shot. The suits wanted to know if I got a clear look at the face of the first tango.

"No, not really"

"How did you know he wasn't an Arab?"

"He was white, and—you could tell from the back—cleaner and moved differently."

"There are white Arabs."

"Yes, but his particular traits stood out. He was European, he moved more like he knew what to do, and was smooth. Most Arabs are uptight and excited when they're in a fighting position, ready to meet Allah. It's just how they tend to be trained."

---

26 (P. 431) Marine Sniper with M40 and spotter at Embassy providing overwatch for return.

Or what they sometimes believe.

They let me go on from there, and at the end wanted to know why I didn't go out to confirm the kill. These guys must have been born stupid.

I just looked at them like they were a piece of shit on the bottom of my shoe. "Who does that?"

My suit skips on in before things get out of hand. "Ski, you and your team did a great job! Let me take it from here."

You got it, Cowboy, I need to sit anyway.

My suit just kept me from going full-on blowback on his buddy's face.

Fortunately, this is where it gets exciting. My suit explains in a very Drill Instructor way his take on things and was questioning the birth of each of the other suits. He also explains that when the mission started, no one cared about the teams sent out to kill the Senator, they wanted to plug a leak, and all of a sudden, the sniper that was killed is now top priority? Then he told them to send out a couple of squads to clear the area and find what they wanted.

Our job was over, and we were tired, hungry, and needed sleep.

He smiles again at me and tells the team, "Let's go eat." He must have been high up because no one said a word and out we went.

I enjoyed this little demonstration of non-political correctness. We didn't get to see this very often this far down the shit pile. I now have learned a little respect for an officer, or whatever he is. Now that he is our guidance counselor, we let him lead the way to chow. The smells from the mess, our Fourth of July meal, and good company to eat and talk with.

The suit opens up to us and gave us his real name, Dan Myers, and yes, he is CIA. He was a Captain in Vietnam and retired as a Lt. Colonel early. There was a rumor that he was a Colonel, and he admitted he was still in the reserves as well. He stayed Infantry and seemed to be a damn good leader. Always doing what the troops did, and instead of leading from the rear, he was in the front.

Dan proved that today by being with us in the shit, doing his job, and afterward, protecting us from dickheads. I liked him and tried to forget he was an officer.

His reason for being here is that he joined the special operations of the CIA and was looking for Soviet involvement in Beirut. The intel on the ground is that instead of just arming the insurgents, the Soviets had "advisors" out in the field. Dan confirmed they did this in action against the Israelis, and even had fighter pilots go up against the Israelis. The Russians got their asses handed to them by the Israelis, and Dan had seen camera footage that proved it.

I just asked him all sorts of questions since he was talking.

Dan said that what we saw today was direct action possibly by the Soviets against U.S. troops. This would be a shit storm in Washington if we could prove it. Normally, proof would be hard to come by, but that proof had been part of his plan.

This was why his buddies wanted us to go recover the body. It was so we would have proof of Soviet intervention. He wasn't about to tell us to go do something he was unwilling to do, he saw too much of that in 'Nam and it wasn't going to happen on his watch. Good for him.

Dan said there would probably be some others coming around and to just answer the questions as best as the three of us could. I thought that would be the last I saw of him, but before he left, he took me half an inch aside and gave me a business card.

"Look me up when you're done with the Corps," he said.

Done with the Corps?

I couldn't imagine a time beyond this. A life outside the Corps. A moment when I was anything but a Marine.

I wonder if somehow, he knew. Gunny Hardin and I had submitted all the application paperwork several months before I left stateside for the Air Force Academy, West Point, and both Army and Air Force ROTC, and the Marine OCS program. I had interviewed already and was waiting for the yes or no, but the field had taught me that nothing is certain. Not even hand grenades.

If all of my options fall through, the CIA might accept people without college. I could wear sunglasses as well as any of the ones I've seen so far, and they might welcome a change in tone. I was tougher and meaner than all of them.

Chapter 39

7 July 1978

We were now practicing overwatch on patrols that were going out. I hadn't done that before, and it was a good learning experience. The ragheads lost credibility after the last go around and we put the fear of God, or Allah, into them.

We were told through the rumor mill they were looking around to find the white guys who were killers. A bounty was placed on our heads.

That's messed up.

The Zeb's have no idea Danny is black and Johnny is Hispanic. I am the only guy they are looking for! No, we have 15 other shooters and ten are white, four are black, and one Asian dude. The Asian talks like he's from Texas, which he is. So this 5'7" Asian with a strong Texas drawl ... that is weird. The bounty is on a white guy so it's nice there are a few of us around, this also gives me some leverage with Danny since I can claim he didn't do shit.

I felt like a long gun sniper on my few overwatch missions for the men on patrols. We would get the route from the platoon leaders running the patrols, and they would tell us the areas they were concerned with. We coordinated coverage to those bottlenecks or open areas and would set out earlier to get into positions. The platoon knew where we would be as well, in case we needed help. There would usually be three teams set up for patrol, and once they cleared our area, we would return to base. No way for us to leapfrog ahead, it was just too congested in the city.

I never was able to shoot again during those last days. No opportunity. It felt like a loss—but also a relief.

Several of the other teams had some engagements and took out some bad guys, so it proved that we could do what we were supposed to do. None of the teams were compromised and the bad guys knew that if they went up against us, they were going to die.

We lived up to our motto: You can run, but you will just die tired.

I wasn't born a hunter, but as time went on, facing the enemy had required me to become one. But only toward men. I will never hunt animals, I tried once, and I hated it. Animals are innocent; men are not.

I am now a hunter, and men are my prey.

Chapter 40

9 July 1978

We didn't mingle with the locals in Beirut, it wasn't the type of area that welcomed us because we were supposed to be helping one side, whoever that was, against another, but alliances there changed daily, and we were never sure who our friends were. The Israelis had no issues like that. Everyone was their enemy, and they took that to the bank.

It's too bad I wasn't able to go to Israel to visit family. It was only a one-hour ride away to my relatives, but it wasn't going to happen. The Corps wasn't going to let me go and come back. We never had any R and R off the base and we just spent our time practicing shooting or watching TV and playing Risk or Spades these final days.

Time on the clock was moving along, and before anyone knew it, it was time for us to leave. We knew another group was coming in, and usually, you leave your combat gear in place for the next team, but we were told to take all our gear back with us. We would be gone before they showed up.

Too bad.

It would be nice to brief them on what our mission set was and what they should expect. Our Captain and NCOIC were staying behind for a bit, and they would handle the actual transition, so I guess they would be doing the briefing and handoff.

I know the embassy and staff were going to miss us because we did some awesome things out in the field, saved some lives, and for better or worse, provided a distraction for the available ladies.

I also knew I would probably turn in my rifle when I got back to Quantico. Not because I want to, but because I only have a few options. With any luck, I would be accepted into the elite school. If not, then a posting as a divisional asset and join a battalion as the resident sniper is a possibility. Either of these options would let me take my precious M40 with me to the next duty station.

We finished our deployment and were given orders to our next duty stations. All of us were to be used in our new MOS- 8541. First back to Quantico, debrief by the cadre, and see if any of us would be enrolled in the new Scout Sniper School. I was excited to get back to Quantico, make the school, and then home for some overdue leave. I will have one and a half years to go on my three-year enlistment and then will have to decide what I wanted to do.

We picked up our gear and headed for the busses that were waiting outside the barracks. I felt uncomfortable aware that this would be one of the last times I'd sit under this hot bitch of a sun. It bore down on us and quickly sucked the lifeblood of water out of us. Our only hope is for the Army to send in reinforcements: brand-new air-conditioned busses!

When they showed up, they didn't look much different than what we came in on. As we boarded, the Gunny in charge said we were lucky we had the ACed buses. They were indeed air-conditioned, and never sparing any expense, the Army had installed on/off switches by all the windows. Or rather, the air conditioner *was* the windows. Voila, roll one down and feel that cool air.

Asshole.

All our gear was loaded up on the deuce and a half (2 ½ ton trucks) which followed us. I felt very vulnerable now without at least a sidearm. The entire time here we had a weapon on us and now, when we could be in the shit, we're not allowed to carry. Once we got on the tarmac and saw the beast, we all breathed a sigh of relief. The buses stopped next to the plane and disgorged us like a dragon tossing its cookies. We didn't run this time to the plane. We strolled as cocky as possible daring anyone to fuck with us. Stupid, yes, but we were hardcore, and no one could take that from us. It's one last parting gift from the Marines. Doesn't matter how long you've been out, you have the confidence of what you've done and who's done it by your side. We'll have each other's backs until we die.

Most people say they'd die for another person, but they don't know until they've been in that position. Would they really? God willing, they'll never find out. But for those of us who have found out—who have jumped into battle to give our lives for another—we carry that knowledge and that trust inside of us. We know our limits, and far from those limits holding us back, we can commit fully to our calling—for me, that would become my family—because we know exactly how far we'll go.

The 707 was open and its steps leading up to the cabins. The ground crews were loading up the cargo areas, and when that was done, we were good to go. TWA planes and American girls. Even though the girls in the city were exotic, these girls smelled nice and looked great. A bonus is that they had the most beautiful legs, hair, and a smile for each one of us.

Haven't seen this in a while!

It is going to be a pleasant flight home.

I thought I would put on the charm and talk to the nice ladies more, but I fell out of character. I was like one of those babies in a warm car trying to stay up. My head would fall and jerk back up several times before I succumbed to blissful, relaxing sleep.

We made it to Germany, had a small layover then off to Bangor, Maine and then a hop, skip, and a jump to Dulles once again. I'd seen this movie before but from a different direction. At least I knew what to expect anyway. Happy days, the land of the big PX and hot showers, flushing toilets, and women. No yellow footprints to follow and no Drills yelling.

The three of us were picked up by a Chevy Van, which is better than a bus—real air conditioning! But since there were only three of us, I guess that was the VIP treatment.

The weapons and gear were picked up by some

other guys and brought in later that day. Off we went to some new barracks, checked in, stowed our gear, and got ready for whatever final challenge tomorrow would bring.

Chapter 41

12 July 1978

It's a Wednesday morning and we have been here for a day. The first step is going to the Admin building and getting processed in, check sheets, and directions to the various areas we needed to hit. After this, off to the Doc's to get our physicals and be probed once more. Lunch at the Mess hall in an air-conditioned building with clean tables and food that was American.

Such a deal!

The next stop was another admin area to get our orders. I hope my kills—I mean skills—in Beirut help me to lock in the position at the Elite school. If not, there should be no reason to keep me from being farmed out to the sniper battalion. Sgt. Ornelas is packing up to go home to New Mexico for leave and said he had orders to Okinawa. I am going to miss him chewing out Danny and decided I would have to pick up the slack.

Danny said, "Go ahead, fuck with me and I'll beat the shit out of you now. You don't have your .45 or rifle, Dikorski."

Stupid play on my name or not, I decided I would shut up. He was much bigger than me, and he had a point. With a gun, I was invincible. Without one, I may as well be the Hulk on a happy pill. Smart, fun... but invincible?

Jeff Dixon was the other guy in our unit who

went with us. He was attached to another team and we didn't have a lot of contacts except back at base camp. He is on his way to Camp LeJeune, Jacksonville, North Carolina. He decided being a sniper wasn't what he wanted anymore and would do something else.

It's me and Danny and we report to the staff and personal section after lunch hoping for orders. Danny got his orders and was going to North Carolina, simple as that. He was fine with it because he got one of his two wishes, either the school or Force Recon. He would be part of the MEF (Marine Expeditionary Force) and had further orders to go on and train for Force Recon.

Good for him. He is a badass and deserves to get to be the elite of the elite. Force Recon is the top of the Marine pyramid.

Next we heard from Johnny. He has orders for Hawaii. I told him to look up Frank and gave him what contact information I had on the chopper unit he was in.

My turn and I'm waiting. I'm told to come back tomorrow, and the Battalion Commander would discuss with me my assignment. Everyone else has their assignments but me.

What did I do?

This man is a Lt. Col., and I avoided people at that level at all costs. I quickly went to my Platoon Sergeant and asked if he had been informed on my status. He was a typical career staff person, probably good at some stage in life in the Corps, but somehow hung on long enough for retirement.

He stated that it wasn't his business, and I would find out soon enough and leave him the fuck alone.

Great. This shit for brains was ROAD (Retired On Active Duty). He was just pissing his time away until he left the service and didn't give a damn about who he screwed with. I wanted to get Ornelas in here to jack this asshole up, but it would probably backfire since he was leaving. I had a good idea of how to fuck him up, and I could, but that might mess up my plans. After all, I've gone through, I'm not afraid of too many Gunnies.

I don't want to stress out, but this is a little insane. Everyone else has their assignments and I have to sit out a little more?

Hurry up and wait, right?

The next day can't get here soon enough. Danny is a real friend. He keeps me occupied and goes out with me to Q-town. We get some drinks and talk about life and how we can fix the world. Danny opens up more than he ever had and tells me about how hard it was growing up. His father was abusive and always drunk. He protected his little brothers and sisters. He didn't finish high school and the only way he could help his family was to join the service. The other branches wouldn't take him, but the Marines would. He's been sending over almost his entire paycheck to take care of his family.

Compared to him, I had lived a privileged life. It's an eye-opener when you see the world and think about how people are so poor, you don't even realize that right here in the United States, people can be in the same place or worse off. He wasn't looking for sympathy, just someone he could trust to open up to that wouldn't judge. There are a lot of good, honest men like Danny in the Corps, and I am glad we met.

We leave the bar at about midnight, and we spot some Navy pukes wading down our side of the sidewalk.

Gonna get some!

We approach them and they move over to the other side of the street, lucky for them because I had a little liquid courage in me. I turn to Danny to mention something and fuck me; there is this 230-lb gorilla behind me with muscles on top of muscles. I've never seen him fight or be ready to...except with a rifle. For him to move forward with that confidence in his size tells me all I need to expect. He scared the shit out of me.

I was ready to go to the other side of the walkway, but he put his hand on my back and smiled.

"You sure scared them, Ski," he said. "You a good buddy to have around."

Right...

He better never leave me. If anyone messes with me, all I have to do is make sure they insult Danny too.

Before I drop off to sleep, I started thinking

about the Russian I killed. I wonder if I'm the first U.S. soldier after Vietnam to waste a Soviet.

The next morning my bodyguard and I go over to eat, we sure like to eat and wander around for a bit. It's like that when you don't have a posting or orders. You check in, screw around, and wait. I finally get my appointment with the Battalion Commander scheduled for the afternoon. We have ourselves another good meal at the Mess, and after, Danny wanders with me to the appointment. I enter the headquarters and do my best crisp march and report in.

The jarhead behind the desk tells me to take a seat and wait. Danny tells me he is going to the PX and he will come back in about an hour and if he misses me, he'll see me back at the barracks. I'm left alone with this POG (Personnel other than Grunts) to ponder endless questions.

What did I do? How did I get in this situation? Am I the only person who has to meet the Battalion Commander?

The POG picks up the ringing phone and then gets up and tells me to follow him to the office. Opening the door, he shouts, "LCpl Sikorski reporting, sir."

I step in, salute, and shout, "Reporting as ordered, sir."

"At Ease, Corporal." He leaves me standing for just a bit and then states, "Take a seat."

How nice of him.

Maybe I'm not in trouble.

Looks like I'm back in the stateside Corps. The Colonel has pressed utilities, gloss shined boots, crisp short haircut, and not a spot of grime on him. Central America and Lebanon, we were lucky to have clean utilities and we wouldn't be caught with spit-shined boots. You didn't want to create any reflections, but here, a different story.

The Lt. Col. says, "Do you know why you're here?"

Fuck no.

Kind of like when a cop pulls you over, right? Let them tell you what's up, otherwise you will mention something stupid. That's when you'll find out it doesn't matter if they had a real reason to pull you over. Their fishing hook is ready to catch whatever you'll throw at them.

My dad used to do that shit to me, ask me if I knew why he needed to talk to me. I would try and guess and give him all sorts of ammunition.

I learned the right attitude quick.

Nope, what's up dude? You tell me!

So I truthfully told the Lt. Col., "I have no clue, Sir. Hopefully, it's about my orders."

He smiled (these guys like to do that when they set you up) and said, "It seems, Corporal, you put the Marines into a quandary as to reassignment. You were going to get a shot at the elite school, but it's now going to be put on hold."

I take a deep breath. If I've somehow lost every shot at the future I imagined, I don't know what I'll do.

I must have messed up somewhere. I wracked my brain trying to think of what officers' daughter I might have been caught with! None that I knew of.

"Devil Dog, a notice came down from higher headquarters that informed me that one of my Marines that just arrived in country has been nominated to the Air Force Academy as well as West Point. Not only that, but this Jarhead is considered for Air Force ROTC, Army ROTC, and Marine OCS. This young soldier needs to report to the hospital to undergo a full physical, has to take all the qualification tests (physical), and needs to go through full interviews by each of the reporting agencies. Also, I was told this jarhead needs to explain why the Naval Academy and Navy ROTC were excluded from this list." Then he just became quiet and stared at me.

I am guessing this Devil Dog must be me. I didn't know what to comment and didn't expect anything like this. I had to ask, "Sir, would that be me?

He looked genuinely perplexed, my first sign that he wasn't pulling a fast one on me after all. "You're fucking kidding me. How would you not know?"

I explained that more than a couple of Gunny's were taking care of me and had moved this along without me having too much input except to either fill out forms or sign forms. I had been moving around quite a bit the last year and a half and didn't have time to follow up on that stuff because I had been in the field most of the time. He was impressed that the NCO's would follow up and take care of someone like me and said that I must have been special. I didn't want him to know how special I was! It looks like I might have a real chance to go to college, learn something, and make something of myself. That might mean giving up the Corps, or not, depending on what route I took. This is fantastic news. I had already talked to my parents to let them know where I was and that I probably would take some leave time and visit. Now, I wasn't sure I would be able to.

So, what was the Colonel to do with me?

He stares hard. "Son, the Corps has invested a great deal of time, money, and energy into making you a Marine. The Corps now needs to know if it was a waste of money and time. Will you be thinking about leaving this institution?" He sets me straight with a look. "You thinking of leaving this brotherhood?" Before I could answer, he adds in a low growl, "I want to know why you failed to answer my question about the Navy."

I have no idea what to tell him to do with me, so I say, "Easy Sir, let me go to the Elite school."

"Nope. That slot is for real Marines. And real Marines don't take the slot from someone else and then decide to leave the Corps."

"But Sir, I wouldn't—"

"Nor would a real Marine let you risk making the wrong choice. Maybe you would, maybe you wouldn't. The fact that it's a question, though? Real Marines don't make any commitments they can't

376

guarantee they'll honor."

I want to tell him he's wrong, but he knows me better than I know myself. "Then send me somewhere stateside where I can help train shooters. Or send me to a staff training position where I can at least give some of my lessons learned to units that might be deployed to areas that I have been."

"A good idea Marine, but it seems the Corps has already given me the answer."

"Sir, yes Sir! Might I ask what the answer is?"

"I have orders, in my hands, for you to report the OCS PLC[27] class that will start in six days. I am hesitant now to send you there since you don't know what you want to do. I will not rescind the orders, which means you will report to OCS as ordered."

This means he is leaving it up to me. OCS. Hot damn, I can become a Marine Officer.

Since he's not in the mood for chit chat anyway, I should get out of here.

Before I can ask if I'm dismissed, he remarks, "Now, you have yet to answer about the Navy."

I took a chance and looked at him and smiled. "The Navy sir? Really?"

He gets up and I shut up and stand up quickly. He smiled, put out his hand, and shook mine. "I had to ask, I'll put in some bullshit answer for you, good luck, come see me tomorrow if you want out of OCS."

That was it. Dismissed and out I went.

Holy Shit! It might be happening!

_____
27   (P. 432) Orders for OCS/PLC

The paperwork said I had two Vice-Presidential Nominations for the Academy's and several recommendations for the ROTC's. I had already been accepted to OCS.

I knew I was super smart! Wait till I tell my disbelieving Dad!

I did want OCS, but I need to sit down and look at the benefits of each offer. My Dad has to declare he is proud at this point. Danny never showed up and instead of going to the barracks, I went to the PX where they had payphones.

"Collect call from Mark Sikorski," the operator says. "Will you accept charges?"

"Who's calling?" questions my mom.

"It's Marco, Mom."

The operator repeats the question, and my mom sounds confused. She yells, "Joe, Marco's on the phone."

"What the hell's he want?" Then I hear grumbling on the phone, followed by my dad's voice. "What's up, Marco?"

The operator repeats the question—whether he'll accept my collect call.

My Dad laughs. "Sure."

And we're finally put through to each other.

"Dad, I've been accepted to OCS! How about that, I told you I was smart!"

"That's real good son, really good."

I took that as a win! Crumbs for some, but for me, it was all I'd ever wanted to hear from him.

I go on in a long ramble. "Dad, I also have been accepted to the Air Force Academy, West Point, and both Air Force and Army ROTC[28]." See your son's not a complete dumbass!

"What are you going to do? That's a lot of places and a lot to think about."

The question is as new as his kind words. I am a man now, and he wants to know the exploits and intentions of the kid he saw as a prodigal son. But instead, I've come back a Marine, not rich with money, but rich in a way most others will never know.

"I don't know," I say. "I want to check out ROTC units in the California area so that maybe I could save a few dollars and live at home. As far as the Academies, I'll go visit them and see what they are like."

He was all for that and said if I lived at home, there was a lot of work around the house that needed to be done. I guess that would be better than paying out for an apartment or dorm. The best bet was going to one of the Academies.

I found Danny at the barracks waiting for me and told him to change clothes, I was paying, and we were going out to dinner. It's not like he was going to answer no. A big boy like him would eat me alive, so I made sure I named the place, a funny named place called Generous George's Positive Pizza. This would keep me from spending an arm and a leg.

He kept bugging me about why I'd asked to get

28   (P. 432) Army ROTC Scholarship paperwork

together, but I wouldn't tell him anything until we sat down to eat. My way of explaining it was that I am going to become an Officer and a Gentleman so that he should enjoy dinner because soon I would not be able to be seen with a low life like himself. That started a good laugh, and then he good-naturedly punched me in the arm.

Being the stud I am, I acted like it was a tap, but I must have moved about six inches. My arm had to be bruised, but I just shook it off and said he needed to enjoy my wonderful presence for the time being.

I'm going to miss him.

He is always good to have around, especially if I was picking a fight. One look at him and most others would back down thinking he would be backing me up, and they would be right. I promised to try to keep in touch with him and said he needed to do the same.

Later the next day I was able to track Garza and Harding down by phone tag and thank them. I was glad I could use the military phones for that. They wanted to know how the deployment went and said they had talked to some people that said positive things about my time in the field.

It was a great lesson in networking. The NCO grapevine extends far so if you develop a good reputation, it can get you places. I know I was going nowhere until I joined the Corps, and now the Corps was helping me get somewhere greater. My next mission would take me through all the new regulations and qualifications to be an officer candidate. I just need to figure out which route I wanted to take.

What a leap, from video games at Castle Park to maybe going to college. Enduring Basic to end up in a jungle, enduring the jungle to end up in a rocky desert, and now, after all that, being able to go someplace that really scared the crap out of me, school.

Knowing I wasn't the sharpest tack in the box made my previous decisions easy, or so I thought. I figured that I just had to listen and do what I was told, but looking back, that wasn't the case. Each time, each situation, I had to learn. Not learning would cost lives, mine or someone else's. I mentioned earlier, hopefully I would learn by other people's mistakes. That only works in training. If you had to learn in combat, well, that is a much harder and less forgiving classroom. Now, I am going to learn something different, in a different world with different people. Will I be able to?

At this point, the possibility of failure stares me in the face. Digging down deep and being honest with myself, I acknowledge that I was never good at school. Was it because I didn't apply myself? I was distracted? Or maybe I was as dumb as my dad had joked.

The Academies scared me. They would expect good grades, or you would find yourself back in the military quickly. In ROTC, you at least had some time and could fix grades possibly without all the military stuff hanging over your head as well.

Staying in the Corps was the best answer because it was something I knew, and all they would be doing is preparing you to be a Marine Officer. The Marines expected you to go to school, but, they were not going to be on your ass full time. But then there was the whole business of being a Marine.

None of them would be easy ways.

More than that, even in the Marines, I would still have to graduate college. That was the problem. This was stupid, I could be shot at, knifed, blown up, thrown around in a vehicle that shouldn't fly, and here I was, afraid of going to school.

The next day I went to see OCS school administration counselor. I didn't know they had those, but that's where the front desk directed me. Being on base and having the school right here made things much easier.

I was escorted to a lieutenant who was easygoing, and I explained my predicament. He had my military jacket (personnel file) in front of him and listened to my concerns. Being a good listener, he addressed my concerns and went over each of the programs.

The Marine OCS/PLC program would pay me 100 dollars a month while I was in school, and I had to pay expenses. That was just the basics. There were good things and bad things.

The positive? I would remain in the Corps and be paid for my reserve training.

The negative was that the costs are all mine.

I could also stay in the Corps and take night classes to finish up my associates degree, and then after phase two, be commissioned as a Second Lieutenant. That would give me a few more years to finish my bachelor's degree. I already had quite a few credits because I went to Junior College and took courses by correspondence.

The Academies program would be all-inclusive and I would remain on campus. The military would pay for everything. The ROTC's were anywhere I was accepted for school. They, too, would pay for school and give me 100 dollars a month. In those days, that would be enough for poor but comfortable living with my eye on the future.

That's a lot of thinking and planning!

The Lt. was kind and gave me insight as to what he felt I should do. "Go OCS/PLC."

He explained that I would have a much easier time of things than most all the incoming class. Even the NCOs that were running the program, they still would give me shit, but probably would not ride me real hard. And in exchange, they would expect me to help the other recruits. It would be just like boot all over again, but the classes would be more geared towards leadership and understanding small unit tactics.

I wasn't quite decided, but the thing he said next sold me. I could take OCS over six weeks with no commitment to going back. After I finished phase one, I could go back to the Corps, or I could accept any of the Academy's or ROTC offers given to me. I would have my time obligation transferred to the other Service and then continue with whatever school I had decided on.

What little doubt remained then disappeared. I was a Marine after all.

Over the next few days, I packed my gear, went out to Q-town a few more times, and said goodbye to Danny and a few others. Little did I know, those yellow footprints would be coming for me.

Chapter 42

17 July 1978

My decision has been made. I am reporting to the USMC OCS/PLC class and have every intention of becoming a Marine Officer. I talked to Gunny Garza and Harding about what I should do, and then located Gunny Davison for confirmation. Everyone agreed that this would be the best course. I would complete OCS/PLC and then take leave to visit some ROTC schools and also the Academy's. After those visits, if the course of action is to go ROTC or Academy, then the Marines would let me leave.

The process would be to accept the scholarship and sign enlistment papers for the Army or Air Force. My Marine commitment would continue under the new service agreement. If I were to fail college or the Academy, I would finish my time in the Army or Air Force, enlisted at or above my current rank. This seemed like a no-lose proposition to me.

I had to report to the school and was told when the busses arrived, I was to go stand in line with the others as they came off the bus. Okay, I picked up my gear and waited. Here come the busses, looks like Greyhound buses that were nice and air-conditioned.

Wait till these college boys get off and feel this heat!

I couldn't wait to see how high-tech the AC system would be. Was it rustic and you had to lower the window yourself? Was it even more basic and the windows didn't even open—just a little gap opening like we're prisoners?

Off they come, and over I go. I find some yellow footprints to stand on. An intense déjà vu sweeps over me. Am I back in boot camp? I am not happy.

They lied to me. Again.

The Drill Sergeants specialize in yelling, pushups, and throat chokes. I don't think these Drills have ever been in combat. Some look just a few years older than me. Next thing I know, one Drill is yelling at me about being prior service.

I get ready to stomp his ass bad, but another drill comes up and pulls him away. Lucky for him, I would have fucked him up. Shithead. I probably shouldn't be here. I will kill the motherfucker.

I will play this game for a bit. I know the drill.

As the weeks progressed, a few Drills told me to just hang tight, do my time, and take care of the recruits. They did leave me alone most of the time, and I helped out the best I could. A change in the Drills attitude here at PLC versus Boot is this time instead of NCO's worried about you serving under them and screwing up, they were more worried about you having to lead them and getting them killed. That was an ironic twist of fate for me. I would be in charge of guys who had trained me.

I guess that is a smart way to do things. Most of the Drills would have to look at the next Lieutenant they had and know another Drill passed them on. If the LT didn't cut it, the Drills only had themselves to blame.

One thing is that during the physicals, I didn't have to worry about shots. I blew through most of the other training. Marksmanship on the range was the greatest, though me being the best shot helped—I shot better than all the instructors, so they made it a game for me to try to shoot pennies and dimes off the targets. We used iron sights and no scopes, and the range masters knew who I was. It was good to have friends in low places!

Drill and Ceremony were fun. During Boot, I never was able to lead it as a private, but now I was starting as the platoon Sergeant and Squad Leader from the beginning. My job was to get everyone trained up. Might sound like hard work, but for me, this was a little bit of a vacation. If I didn't have to go to a real school and have to learn something, then this would have been great.

The military classes were good. I have a better understanding of why some of the leaders did what they did. As a young boot, we were taught not to question why we would do things. It was more of the tear us down and rebuild us in a killer mold—and a desperate prayer that the monsters they created could be controlled.

All the classes in hand to hand, rifle ranges, and tactics on near-and-far ambushes were designed so that leaders knew that when they pointed in a certain direction, we would go in that direction and kill all surrounding enemies. This new perspective was more about how to point the killers in a direction that needed to be killed. Not "police action," "riot control," or "crowd dispersion." Those things were left to the Army.

Something else that came home hard was to learn that you will put good people in harm's way knowing they would be killed, but those sacrifices were in service to our greater mission to the defeat of the enemy in total. It wasn't enough that we sent them back wounded and suffering. Our victory had to be overwhelming, and sometimes you had to sacrifice good combat troops in the hopes they would succeed or buy time for everyone else.

As Chesty Puller said: "They are in front of us, behind us, and we are flanked on both sides by an enemy that outnumbers us 29:1. They can't get away now!"

If you're wondering who Chesty Puller is, he's one of the most revered Marines to ever strike fear in the hearts of the enemy. Lewis Burwell Puller, known affectionately by all Marines as "Chesty," served in the United States Marine Corps in World War I, leading countless skirmishes in Central and South America, World War II, and Korea. He enlisted as a Private in 1918 and rose to the rank of Lt. Gen. before being medically retired after suffering a stroke in 1955.

I tried not to say anything like "when I was there" or "well the way *we* do things," because I would come off as a smartass undermining the leadership.

This worked out well because I was asked my opinion a few times—and it was taken.

All the things we did in Boot, we did here in PLC, but not as much. We had more class time than in Boot, but that's to be expected when these boys would be paid to think.

Wait, that means me too!

Not good.

Maybe I could be a shooting instructor when I was done rather than a shooter. I don't know, but it was food for thought, and it opened another door in case my dumb ass lost the keys to the others.

Chapter 43

24 August 1978

We graduated on 24 August 1978 and did our marching around. We looked good for all the families that were able to attend. I wish this had meant a lot to me, but at the time, my heart only had room for pleasant distractions and the real work ahead of me.

Before I left Quantico, I was able to go and visit my dad's family in a suburb of Pittsburgh, Pennsylvania called Carnegie. I was able to see my Grandma Rose, Grandpa Joe, Uncle Norbert (Dad's little brother), and Aunt Pat.[29] All three of my cousins were there, including Mike, P.J., and Cindy. As time went on, Mike joined the Marines, P.J the Navy and Cindy (the smartest of all of us) Went to college through the Navy program and became a Medical Doctor.

It was good to see my aunt and uncle, and I think this is the first time I met the cousins. We spent the week visiting and telling stories—including stories I'd heard before but now saw right through. They were stories about my father, things I'd suspected were lies all along but now had the experience to understand.

---

29   (P. 433) Grandpa Joe, Grandma Rose, and Cindy
    Sikorski on leave in 1978.

Chapter 44

September 1978

I had official orders to visit West Point in New York as well as the Air Force Academy in Colorado. After those stops, my trip would be to check out ROTC universities in Southern California and take some much-deserved leave time. There were a couple of schools that contacted me, but they were not near my parent's house. I would visit them, but I wanted to be close to my parents' house so I could sponge off them if I chose ROTC.

Just because I'm a Marine doesn't mean I'm not still their son!

My children will get free meals and laundry services for life, too. It's just my way.

There were a couple of Air Force ROTC programs I could go to, and all within driving distance. The one I decided on was University of Southern California (USC). I thought about Cal State, but USC looked better on paper.

Because of the OCS program, I had missed the start of all these schools for the current semester. The schools would allow me to start in December, after the winter break, and get my credits. The one exception was the Academy. Thanks to transfer credit from my military service, the Academy had a prep school I could go to for half the year that might get me up to speed on life at the Academy quickly. There was only one Army ROTC program, and that was at Claremont Men's College in Claremont, California. I could go there for just ROTC and attend normal classes at the University of California, Riverside.

I started my search and went up to West Point since it was the closest. I knew whatever I did, I wasn't coming back to Quantico for some time, so I sent all my stuff home to Riverside. My visit entailed young men being yelled at, marching, and being braced non-stop.

Let's see, get yelled at, attend classes, get yelled at, made to perform chickenshit things, get yelled at some more ...

Nope.

There was no reason for this display except to prove who had more power. At least in Boot, the people doing the yelling had some experience, these turds looked like a bunch of assholes yelling at everyone because they could.

Next up was the Air Force Academy. They had airplanes on display at the campus. I liked that! They had to march around and get yelled at as well, but they looked a little happier. Maybe their loves for the birds made up for the rest.

Can't say that either place excited me. I had my fill of discipline for a while. If they would accept me here, my lifelong dream to fly would come true. The problem is, I couldn't pass the flight physical because of my eyes.

Wait...what's that? The world's greatest sniper

failed a vision test?

I did great in the spatial and reaction testing, but the eye exams failed me. How can this be? I shoot at the expert level without glasses!

The Doc even tried to cheat for me, but the depth perception was off. There was nothing he could do about that. And just like that, I couldn't fly.

Damn. If that isn't a disappointment, I don't know what is.

I left there frustrated and feeling like a gutshot had taken the life out of me. That's okay, now it was to take some leave time and catch up with some friends. I would also look at the ROTC programs but had settled on finishing out the OCS program with the Marines.

I went home and tried to kick my brother out of my room. It was not going to happen unless I decided to stay home. Fine, I will sleep on the sofa in the living room. My brother, the Zeb.

Since I had a few more dollars in my pocket, I decided to buy a real car and replace the little convertible I still owned. What I picked up is a real sweet 1974 Dodge Dart Sport. It has a 318ci, 3 speed. I added a Hurst shifter and a four-barrel Holly carb with Hooker headers. Next was a lift kit for the back end with hydraulics because I put in racing tires, T/A Radials with Cragger mag rims. Then for the final touch, two tone blue paint with gold pinstriping. The engine was clean enough to eat off of and now I could race this new car on the street.[30]

---

30   (P. 434) 1974 Dodge Dart. License Plate "Mark Ski".

Fixed up with a new ride, I went to see the whole crew. First, I saw Tim, Bob, Pat, and a few old girlfriends. I gave Tamese (just turned seventeen in May) a call and was hoping to date her once again.

I went to see Mr. Williams, and he asked if I was ready to come back to work. He had the snack bar manager job open for me. We had a good visit and I went over my plans. He listened and said I should probably go to school if the Military was going to pay for it. As much as I liked the Marines, the Air Force or Army seemed like the smarter thing to do.

I'd changed my mind about a hundred times in the last twelve months, but by now I saw that as its own kind of mission. Fighting through chaos taught me that. All I can do is take an honest assessment of my current situation, the obstacles to overcome, the enemies coming at me—then take aim, fire, and reload for the next challenge.

He said a few more things and was very convincing. I told him I would come back and visit some more. When he told me to do so, I could hear it in his voice. He knew as much as I did that the person I'd talk to next was the real challenge.

My dad appeared to be happy that I had come home, and we were able to spend some time talking about options and opportunities. He was convinced that the Air Force Academy or ROTC was the way to go. So what if there were no flight options? A navigator was just as good and paid just as well. It is the degree that matters afterward and would help me in the civilian world.

It was time for some distractions. Time for entertainment and to put my leave time to good use. I went to the beaches, caught up with girlfriends, even went to a homecoming dance with Tamese, things were looking up.

Maybe I needed to stay here. It was a heck of a lot more exciting—and less painful—than training or fighting. But I knew where both paths would take me and that neither were where I wanted to go next. It was time to take aim and fire. No matter the consequence, I could always reload for what came next.

I just could not bring myself to go into the Air Force if I couldn't fly. I know that is egotistical, but being on the ground and watching others fly just wouldn't cut it. With all the experience I had in combat and the field, there was no place for me in the Air Force. Making my father happy was important, but regretting a life decision would be worse. Because right or wrong, I need to have the possibility of combat.

Maybe I was sick, but I couldn't see a way around it.

In my mind, the Army was a great choice. I had visited all the campuses. West Point was too much bullshit and not even close to the Corps but they wanted to act like they were. On the other hand, I went to several campuses for ROTC. It did not matter which one I went to, they *all* had girls. Even Claremont Men's College (CMC)!

My head was spinning now. I would have school paid for, $100 a month, and plenty of work. I had to give up one weekend a month and part of the summer, and I could have all the girls I wanted?

I met with Captain Muergia and Captain Bush at the CMC's ROTC Detachment. SFC Potter who was a former Marine and hated the Corps, or so he said and Colonel Giboney, who was in charge of the overall program. I really liked the campus and met a few of the cadets as they were called as well. One of these young cadets was going to become one of my best friends forever although neither of us knew it at the time. The other thing I didn't want to bring up but...the Army said I could fly helicopters! I had been burned once, but these guys were officers and they wouldn't lie.

Would they?

Even better, I didn't need to drive to CMC every day, just one day a week for classes. They had a sister program agreement with the University of California, Riverside, which was about 20 mins from my parent's house. Free room, free food, car, girls, little brother... wait, forget the brother part. This was going to work out great.

I applied to UCR and Claremont, and once accepted, turned down all the others including the Academies. There was one fly in the ointment though, there always is: I didn't have the credits to get into the third year of UCR. I wouldn't graduate with the class and would have my graduation in December

1981 instead. There were all sorts of hoops I had to leap through because of this. The approvals came, but the scholarship would be delayed until July 1979. My mission would now be making up classes that I had missed which totaled to about six months' worth. I wanted to progress faster by taking more courses, but I wouldn't be able to take full class loads and still be on active duty.[31]

The gods of war took pity on me. It all worked out and was meant to be. I signed my obligation to the U.S. Army and entered the reserves. Until July of 1979, I would attend drill and be paid for that time and get credit. My classes would start full time in December 1978 at the Riverside Community College (RCC). I had to pay for these classes myself, and thankfully, the ROTC program allowed me to take Military Specialty classes at Claremont in the preceding months to catch up. This is the time where I met my best friend forever, Steve Moran. Many more stories are in the hopper of our exploits as cadets.

Mr. Williams held to his word and I started up as the assistant manager/snack bar manager so I could earn some extra money to help pay for classes at RCC. This was an exciting time as it turned out that being an expert marksman didn't mean squat in the real world.

Don't get me wrong. I learned a lot, but I went into the service knowing nothing and learned an art form that does not translate well in the civilian

---

31   (P. 434) USMC Honorable Discharge 1979

world. Now I would get new continuing education from people I knew to prepare me for the community where I belonged. In some ways, I was just buying time, because eventually, civilian life was an obstacle I had to put in my sights.

Chapter 45

Life After the Marines

A few things followed me into civilian life. Most of them involved fights. There certainly wasn't any Edge of Silence when it came to my mouth in the civilian world.

It's not that I wanted to get into fights. I *need* to get into fights. I don't pick them, but I certainly don't shy from them. And if I encourage some punch-happy dummy to throw the first fist, I can't be blamed for defending myself.

The Drive-In allowed me to get into fights. Most times they occurred at the Swap meet on Saturday and Sunday, but some happened in the late evening when working the "back gate," also known as the exit for most people.

There were many instances of getting into it with other people, but two stand out. The first one occurred when five Hispanics came into the theater on a Saturday night. One was driving, and the other four were in the trunk. They came correctly through the front, paid for one ticket, and decided since the car was a low rider, no one would guess more people were hiding just out of view.

I followed them in and as they were getting out of the trunk, I stepped up, not the smartest thing to do, and said," you all need to leave now and go back through the front. You have two choices, pay for the other four or get reimbursed."

The biggest guy gets out and roars, "How about we kick your ass?"

Next thing they all pull out these three to six-inch switchblades. Two years ago, I would have gone to get Mr. Williams. Now, I figure maybe one or two of these guys have been in a real fight and if I take out the biggest one, the rest will turn coward and leave.

Of course I also carried the weapon that had served me better than anything. I also had my knife of choice, buck knife I called the "General." The blade is almost eight inches, and with the handle, you have a foot of death in your hands.

As the turds surrounded me, I pulled out the buck and asked, "Which one of you wants to die first?"

I didn't give them a chance to answer anything. I smiled, screamed "Ohh Rah," and charged the big guy. Just as I thought, he screamed, turned, and ran while the others scattered. Now I had two choices: go back and take out his friends—or keep moving, get reinforcements, and come back with an army. I kept moving to the office, called Mr. Williams, and went back out with a few more guys to finish the job.

But by then, all of the guys were gone—least of all the first one I'd sent running.

Mr. Williams asked, "What would you have done if you caught him?

"Probably would have killed him."

"It's good you didn't catch him then."

"Yep."

For him, the fight was over. But for me, it had

never stopped.

The next morning, the first place I went was to see if the car was still there. It was. I pulled out the "General" and cut all four valve stems from the tires and figured that would call things even. I could have cut the tires so there was a bit of mercy left in me.

The next event occurred when someone did come in the back gate and when he stopped with his two friends, decided that I needed a good ass-kicking. Most people get pretty brave when they have others with them. Me, I'm just stupid and told them to get out and prove it. There were two big guys and the guy my size was the talker.

I didn't want to talk or fight. This was one of the few times I had brought a BB pistol to work. Having a short fuse, I pulled out the gun, shot him in the face about half a dozen times, and told the others they were next. They plucked him up and jumped back into the car and sped out with squealing tires.

Mr. Williams heard the commotion, tires burning rubber, and came out to talk to me. "What was that about? Do you need help?"

"No, I've got it covered, just some guys trying to get into the back gate."

"I thought I heard someone screaming."

"Yeah, I had to hurt one of them."

"You shouldn't be doing that."

"You do."

"I'm the boss, you're not."

Steven, who worked as an X-Ray tech during

the day and at the theater at night said some guys took their friend into the ER he worked at, stating that someone shot him in the face at the Drive-In. He was wondering if I knew anything about it, because he knew I carried both a knife and a BB gun.

I told him maybe, but it didn't matter unless they came back. He wiped his forehead and his neck.

I told him not to worry, they were cowards anyway. Guess I confirmed something if anyone read into it.

The bad thing, or maybe good, was that I didn't care. I could have killed them and not thought twice about it. Maybe my ethics were getting messed up here in the civilian world. No one should die just because of something stupid like this, but on the other hand, you shouldn't be so stupid to challenge someone who you have no idea of their mental state. I will just chalk it up to defending myself against harm. No sins here, just move along, please.

The one time I guess I did care was when Tim, my buddy from before, and I went cruising in his '72 Dodge Challenger convertible. We were visiting Olivia, one of my old girlfriends from before.

Did I tell you she lived in a Hispanic neighborhood? As we were leaving, a bunch of, and I mean a bunch-10 to 15 young guys started yelling at us and asking why a couple of white guys were in the area. Me being me shouted a few words that came to mind in Spanish from Central America and gave them the bird fully believing that we could zoom away and laugh. Well, as the gods of war will show you, you better be careful what you say.

Tim's car stalled. In his worried state, he flooded the engine (too much gas went into the carburetor and would not let the car start). The top was down, the Mexicans were grinning at the stupid Gringo's, and I thought this was a shitty way to die after all I had been through.

As I pounded on Tim's head to get us the fuck out and he was screaming something back at me, the car finally roared to life! We left about an inch of rubber on the road burning out the tires as we left. Yep, I forgot where I put that tough Marine that day!

Dreams are the second thing that came out of my time in the Corps. I used to have great dreams, fantasy, flying, racing, etc. Then a period of no dreams while I was enlisted but then near the end, I started having dark dreams. Now that I'm out, the dreams are still there, but time is slowing their impact. I just tell everyone I don't dream, makes it easier.

In some ways, that's true. I have fewer dreams—but the ones I do have are stronger than ever. I have this recurring dream that gets more real as time goes on. This was the first time my dreams manifested with my family present to see the horror escape from me into the waking world.

My father caught me in this dream recently. I made fun of myself, but it did scare the shit out of me. It is the first time I actually woke up and still thought I was fighting. It was a dark evening with the moon shining through the window. A slight breeze came through the screens and moved the curtains. I was back in Central America and had just killed this guy with my bare hands and I was trying to get away from him.

But he was still alive and clutching me, trying to take me down to hell. All I could do was grip him and shake his arm loose. The next thing I know, I'm yelling at the top of my lungs, not sure what I was screaming and throwing his arm everywhere—

A light turns on and I'm standing in my whitey tighties, shaking my own arm violently and yelling. Can you even picture this, a grown ass man screaming and tossing his arm all over the place using his other arm and hand. It must have been something to see!

My dad is standing there in his whitey tighties. "Marco, what in the hell is wrong with you?!"

Shit, I don't know.

I have got to make something up fast! Glad I have been always quick on my feet. I tell him I saw someone emerging from the closet and getting close to me. When he got within an arm's reach, I snagged him, and here we are.

I didn't want to tell him the truth. I had slept on my arm, and it was numb, so I never felt myself shaking it. Certainly not hard enough to wake up before anyone saw that the things I'd locked inside on occasion found their way out. Instead, I told him the most plausible story I could come up with. The guy in the closet is the story I'm sticking to. I don't want to go into a psych ward.

Hopefully, these nightmares will go away. I swear I locked the box tight.[32] I'd find some relief by talking to Gunny—but back home, I don't have a Gunny. I really don't have anyone. It might take years before I'm ready to talk about it with anyone else, if ever. It may take until now that I'm writing this memoir.

Along with all this going on, one summer evening while working, I reflected on the last two years in the Corps, and how far I had come. A car drove up and broke my train of thought. It was one of my workers, a young lady named Vicky. Unfortunately for her, she was known as Icky Vicky—I know, sounds bad, but she was Icky. It's not gentlemanly for me to explain why.

She unrolls her window and in a shrill voice tells me, "Hi Mark, here to watch a movie with my girlfriend."

Ha! Always thought she might be a lesbian.

I look at her "girlfriend" and holy shit, what a princess. Blond hair, blue eyes, and from what I could see, a tight little body to boot! Just my type. This will be an interesting competition, but I've trained my whole life for this moment.

Vicki keyed in on that pretty quick. "Quit looking asshole! She has a boyfriend and is seventeen."

Never stopped me before!

How was I supposed to know I was now lusting after my future wife?

---

32   (P. 435) "Ask Me What I Was"

Chapter 46

Three and a half years later...

12 April 1982

I arrived at the battalion 4/61 ADA that morning to report into the S-1 (the personnel office). After getting my paperwork done, I was told to report to the old man, a Battalion Commander called Lt. Col. Jay Martindell.

The old saying is first impressions are lasting impressions. Just so, my father told me that when I report in, I need to understand that the commander's first impression of me will be extremely important. Be very conscious of what I say and do in front of him.

No problem, I could ace this better than anyone. After all, I am a Marine with an Army wrapper.

After being given directions to his office, I went to the outside door, but a man was standing in the way. He had his back to me and would not move out. No problem, I'm used to telling people what to do now.

"Excuse me, I need to get by."

No movement.

Again, a little louder, I say, "Hey, please move, I need to get by you."

This guy ignored me and kept talking to someone on the other side of the door. Asshole.

Okay, let's have the Marine come out and move

this guy, right?

"Hey! Would you get the fuck out of my way?"

His shoulders stiffen up.

Yep, bet no one talks to you that way, huh?

Then he turns around. He's not a big guy, and he's kind of old, probably in his early forties, but he looks pretty wiry and strong. He probably has some experience behind him. These tough old Army sergeants have seen some shit.

Starting with Marines who are better at taking shots than making first impressions.

Oh, shit, Sikorski. You did it again.

When I went to look at his rank, all I could see was the blue oak leaf of a Lt. Col. and the name tag that read Martindell. Fuck.

This guy smiles like the Cheshire cat. Where have I seen that before?

He looks down at the name tag that I can't cover up. "Now tell me, Lieutenant—" he looks down at the name tag that I can't cover-up "—Sikorski, who are you here to see?"

I should run. I should definitely run.

But he's already seen me.

"Sir! I am here to report to you, Sir!"

He smiled an evil fucking smile. "I was hoping you would say that."

Epilogue

This is a far cry from the end of the story. Some of you already know what happened next.

The associates degree I earned at RCC allowed me to get a BS degree in Business at UCR. I finished the ROTC program at CMC (the school's new name is Claremont McKenna), and I went into the U.S. Army as a Second Lieutenant, Air Defense Artillery, and let me tell you, there's a story there. But that's for another time.

I have just as may stories, if not more, of the trial and tribulations of leading combat soldiers. I remained in the Army Reserves through Desert Storm and had a small deployment during that time as well.

After my military obligation was over, I started a very successful career as a stockbroker with a company named E.F. Hutton. I've been a stockbroker for over thirty-six years now.

And somewhere along the line, I attempted to raise four children while inheriting another two. I'd fought for my very life, but raising them was harder than any combat operations. But what a victory raising them has given me. It's led to forty years of marriage and 12 grandchildren.

Which brings me to the woman I pointed out earlier. The one I promised to fight Vicki over if it came to it.

The girl who drove in with Vicki turned out to

be the girl of my dreams. More than that, she became my wife. If Vicki wanted a fight, she saw that this was one she'd never win. Making a family with this girl became the mission that defined the rest of my life.

The End

Acknowledgments

Now that the Edge of Silence has been broken, the words are out there and part of my life has been shoved into the light I feel I should at least recognize the individuals that pushed me kicking and screaming, not to shots like the nurses did, but to the paper to begin this tale. The major twisters of my arm begin with my wife, Robin, as of this writing, has stuck with me for over forty years. I have been less than the perfect husband and hopefully, this helps her understand a little of why having to deal with me was harder than it would be with most men.

Next would be my kids. Michelle Dockter, Sara McConnell, Robert Sikorski, and Michael Sikorski. I have no idea how they survived growing up with me as their dad, especially when they had to answer that most dreaded question.

"Do you want the Marine to come out?"

No one wanted to see him.

Then there are my inherited kids, Sarah Fidler and David Collins. Even though they didn't grow up as youngsters in my house, they have had to deal with some of my "control issues." Hopefully, this helps all of them get over their nightmares and gives some understanding and closure to their life with me.

This memoir tells about some people, now deceased, that brought great knowledge to me over the years and helped shape me. My father, Joseph Sikorski, and my former boss and friend, Fred

Williams. Both great men who I will always answer to. The third mentor is still kicking because he is so ornery—neither heaven nor hell will take him—and that is Colonel Jay Martindell. Although he does not play a part in these early years, he was very important in my Army life and after.

My boyhood friends Tim, Bob, Pat, and Gary—along with a whole host of young ladies, of course, starting with Tamese, Donna, Tracy, Mary, Olivia, Tammy, Bonnie, Janet, Mellissa, Terri—and the list goes on, so I better finish before my wife starts asking questions.

Then, my brother, David. Without him guiding my ethics and sense of honor, I probably would not have been able to see myself through hell and come out that crucible intact.

And lastly, the ones who call me a brother now, Guenther Polok, Steve Moran and Darel Maxfield. I'm proud to call you my brothers as well as my friends.

Photos, Orders and Certificates

Figure 1, P. 11, Staff Sgt. Joe Sikorski at Tan Son Nhut Air Base, 1969

*Figure 2, P. 19, Joseph Sikorski and Rachel (Kiki) Pimenta wedding
in Casa Blanca, Morocco 1958*

Figure 3, P. 19, Kingdom of Morocco Report of Birth

Figure 3, P. 19, Kingdom of Morocco Certificate of Citizenship

Figure 4, P. 19, Joe and Mark Sikorski, Casa Blanca, Morocco, May 1959

Figure 5, P. 24, Leaving Pittsburgh, 18 years old, 1954. Brother Norbert and Mom Rose Sikorski

Figure 6, P. 35, Me and my 1970 Fiat 850 Sport Spyder

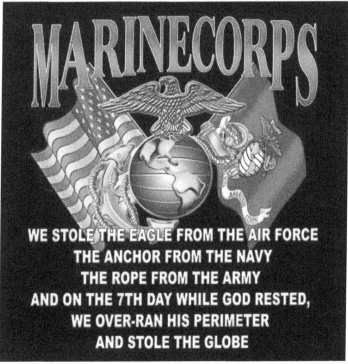

MARINECORPS

WE STOLE THE EAGLE FROM THE AIR FORCE
THE ANCHOR FROM THE NAVY
THE ROPE FROM THE ARMY
AND ON THE 7TH DAY WHILE GOD RESTED,
WE OVER-RAN HIS PERIMETER
AND STOLE THE GLOBE

Figure 7, P. 37, Marine Corps saying

Figure 8, P. 67, Varsity Rifle Letter Team (1 yr JV, 3 years Varsity)

Military Training Certificate

RESERVE OFFICERS' TRAINING CORPS

This is to certify that MARK G. SIKORSKI

successfully completed four *years of instruction in the* Army Junior

Reserve Officers' Training Corps, on 16 June *, 19* 77.

Given at the Army JROTC Department, Polytechnic High School, Riverside, California,

this 16th *day of* June *in the year of our Lord,*

one thousand nine hundred and seventy-seven. He is recommended for enlistment in the regular or reserve components of the U. S. Army in pay grade E-3, and provided he achieves a qualifying score on an appropriate MOS test, for enlistment in pay grade E-4. He is further recommended for constructive credit for MS I and MS II in the Senior Army ROTC program. He is further recommended for enlistment in the regular or reserve components of the U. S. Navy, Air Force and Marine Corps in pay grade E-2.

ROBERT G. SAGONA, MAJ, AUS Retired
Senior Army Instructor

DA FORM 134, 1 JUL 71   PREVIOUS EDITION IS OBSOLETE.

Figure 9, P. 72, Graduation from Jr. ROTC

Figure 10, P. 95, Joe Sikorski's Medals

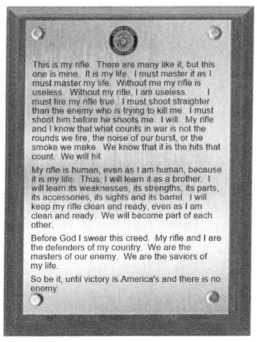

This is my rifle. There are many like it, but this one is mine. It is my life. I must master it as I must master my life. Without me my rifle is useless. Without my rifle, I am useless. I must fire my rifle true. I must shoot straighter than the enemy who is trying to kill me. I must shoot him before he shoots me. I will. My rifle and I know that what counts in war is not the rounds we fire, the noise of our burst, or the smoke we make. We know that it is the hits that count. We will hit.

My rifle is human, even as I am human, because it is my life. Thus, I will learn it as a brother. I will learn its weaknesses, its strengths, its parts, its accessories, its sights and its barrel. I will keep my rifle clean and ready, even as I am clean and ready. We will become part of each other.

Before God I swear this creed. My rifle and I are the defenders of my country. We are the masters of our enemy. We are the saviors of my life.

So be it, until victory is America's and there is no enemy.

Figure 11, P. 125, Rifleman's Creed

Figure 12, P. 129, 1st Battalion, 5th Marines, 1st Marine Div

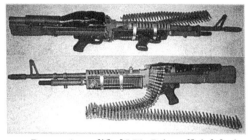

†*Figure 13, P. 130, A modified M60B (unofficial designation)*
"free gun" as used by the door gunners of Light Attack Helicopter
Squadron THREE [HA(L)-3]. Gunners would attach themselves
to the airframe with their gunner's safety belts and hang out the
door firing these guns to protect the belly and tail of the UH-1 when
suppressing ground fire. This particular gun has a mechanical
buffer fitted to boost its rate of fire. The buttstock of the ground gun
has been replaced by the sheet metal cover from a M60C. The bipod
has been removed from the barrel and a second pistol grip fitted to
the forearm. Extra springs have been added to the inside of the feed
cover to help draw the belt. On some guns, the forearm was removed
and the pistol grip was attached to the operating rod cylinder. In
action, the gunner flipped the gun on its side so that the belt draped
over the feed cover and the links and brass ejected downward.
(Photo: www.seawolves.org)

421

‡§Figure 14, P. 131, M60 Bungee System

Figure 15, P. 137, My brother David

MILITARY OCCUPATIONAL SPECIALTY

0331
MACHINEGUNNER

THIS IS TO CERTIFY THAT

PRIVATE FIRST CLASS SIKORSKI, MARK

HAS COMPLETED ALL TRAINING AS PRESCRIBED BY THE COMMANDANT OF
THE MARINE CORPS AND HAS BEEN ASSIGNED TO A MARINE RIFLE COMPANY
WITH THE (MOS) RATING 0331 MARINE MACHINEGUNNER

GIVEN AT MCB, CAMP PENDLETON, CALIFORNIA

ON THIS 3RD DAY OF AUGUST 1977

Figure 16, P. 145, MOS 0331 Machine Gunner

Figure 17, P. 154, Me (age 18) and my gear ready for action

425

Figure 18, P. 157, My Chopper and our flight

†*Figure 19, P. 187, Designated 282nd Assault Helicopter Company, what it looked like after we landed. You can see the flak jacket on the seat and the belt feed for the M60 go under the seats.*

‡ ††Figure 20, P. 261, Chuck Mawhinney shooting the M40A1, confirmed kills, 103

MARINE RIFLE EXPERT

SNIPER QUALIFIED

THIS IS TO CERTIFY THAT

LANCE CORPORAL SIKORSKI, MARK

HAS QUALIFIED EXPERT

USING THE REMINGTON M40A1 SNIPER RIFLE

GIVEN AT QUANTICO, VIRGINIA

ON THIS 21ST DAY OF APRIL 1978

Figure 21, P. 263, My Qualification Certificate on the M40A1

SPECIAL WEAPONS TRAINING COMMAND
MARINE CORPS BASE, QUANTICO, VIRGINIA

MOS RATING 8541

SCOUT SNIPER

HAS BEEN ASSIGNED TO

LANCE CORPORAL SIKORSKI, MARK

HAVING SUCCESSFULLY COMPLETED THIS 10 WEEK COURSE AND ALL NECESSARY
TRAINING MATERIAL AS PRESCRIBED BY THE COMMANDANT OF THE MARINE CORPS,
THE ABOVE NAMED MARINE HAS GRADUATED WITH HIGH HONORS.

GIVEN AT MCB QUANTICO, VIRGINIA

ON THIS 10TH DAY OF MAY 1978

Figure 22, P. 267, My Graduation Cert MOS 8541 Sniper

‡‡ §§*Figure 23, P. 273, Beirut, 1978. SeaCobra providing overwatch*

¶ °°°Figure 24, P. 321, Resemblance of Beirut war zone, 1978

†††Figure 24, P. 321, Resemblance of Beirut war zone, 1978

‡‡‡Figure 25, P. 353, Lebanese Militia with a RPG posing

§§§Figure 26, P. 356, Marine Sniper with M40 and spotter at
Embassy providing overwatch for return. Notice the shorts!

Figure 27, P. 377, Orders for OCS/PLC

Figure 28, P. 379, Army ROTC Scholarship paperwork

Figure 29, P. 391, Grandpa Joe, Grandma Rose, and Cindy Sikorski on leave in 1978.

Figure 30, P. 395, 1974 Dodge Dart Sport. License Plate "Mark Ski"

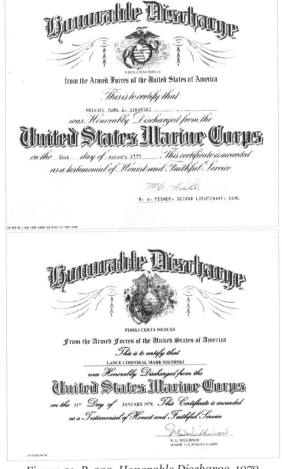

Figure 31, P. 399, Honorable Discharge, 1979.
Original top, Corrected below

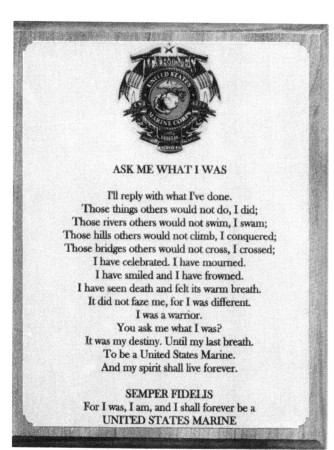

Figure 32, P. 407, "Ask Me What I Was"

Endnotes

Cover images

ali wannous, Destroyed city in Syria, 16 October 2022 < https://www.pexels.com/photo/city-landscape-street-building-10932618/>

Hippocamelus, Wikimedia Commons, UH-1 H Iroquois Chilean Air Force (FACh), 11 October 2022 <https://commons.wikimedia.org/wiki/File:UH-1_H_Iroquois_Chilean_Air_Force_(FACh).JPG>

Interior references

* USMC eagle globe and anchor poem, Poem Searcher Discovery Engine, 26 April 2022 <https://cdn-0.poemsearcher.com/images/poemsearcher/s_a7/a703dc97aedf5ee0d0b6abbc6bafa15a.jpeg>

† Bob Stoner GMCM (SW) Ret., 2005, modified M60B, Warboats.org, 16 April 2022 < https://www.warboats.org/stonerordnotes/M60%20GPMG%20R5.html>

‡ Ben41, 2010, A door gunner fires the M60, IMFDB, 16 April 2022 < https://www.imfdb.org/wiki/File:Vlcsnap-106362.jpg>

§ M60 Bungee system, 16 April 2022 <https://i.pinimg.com/564x/07/f5/bb/07f5bb8beecbd36e3f3342cad1607029.jpg>

¶ manhhai, Helicopter after landing, Flickr, 16 April 2022 <https://www.flickr.com/photos/13476480@N07/22217600344/sizes/l/>

** John Pike or Robert Sherman, 1999, M40A1 Sniper Rifle, FAS Military Analysis Network, 16 April 2022 < https://man.fas.org/dod-101/sys/land/m40.htm>

†† Chuck Mawhinney shooting the M40A1, Pinterest, 16 April 2022 <https://pin.it/J68wpt9>

‡‡ Knight Manjikian, 2015, Beirut 1978, 16 April 2022 <https://www.aztagdaily.com/archives/238898>

§§ USMC, 2012, A U.S. Marine Corps Bell AH-1T Sea Cobra helicopter on patrol outside the city of Beirut, Lebanon, Wikimedia Commons, 16 April 2022, <https://commons.wikimedia.org/wiki/File:AH-1T_SeaCobra_in_the_outskirts_of_Beirut_1983.JPEG>

¶¶ 2012, Beirut car bomb resembles 1978 war zone, Seacoastonline, 16 April 2022 <https://www.seacoastonline.com/story/news/nation-world/2012/10/19/beirut-car-bomb-kills-top/49338756007/>

*** Resemblance of Beirut war zone, 16 April 2022 <http://www.studioguenzani.it/artist/gabriele-basilico/>

††† Resemblance of Beirut war zone, Google Images search, 16 April 2022 <google.com>

‡‡‡ Langevin Jacques, Lebanese Militia with a RPG posing, ThoughtCo., 16 April 2022 <https://www.thoughtco.com/timeline-of-the-lebanese-civil-war-2353188>

§§§ Don Mell/AP/Shutterstock, Marines Beirut 1983, Shutterstock, 16 October 2022 < https://www.shutterstock.com/editorial/image-editorial/marines-beirut-1983-beirut-lebanon-7360557a>

437

Authors Bio

Mark grew up in a nice Jewish family and was unable to find a good Jewish girl, so he converted one to be his wife over 40 years ago. He has four kids, inherited two more, and twelve grandchildren (those produced at the time of this writing). To say he is blessed is an understatement. This book was written to take his oral history and attempt to put into words, a sliver of time in his life. He is an avid, though not really good, racquetball player, owns and rides horses but should probably be bubble wrapped when he does run the horses. He enjoys painting for the grandkids and friends and is going to retire as soon as his eldest daughter lets him. The one goal in life he has now (besides staying alive) is to be the best grandfather he can be.

Made in the USA
Monee, IL
03 February 2023